THE STRUGGLE AGAINST HIGH FINANCE

GOTTFRIED FEDER

INVISIBLE EMPIRE
PUBLISHING

Hardcover ISBN: 978-1-963591-20-0

Trigger/Offensive Content Warning and General Disclaimer:

"Let me issue and control a nation's money and I care not who writes the laws."

Mayer Amschel Rothschild

CONTENTS

CONTENTS

PREFACE

We stand in the tenth year after the memorable November 9, 1923. On the eve of that day, November 8, our leader wrote the foreword for my book: *"The German State on National and Social Foundations,"* and in it the sentence: *"The literature of our movement has thereby received its catechism."* A small span in the life of a people, but when one considers the development of our movement and the history of our people in this span, a highly significant and decisive one. For in these few years, the vast majority of nationally minded Germans recognized salvation in National Socialism, and step by step the effects of the disastrous Treaty of Versailles proved the justification and the correctness of our demands. Our leader stood before us in these decisive years with exemplary steadfastness. The programmatic goals of the movement, which were established at its inception, remained unchanged.

It is, I believe, a duty to account to the German people, as far as it has been granted to us personally in these years, at least in the main points, what we have been able to contribute to the movement. I must go back to the beginnings, which date back to the year 1919, and it may be of interest to note that even then the fundamental lines were already drawn. With intention, only what has been printed is given here. To also publish the handwritten expositions, which have only been submitted in manuscript, would not yet be the right time.

It was in May 1919, shortly after I had published my essay *"The Radical Remedy,"* that I spoke at a gathering of soldiers, among whom was Adolf Hitler. Adolf Hitler writes about this in his book *"Mein Kampf"* (I, 220 ff., People's Edition p. 229 ff.): *"For the first time in my life, I heard a principled exposition of the problems surrounding the international stock exchange and loan capital. After I had listened to the first lecture by Feder, the thought immediately flashed through my mind, that now I had found the way to one of the most essential prerequisites for the establishment of a new party. In my eyes, Feder's merit lay in the fact that he with ruthless brutality established the speculative as well as the nationally harmful character of stock exchange and loan capital, thereby exposing its irreconcilable prerequisite of interest. His expositions were fundamentally so correct, that the critics of them from the very outset, disputed less the theoretical correctness of the idea, than rather called into question its practical implementation. But what was considered a weakness in the eyes of others, I saw as the strength of Feder's presentations."*

And further:

"As I listened to the first lecture of Gottfried Feder on 'Breaking the Thraldom of Interest', there immediately dawned on me, that here was a theoretical truth of immense significance for the future of the German people. The sharp distinction of stock market capital from the national economy offered the opportunity, to counteract the internationalization of the German economy, without at the same time threatening the very foundation of an independent national self-preservation, which would have been otherwise endangered in a struggle against capital in general. The development of Germany already stood too clearly before my eyes for me not to realize that the most bitter struggle would no longer be fought against foreign peoples, but against international capital. In Feder's lecture, I sensed a powerful prelude to this coming struggle."

In the following pages, the main issues of National Socialist finance and economic policy are discussed. This book does not intend to replace my work *"The German State on National and Social Foundations,"* which rather remains as a fundamental summary of the subject alongside it, nor does it attempt to provide a comprehensive systematic treatment of the field. It may be that the closer connection of the individual pieces to historical events lends them greater liveliness, and in their historical sequence, they may also serve as a not unwelcome contribution to the history of our movement. To avoid repetitions, I have truncated some of the essays. As with *"The German State"* in its reissue in the *"National Socialist Library,"* the individual writings in this republication remain essentially and in all fundamental points unchanged. The locations of the first print were indicated.

Murnau, October 1932.

Gottfried Feder

For the fifth edition

On January 30, 1933, Reich President von Hindenburg appointed Adolf Hitler as Reich Chancellor. On March 5, the German people demonstrated their faith in the Führer. The German Reich is National Socialist. It has become possible, step by step, to fulfill the demands we have made for fourteen years.

This book, which was conceived as a documentary when it was created, is now a document for a movement that has turned from a hope and a vision into reality. Therefore, it appears unchanged.

Murnau, September 1934. Gottfried Feder

CHAPTER 1

THE INNER HISTORY OF BREAKING OF INTEREST SLAVERY

For Introduction

First print in the *"Völkischer Beobachter,"* 1920, No. 72

Happy is he who has seen the deep reasons of things. Virgil.

"How did you actually come to the idea of breaking the bondage of interest?" I am often asked these days. I do not know whether Columbus was frequently asked: *"How did you actually come to discover America?"* The answer to such a question can and will vary greatly depending on the position the questioner takes on the matter and the person being addressed. Nevertheless, I will try

to give an answer that satisfies the questioner and—what I consider even more important in such cases—the person being questioned himself in good conscience.

In the recognition of very important, perhaps the most important connections in major world issues, it is always a matter of a sudden intuition, of creative insight into previously obscure connections, illuminated by a fortunate glimpse into the future. The birthplace of an idea, this sudden bright recognition of a truth, stands at the intersection of the inner and outer history of the thought. The inner history often remains dark and veiled; it partly unfolds entirely in the subconscious, but in any case, with a thorough immersion into the inner experiences, points of reference for the psychological development of a thought can be found, just as naturally a certain intellectual attitude is a prerequisite for the correct evaluation of the psychic experiences.

The intellectual prerequisite must by no means lie in engagement with a specialized field, but rather is much more general in the right instinct for certain relationships.

In my case, a good sense for the order of magnitude was likely the prerequisite for the conclusive composition of the series of facts that were first correctly sensed and then scientifically verified. And in my professional occupation as an engineer, this confident sense of the order of magnitude was always more important and reliable for calculation results or for the dimensioning of construction elements than the results from the slide rule and logarithm tables, which, although they provide much more precise numerical results, do not indicate the correct *"comma."* But it is on the correct *"comma,"* i.e., the order of magnitude—whether ones, tens, hundreds, or thousands—that the answer to economic political questions of the greatest scope depends, and not on the second, third, or fourth digit of the numerical series. What matters is not whether Germany's fixed-interest debt amounts to 275 or 320 billion, nor whether the total capital of all German joint-stock companies is 13.8 or 14.6 billion, but rather that fixed-interest securities require an interest service of roughly 15 billion, whereas the total dividends of German industry in its best year amounted to only around 1 billion; thus, it is a matter of the ratio 1:15, the relationship between the two best-known forms of securities: fixed-interest securities and profit-sharing securities.

The impact of not always easy life and professional experiences on the spiritual attitude toward comfortable income from pure capital ownership, from interest and dividends, manifested itself through increased attention to general economic and social relationships. As a young engineer and entrepreneur with too little capital for far-reaching ambitions, I soon learned of the iron, merciless grip of impersonal money power, which first offers and grants the desired *"credit,"* but then acts solely out of selfish capital interests during every economic crisis. Abroad, I observed how the credit needs of smaller states were carefully nurtured and then *"generously"* granted credit, for example, the 600 million of the Disconto-Gesellschaft to Bulgaria in 1913/14; but also, the demoralizing relationships of dependency that arose from it. In this way, the bridge from narrow personal experience to broader recognition of international relations was already built. The recognition of the strong, inseparable financial and moral connections was present in the subconscious but was not yet clear.

The great war, with its immense impressions, initially blurred the pursuit of these financial problems until the colossal financing of the world war through our war bonds heightened my attention and—my discomfort over the progressive indebtedness of the people to such an extent that I repeatedly spoke out against the form of our much-praised *"secured debt"* in contrast to the *"floating debt"* of France and England. Admittedly, at the time, I was met with more or less pitying smiles, although I was already then given the admission that *"of course, with ever-increasing indebtedness, there could no longer be any talk of a real 'security' of the war debt."*

I would have considered indebtedness of the Reich through the printing press alone sufficient, without burdening the entire people with the high interest, which—like the debt itself—given the colossal figures being considered, could never be seen as covered by the real wealth of the Reich but would always only be covered by the tax power of the entire people. As long as a victorious end to the war left the possibility of full or partial repayment of war burdens, a more thorough examination of these relationships was omitted. When our poor German people in those dark November days suffered the full force of their fate, all those conscious and unconscious, emotional and intellectual experiences rose again, and my abrupt, clear answer to the pressing question *"What now?"*

Was:

Breaking the bondage of interest!

In one night, the first draft was composed, and on November 20, 1918, I submitted to the government of Bavaria my guidelines and demands for breaking the bondage of interest.

I emphasize that in this, no actual socialist thought processes played a part.

Contrary to the revolutionary slogans of freedom, equality, and fraternity, the idea of breaking the bondage of interest found very little understanding among the Marxist ministers. Not to mention that the capitalistic press initially shrouded itself in eager silence.

With this introduction of the thought into the public sphere begins the external history of the idea, which will then provide the answer to the often-asked question: *"What has been done so far for the realization of this idea?"*

CHAPTER 2

THE RADICAL MEASURE

First print in the February 1919 issue of *"Süddeutsche Monatshefte,"* Munich

Nummus non parit nummum! Money should not be able to give birth to money. An ancient problem of humanity—the interest problem—is expressed in the concise words of this ancient Roman maxim.—*"You shall not take interest from your brother!"* commands the Bible.

Something within us recoils at the idea that money, as something inherently barren, grows by itself through interest; it contradicts our moral sensibilities that mere possession of money, without the addition of one's own productive labor, increases through interest. The justifications offered by economists for the legitimacy of interest fail to convince, especially where the main argument for interest—the risk associated with lending money—becomes minimal. This is the case with the overwhelming majority of fixed-income investments, which largely consist of values that, through legal provisions for the protection of minors' assets, reach a minimal limit of potential loss, so that with these, there can be no talk of any special risk. With other less secure capital investments—stock companies, LLCs—the greater risk is offset by the possibility of greater profit. With these values, we have already crossed the boundary for the narrower concept of loan capital.

What is loan capital? Loan capital is debt! This is all too often overlooked. One should not say that the German people possess 100 billion in capital in the form of war bonds, but rather that the German people have 100 billion in debt, for which they must pay interest; in addition, another 50 billion in uncovered debts, for which the German people must also pay interest; further, 25 billion in railway debts of the state and national railways, for which they must likewise pay interest; furthermore, 12 billion in bonds from land credit institutions; and 11 billion in mortgage bonds from mortgage banks, for which the people must pay interest in the form of high rents; and finally, 6 billion in municipal bonds from German cities and communities, which the German people must finance. For all this capital, the German people as a whole must work in order to pay the interest.

For over 200 billion of such debt securities, the German people must pay interest. For this, the entire productive population of Germany must toil from here on out for eternity in service of perpetual interest!

It is particularly noteworthy that our socialist thought, from Marx and Engels right up to the Erfurt Program and its most significant interpreters like Kautsky, does not primarily target this loan capital, but instead, with fanatical sharpness, it focuses on industrial big capital as the curse of the working class. The first fundamental question regarding the correctness of such a directed struggle would require a thorough examination of the capital invested in our heavy industry. It will likely come as a surprise to most readers to learn that, as tallied only very summarily above, the 200 plus billion in fixed-interest debt securities stand in contrast to only 11.8 billion in share capital of German industrial enterprises. Keep in mind that, across all sectors—in our industry for iron and coal, for clothing and textiles, for stone, earth, and mining, shipping, wood and glass, in our construction trade, in the massive chemical factories, in our once world-dominating electrical industry, in our machine and locomotive factories, shipyards, and paper factories, in the transport and food industries—in short, in the vast scope of all industries, only 11.8 billion of our national wealth is invested.

With this finding, we have gained a platform for further discussion of our problem. For all such broad-stroke treatments of issues, it is fundamentally important to become clear about the order of magnitude of the factors involved. It is irrelevant whether individual figures vary by 10-20% above or below, but a reliable determination of the order of magnitude1) of the various numerical groups is an essential precondition.

20:1 is thus approximately the ratio of fixed-interest loan capital to industrial capital. This is the first fundamental finding. Roughly 10 billion is required for the interest payments on the existing fixed-income securities in Germany. About 1 billion was the yield from dividends of all German stock corporations. This ratio of roughly 1:10 must also be kept in mind as a second basic insight.

We must also become clear about a third point. This is the growth of the two types of capital. I need to digress further here and hope that through a brief excursion into higher mathematics, I can clarify the problem. First, some examples.

1) In the years 1915/16, according to the Statistical Yearbook for the German Reich, there were a total of 4,761 joint-stock companies in Germany with a total of 15.8 billion marks in share capital. From this, we subtract 397 banks with 4 billion in capital, leaving 4,364 joint-stock companies with the aforementioned 11.8 billion in total capital of all German industrial joint-stock companies. For completeness, it should be noted that there were also approximately 16,000 limited liability companies with a total capital of 3.5 billion. If we add these 3.5 billion in capital of the LLCs to the above figure of 11.8 billion for joint-stock companies, we arrive at 15.3 billion in total large industrial operating capital. Despite this significant increase in the figure for industrial capital, the ratio to loan capital does not change very substantially.

The charming story of the invention of chess is well known. The wealthy Indian King Sherham granted the inventor, as thanks for creating the royal game, the fulfillment of a wish. The wise man's request was that the king give him one grain of wheat on the first square of the chessboard, two on the second, four on the third, and so on, doubling the number of grains on each subsequent square. The king smiled at the seemingly modest request and ordered a sack of wheat to be brought to distribute the grains for each square. It is well known that fulfilling this request would have been impossible even for the richest ruler in the world. All the harvests of the world over a thousand years would not suffice to fill the 64 squares of the chessboard.

Another example: Many will still remember the torment of compound interest calculations from their school days; how a penny invested at compound interest at the time of Christ's birth grows, doubling every fifteen years. In the year 15 AD, the penny has grown to 2 pennies; in 30 AD, to 4 pennies; in 45 AD, to 8 pennies, and so on. Very few will realize what value this penny would represent today. Our entire Earth, made solidly of pure gold, our Sun, which is 1,297,000 times larger than our Earth, and all our planets, glowing red-hot with gold, would not be enough to represent the value of this penny invested at compound interest.

A third example: The fortune of the House of Rothschild, the oldest international plutocracy, is estimated today at around 40 billion. It is well known that the old moneylender Mayer Rothschild in Frankfurt around the year 1800, with no significant personal wealth, laid the foundation for the vast fortune of his house by lending out the millions that Landgrave Wilhelm I of Hesse had entrusted to him for safekeeping.

If Rothschild's growth of money through interest and compound interest had only proceeded at a moderate pace—the two sharply ascending curves are loan interest curves, with the upper curve showing the development of the Rothschild fortune, and the lower curve, initially flat and then rapidly rising, showing the characteristic development of all such curves, where the ordinate values double with every constant interval on the abscissa. The dashed line shows the development curve of our total industry over the last 40-50 years. The finely dashed, varied lines show the development of a series of arbitrarily selected large industrial enterprises, from which the general character of the dashed curve of industrial capital is derived curves of industrial and loan capital.

Curves of Industrial and Loan Capital.

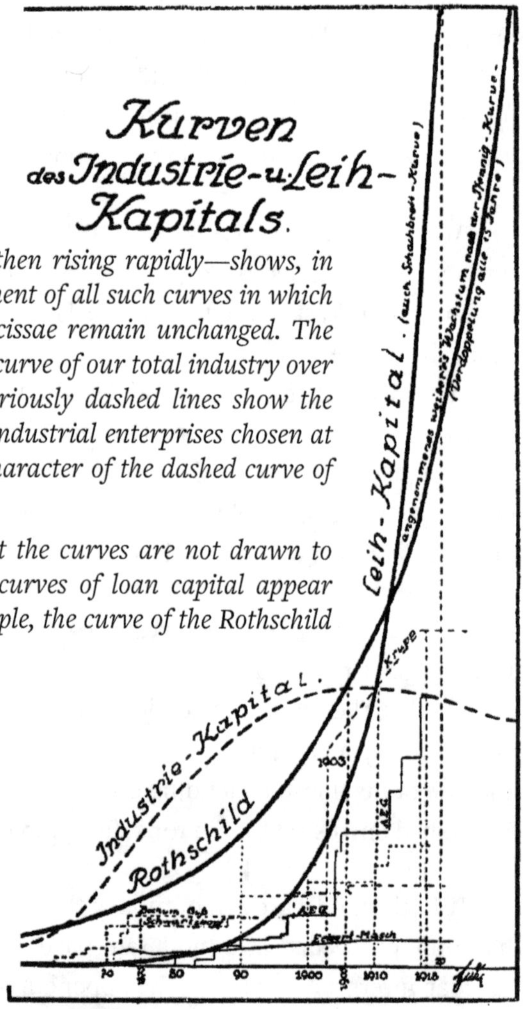

The two boldly drawn curves are loan-interest curves: the upper curve shows the development of the Rothschild fortune, and the lower curve—at first flat and then rising rapidly—shows, in general, the characteristic development of all such curves in which the ordinates double while the abscissae remain unchanged. The dashed line shows the development curve of our total industry over the last 40–50 years. The fine, variously dashed lines show the development of a number of large industrial enterprises chosen at random, from which the general character of the dashed curve of industrial capital is derived.

It must be expressly noted that the curves are not drawn to scale and that, in particular, the curves of loan capital appear greatly compressed. Thus, for example, the curve of the Rothschild fortune would have to be drawn at least eighty times higher than the Krupp curve. The purpose of charting the curves is only to show the fundamentally different character of the two kinds of capital. The curves of loan capital first exhibit a very slowly rising development; the rise then becomes faster, ever more rapid, seizing everything, soaring far beyond human concepts and striving toward infinity.

The curve of industrial capital, by contrast, remains within finite limits! Although the course may show very strong deviations in individual cases, in general the basic character of industrial development will always be such that, after a vigorous initial rise, a certain period of maturity, of saturation, follows, after which decline sets in—more slowly or more quickly.

It must be explicitly noted that the curves are not drawn to scale, and in particular, the curves of loan capital appear somewhat compressed. For example, the curve of the Rothschild fortune would have to be at least 80 times higher than the Krupp curve. The purpose of drawing these curves is solely to illustrate the fundamentally different character of the two types of capital. The curves of loan capital initially show a very slow rise; the development then accelerates until it becomes increasingly faster, pulling everything with it, and eventually surpassing all human comprehension, striving towards infinity. In contrast, the curve of industrial capital remains within the finite!

The course may show significant deviations in individual cases, but in general, the basic character of industrial development will always be such that after a period of strong initial growth, a period of maturity, of saturation follows, after which decline sets in, whether slowly or quickly.

If it had proceeded like the penny, the curve would not have risen so steeply. But assuming that the increase in the Rothschild fortune continues at the pace of the penny, the Rothschild fortune would amount to 80 billion in 1935, 160 billion in 1950, 320 billion in 1965, thereby already far surpassing the entire German national wealth.

From these three examples, a mathematical law can be derived. The curve that expresses the rise of the Rothschild fortune, the curve derived from the number of wheat grains on the chessboard, and the curve that indicates the increase of the penny invested at compound interest, are simple mathematical curves. All these curves have the same character. After an initially modest and slow rise, the curve becomes steeper and steeper and practically soon approaches tangentially towards infinity.

Quite differently, the curve of industrial capital behaves. Also mostly grown out of small beginnings, the curve soon shows a strong rise until a certain saturation of capital is reached. Then the curves flatten and will generally decline slightly in individual industries when new inventions have led to the devaluation of existing factories, machinery, etc. I would like to single out just one example here: the development of the Krupp fortune. In 1826, old Krupp died almost without wealth. In 1855, Alfred Krupp received his first order for 36 cannons from the Egyptian government. By 1873, Krupp already employed 12,000 workers. In 1903, Frau Bertha Krupp sold all the assets and facilities for 160 million to the Alfred Krupp company. Today, the share capital amounts to

250 million. What does the name Krupp signify for us Germans? The pinnacle of our industrial development. The first cannon manufacturer in the world. A sum of the most tenacious, purposeful, and intensive work performance. For hundreds of thousands of our fellow countrymen, the Krupp enterprise meant bread and work. For our nation, honor and weapons. And yet,

What does the increase in the Krupp fortune over a century of tenacious work mean compared to the growth of the Rothschild fortune from interest and compound interest through effortless and endless value increase? It is a dwarf compared to these billions. Nothing shows us more clearly the deep intrinsic difference between loan capital and industrial capital. Nothing can more clearly demonstrate the difference between the devastating effects of loan interest and the operating profits (dividends) of large industrial enterprises based on fixed operating capital.

It cannot be emphasized enough that the recognition of the mathematical laws that loan capital and industrial capital follow alone shows us the clear path where the sword must be placed for a reorganization of our shattered financial economy. We clearly recognize that it is not the capitalist economic order, not capital as such, that is the scourge of humanity: The insatiable interest demand of big loan capital is the curse of all working humanity!

Capital must exist – Labor must exist! Labor alone accomplishes little – Capital alone should accomplish nothing!

Capital without labor must remain sterile! Therefore, the most important demand, the noblest task of the revolution, the most reasonable goal of a world revolution is Breaking the interest-economy of money.

The House of Rothschild is today estimated to be worth 40 billion. The billionaires of American high finance, the series of Kahn, Loeb, Schiff, Speyer, Morgan, Vanderbilt, Astor, are collectively estimated at least 60-70 billion. At a mere 5 percent interest rate, this means an income for these eight families of 5 to 6 billion, which is almost as much as, according to Dieffenbach's investigations in 1912, 75% of all taxpayers in Prussia had as annual income. (There were then about 21,000,000 officials. 75% of this is roughly 15,000,000. Each official had an average of 1.56 dependents, hence 23 million dependents.)

Approximately 38,000,000 Germans therefore had to live on what the aforementioned billionaires earn in a year. – Certainly, the American billionaires are not in the sense pure loan capitalists like the House of Rothschild, nor do I wish to argue whether the American billionaires are *"100-million-dollar billionaires"* or true *"1000-million-mark billionaires"*; in the first case, one would have to add one or two dozen other names. Or let's take the Rathenau's "300", then our estimation certainly holds true.

It is not even essential here to provide an exact figure. The staggering proportion of 300 to 38,000,000 alone opens our eyes to the dominance of international loan capital.

Therefore, it is necessary to shake off with all our might the terrible yoke that must stifle all productive labor, to wrest the power from money to generate interest and continue to generate it until all of humanity has become helplessly enslaved to international loan capital.

Our fatherland is deeply troubled, the whole world is deeply troubled. The poison of Mammonism gnaws at the body of humanity. Bolshevism wants to cure humanity. It seeks to shatter it like earthen pots. A harsh surgery it wants to perform on suffering humanity, believing it can save through operation when the cause of the illness lies in creeping poison. Only the removal of the toxic substance can bring salvation. The idea of breaking the interest-based economy is not directed against human nature; it does not extinguish the spirit of enterprise, nor does it hinder the production of goods—only the effortless and endless inflow of goods from usurious interest must come to an end.

Let us now quickly clarify the most important aspects of this revolutionary demand, and indeed, we will first examine the questions from our national perspective.

First, this requires a clear look at our current situation. State Secretary Schiffer declared it *"unmanageable"* in his great speech in the Berlin Chamber. This is only partially true. The immense indebtedness of our national economy, the unprecedented devaluation of our means of payment, in short, the fact that we have overnight become a poor people, is indeed manageable.

The burdens imposed on us by the peace settlement cannot, however, be overlooked. As we have seen, the existing debt instruments already amount to around 250 billion. Let us assume that the Entente imposes an additional 50 billion in war reparations in some form, bringing the total debt to around

300 billion. Though it is difficult to compress into the narrow framework of this discussion, a few words must be said here about the size of the German national wealth. The investigations by Selfferich and Steinmann-Bucher estimate the German national wealth at around 350 billion. Such estimates, however carefully constructed, can only be accepted with great reservation. They are valid only for times of undisturbed economy. They are also misleading in that they include state and municipal assets, such as road construction, river regulation, etc. It is clear that while the execution of such works has cost enormous sums, they actually have no intrinsic value. A better measure of national wealth is the so-called taxable wealth, as derived from tax declarations for the business tax or the war wealth tax. This yielded a total of 192 billion, which is significantly less than Selfferich's estimates. To this sum, we might add an estimated 10% increment for legally tax-exempt small properties and a similar increment for *"silent reserves."*

In any case, it seems utopian to speak of a national wealth exceeding 250 billion. But even this figure is of very conditional value. The most accurate approach would be to abandon the notion of a numerically quantifiable national wealth altogether and come to the realization that national wealth finds its true expression in the intellectual and physical labor power of the entire nation, thus belonging to orders of magnitude that have nothing to do with the narrower concept of capital. We must also consider another source of national wealth in the existence of mineral resources, forest wealth, and fertile land, but these too cannot be numerically quantified, as they fluctuate between zero and infinity, depending on whether the mineral resources lie fallow or are estimated to contain billions of tons of coal, etc.

We must not forget that Germany is essentially a poor country. It holds almost no monopolies. In terms of mineral wealth, it lags far behind most neighboring countries, not to mention the vast mineral resources of the Chinese and American empires. In the fertility of its soil, it falls far short of the blessed regions of Russian black earth, and the effortlessly productive tropical and subtropical landscapes. In the end, we are always left with only the labor power and the will to work of our people, and we must be clear that under these circumstances, there can be no talk of secured loans or tangible collateral for our debt securities.

Whether it's interest-bearing war bonds or non-interest-bearing Reichsbank notes, the only thing behind them is the tax power of the entire people, and what is tax power other than a function of the labor performance of the entire productive population?

We must now briefly clarify another set of issues raised here, namely the main items of our state's sources of income and expenditures. There is a remarkable contrast between the broad space that the question of raising money occupies in our private lives and the interest we take in the major questions of our state's financial management, and yet there is no fundamental difference between individual households and the national economy.

The main items of state income are: firstly, the net revenues from postal services and railways; secondly, income from mines, forestry, and other state enterprises; thirdly, customs duties and indirect taxes; and fourthly, direct taxes.

To avoid dealing only with theoretical discussions on such eminently practical questions, I will briefly explain the individual items in terms of their scale, using the Bavarian state budget1) for the year 1911 as an example. Postal services, telegraph, and railways brought in 120 million, forests, mines, etc. around 40 million, indirect taxes 53 million, direct taxes 60 million. Another 67 million came from stamp duties, fees, inheritance taxes, ground rents, and transfers from the Reich, etc.

What about the expenditures? Here we find, in the first place, the costs for servicing the state debt, including railway loans, with 85 million. For the Royal House, 5 million. Justice administration 27 million, internal administration 40 million. Churches and schools 51 million, financial administration 13 million, expenditures for Reich purposes 50 million, pensions 36 million. Miscellaneous expenditures 5 million.

1) The following figures on the Bavarian state budget are rounded and taken from the Bavarian Statistical Yearbook of 1913. This is the last statistical yearbook that appeared before the war, providing exhaustive information on Bavarian finances. No new publications have appeared during the war.

An income surplus of 27 million balanced the annual budget in that fortunate year of Bavarian finances.

Within the framework of our discussion, however, only the expenditures that could be eliminated by breaking the interest-based system are of interest. Naturally, the first item here is the expenditure for servicing the state debt with 85 million, along with the largest part of our expenditure for financial administration—about 10 million—and a large portion of the expenditures for the Reich military, which we can estimate at half, i.e., 25 million. Finally, the expenditures for the Royal House with 5 million would also be eliminated, totaling 125 million.

The elimination of these items would make it possible to forgo the collection of all direct and indirect taxes, which, as we have seen, brought in 53 and 60 million, respectively—113 million in total! We are by no means of the opinion that all direct and indirect taxes should be abolished; within reasonable limits, they undoubtedly have both an educational and a regulatory function. It is surely no more than right and fair that income from secured property should remain subject to a moderate, graduated tax, as the state must also use its powers to ensure undisturbed property rights. It seems equally appropriate that commerce and industry should be required to contribute appropriate tax payments from their operating profits, as the state must also ensure the maintenance and expansion of public transportation routes. A corresponding minor poll tax for every eligible voter is also a requirement of justice, as the state is also responsible for the protection of personal safety and property.

In the area of indirect taxes, a strong expansion of all pure luxury taxes could have a regulating effect in the best sense, while all basic national necessities should be kept free from taxes.

The result of such tax policy should not be sought primarily in the high financial gain—this cannot be the focus, as it should not be a real tax burden for the majority of the population, but rather a reminder that humans are not just individuals, but also citizens with civic rights and duties. The yields should be used less for the relief of profit-making state enterprises, whose net yields, as we have seen, are sufficient to cover the ordinary expenditures of the state for education, culture, justice, internal administration, etc. They should instead be used to promote special cultural tasks of the state, for which within the framework of the ordinary state budget, corresponding funds were never available. I am thinking here primarily of convalescent homes, institutions for the blind and disabled, children's homes, maternal care, the fight against tuberculosis, against alcohol and venereal diseases, for the creation of garden cities and settlements, especially for the accommodation and humane care of our war-disabled.

Our view broadens. We see new horizons. The abolition of all taxes could signify the breaking of the interest based economy? It would signify it if we had emerged from this titanic struggle as a victorious people. So let us not rejoice too soon, for the burdens imposed on us by our enemies will see to that. But in any case, we see new horizons based on the very simple consideration of the example of our Bavarian state budget.

In their basic outlines, we find quite similar conditions in the other German federal states, and it is not too much to say that the surpluses of the profit-making state enterprises, i.e., railways, postal services, telegraphs, forests, mines, etc., could cover all state expenditures for the entire administration of justice, for the entire internal administration, including state construction, all expenses for education and culture as well as religious purposes without difficulty. What an almost ideal condition. Why is it not so? The interest has crept in. Because of interest payments, the population's food is made more expensive; because of interest, flour and salt, beer and wine, matches and tobacco, and countless other daily necessities are burdened with indirect taxes. Because of interest, direct taxes must be levied: land taxes, which are passed on through more expensive grain; building taxes, which drive tenants into poverty; trade taxes, which burden productive labor; income taxes, which inevitably depress the standard of living of officials and salaried employees; and finally, at the very end, modest in giving, insatiable in taking, comes loan capital with the capital income taxes. Out of 253 million in capital income in Bavaria based on the tax declarations of 1911, a mere 8.1 million in state taxes were paid. We have seen that every capital income, every capital interest must ultimately be raised exclusively through the labor of the entire people. We have seen that the interest payments for state debts constitute the largest item in our state budget, and we have seen that those liable for capital income taxes contribute only a very modest portion to state revenues.

In terms of scale, the capitalist pays 8 million out of 60 million in direct state taxes—only a tenth to a sixth. The direct taxes represent approximately one-fifth of total state revenue. Thus, loan capital contributes only about a thirtieth to a forty-second toward the total state needs.

The picture becomes truly horrifying when we consider our Reich budget. Here, the conditions are already much more unfavorable. The Reich does not have the same sources of revenue as the individual federal states. The direct taxes are reserved for the federal states; the profit-making enterprises of the Reich are limited to the Reich postal services and the Reich railways (thus excluding the Prussian state railways), and thus only customs and indirect taxes remain.

The scale of these Reich revenue sources (see the Statistical Yearbook for the German Reich of 1917 and 1918) in 1915 was 1 billion from Reich postal services and railways, 0.7 billion in customs, 1 billion in indirect taxes, 0.8 billion in special revenues (defense contribution, matricular contributions), etc. Here again, the same picture. More than a third, namely 1.3 billion, was consumed in 1915 by the interest payments on the Reich debt. Here too, loan capital has forced its way in. Here too, it draws on all indirect taxes to satisfy itself. Sugar contributed 163 million, salt 61 million, beer 128 million, tobacco, spirits, wine, lighting materials, matches, playing cards, and countless other little tax items had to pitch in to raise a billion, which then flows entirely into the pockets of the capitalists.

Today, even the mere raising of the Reich's debt interest is a mystery. 5 billion alone are consumed by the interest payments on our 100-billion war bonds. The revenues from the post and railways can hardly be increased further. We will scarcely be able to raise customs duties much more. So, there likely remains only a fivefold or tenfold increase in indirect taxes—an impossibility—or the clear insight that the only salvation lies in breaking the interest-based economy of money. The entire war bond economy was an enormous monetary fraud. 100 billion has the German people borrowed from itself for its war. 5 billion in interest has it promised to itself; thus, it must pay 5 billion in taxes. Only the big capitalist benefits, he who draws so much capital income that he can never possibly consume it all; through the capital income tax, only a very modest percentage is taken from him, as we have seen.

I hope already now, through the broad lines of my argument, to have dispelled the all-too-human fright of many readers regarding the possible loss of their interest from their beautiful securities. Only very briefly shall it be shown by an example that the entire interest economy is a great monetary deception, and I will go to the very limit here with respect to decent bourgeois income conditions. Suppose the labor income of a family head is 10,000 marks, plus 5,000 marks from capital income. From this, approximately 1,500 marks in direct taxes must first be paid. Furthermore, in the form of expensive rent, at least 1,000-1,200 marks must be deducted for the eternal rent; another 1,000 marks may well be consumed by indirect taxes for a family of five to six members, and already it is apparent that even under the favorable tax conditions of earlier years, little remains of the beautiful capital income of the small and middle capitalist. Today, there can no longer be any talk of "*something remaining*": on the contrary, significant portions of labor income will also likely be taxed further, if one considers the fantastic tax plans of the present. Matters naturally look entirely different for the big capitalist who, let us say, draws 1 million in capital income. (There are quite a few such golden people in Germany today.) In capital income tax, this fortunate person pays at most 50-60,000 marks. In indirect taxes, he pays no more than the family man in the previous example. For his household, even in today's expensive times, he can still live quite comfortably on 40-50,000 marks. He keeps a neat round 900,000 marks net, from which next year at 5% interest he can draw new loan interest of 45,000 marks, and this of course rightfully at the expense of the working population.

The small renter, who lives solely from his interest, would undoubtedly be harmed. If he is capable of work, he would of course have to resolve to secure a labor income. In this way, he still positions himself much better than the millions of his compatriots who have nothing but their physical or intellectual labor power.

If he refuses to do this, he must consume his wealth. For 20 years, he can still subsist on it, should he, as before, consume at 5% of the interest as living expenses henceforth. For persons who are not in a position to work or are weakened by illness and age, it goes without saying that an appropriate existence must be provided through the extension of social welfare for all sections of the population. It would go far beyond the scope of this essay to delve in details into the personal interests of particular layers of the population. A demand as ground-shaking as this cannot in any case concern personal interests, and yet in the actual implementations of the idea, one will make the experience that its salutary consequences will finally accrue personally to everyone's benefit.

On the problem just broached concerning the eradication of interest on war bonds, I have indeed endeavored to clarify that the small capitalist, i.e., all those hundreds of thousands who through more than American sales pressures for securing the issue of war bonds were induced to offer their savings, get nothing out of the interest not only that they themselves must indeed pay taxes for, but, under a taxation custom-tailored to spare the big capital, must pay part of these taxes indirectly again out of their pockets for the interest on their million-mark subscriptions. I imagine that, apart from these most material considerations, the general moral appeal alone to the concern of all anxious parents for the welfare of their posterity should suffice towards accepting the renunciation of eternal interest on the government bonds as quite natural. After all, what is the patriot, who gave his fatherland in its utmost need 10,000 marks, losing in this case but only a mathematical pretext to receive 50,000 marks in interest over the next hundred years—an entitlement which would not even remotely have made inroads upon the reduction of his capital? My children and grandchildren will have to work so that only these interest payments can be made in the first place.

The question of repaying the borrowed sums can be solved in various ways. In my brief outline of this problem, which I submitted to the government of the People's State of Bavaria on November 20 of last year, I made the proposal to simply replace the payment of interest with repayment in 20 annual installments of 5%. I believe I can make an even better proposal in the following, which, due to its simplicity, certainly deserves preference: "*The war bond certificates are declared as legal tender, with the annulment of interest.*" That is the egg of Columbus. The advantage of this measure is first that no one really notices it. The bond certificates remain quietly in the depositories, but they bear no offspring, just as little as a book or a wardrobe or any other consumable item that one has lent to a friend.

If one needs money, one simply takes a certificate and pays with it. In terms of beauty and paper value, our war bond certificates are just as good as our other 10-, 20-, 100-, and 1000-mark bills. There can be no talk of flooding the market with payment means in such a seamless transition from the interest-based economy to the interest-free national economy. The war bond certificates are already safely stored and well-guarded in bank vaults or other places considered thief-proof by the people, such as the woolen stocking or the manure heap. The fact cannot be denied that the paper payment means issued to the amount of approximately 40 billion are also not in circulation, but are instead hoarded in the manner described above. Our need for payment means even during the peak of the pre-war boom was only about 4-6 billion, and there can be no talk of needing more than double that sum today, given the increasingly established cashless payment economy.

In exactly the same way, the annulment of interest for all fixed-income securities must naturally also be carried out. For these securities as well as for dividend-bearing securities, the originally proposed *"repayment"* in place of interest payments will be more advisable, especially for mortgages. The breaking of the interest-based economy for mortgages undoubtedly means the solution to the housing problem. The liberation from un-affordable rents. It is equally incomprehensible why the holder of a mortgage should have eternal interest enjoyment from the once loaned sum, why an easy and endless flow of goods should be granted to him, why the great mass of the people should pay high rents year in, year out, for the sake of this unhealthy principle. Only briefly should it be noted that, of course, a complete abolition of rental interest is out of the question, since the administration and maintenance of buildings constantly require work and money. Therefore, a reduction of rents can only occur as far as it results naturally from the facilitated repayment of mortgages.

It is neither possible nor the right place here to go into detail on the countless questions raised by the implication of this idea. At least the most important ones should be mentioned: the question of capital procurement in general, the treatment of all mortgage securities, the mortgage system, the issue of banks and banking, the entire reorientation of our social policy, and finally the overall reshaping of our financial system necessitated by this.

But one thing should be emphasized with utmost clarity: that the breaking of the interest-based economy has anything to do with our entire value-creating work, insofar as it does not hinder the entrepreneurial spirit, productive work, the production of goods, the acquisition of wealth; on the contrary, as we have seen, the entire productive nation is freed from a gloomy, inexplicable, heavy burden; our spiritual life is purified of an intoxicating poison. How correctly throughout history the fertility of the interest problem has been recognized can be seen from the fact that in all times and among all peoples, the interest problem occupied the minds.

In the Old Testament, we find in various places, such as Leviticus 25, Deuteronomy 15, provisions on interest remittance in the form that every seventh year should be a year of release or jubilee, in which all debts to fellow countrymen should be forgiven.

Solon in the year 594 BC. Through legislation, the personal debt servitude was abolished. This law was called the great Seisachtheia.

In ancient Rome, the lex Genucia of 332 BC prohibited Roman citizens from taking interest altogether.

Under Emperor Justinian, an interest rate ban was issued with the stipulation that no more interest could be demanded if the accrued interest had reached the amount of the originally loaned capital.

Pope Leo I the Great issued a general prohibition on taking interest in the year 443; until then, only clergy were forbidden to demand interest on a loan. Now the prohibition of interest became part of canon law and also a binding regulation for the laity. Gradually, secular legislation also adopted the canonical views and even punished the taking of interest. This is found in the imperial police ordinances of the years 1500, 1530, and 1577.

However, such laws were fiercely contested and often circumvented, and we might just note as a remarkable historical fact here that, while canon law prohibited Christians from taking interest from the 11th to the 17th century, this was permitted to the Jews.

It would be extremely interesting to investigate what economic developments led to these violent debt relief measures. It would be particularly valuable to see what powers and forces continually overrode the interest bans.

In the Middle Ages, usurers were often summarily dealt with; peasants or embittered citizens banded together and killed the usurers. Today, we have entered a completely different stage in the development of the interest problem. Protests against usury are deeply disapproved of. It is no longer just about localized abuses that could be combated by removing the source of infection; it is about a severe affliction of all humanity. It should be particularly emphasized that in our current culture, it is precisely the internationality of economic relations that makes the principle of interest so deadly. This historical review is not intended as an analogy for today's conditions. When the Babylonians defeated the Assyrians, the Romans the Carthaginians, and the Germans the Romans, there was no continuation of the interest economy; there were no international world powers. Wars were not financed through borrowing but by treasures accumulated during peacetime. A particularly noteworthy discussion on this is provided by David Hume in his treatise on state credit. Only the modern age, with its continuity of conquest and international law, allows loan capital to grow immeasurably. The penny placed on interest at the time of Christ's birth no longer exists, because in the meantime all property rights have repeatedly succumbed to force; on the other hand, the penny that old Rothschild placed on interest still exists and will continue to exist, if there is such a thing as international law, into infinity. It is also noteworthy that vast regions of the Earth only transitioned from a natural economy to a money economy in the modern age. Furthermore, only in the 19th century were all restrictions on interest-taking abolished (England 1854, Denmark 1856, Belgium 1865, Austria 1868).

We must finally break with the idea that loan capital has been granted a superhuman power, the ability to grow eternally out of itself without any productive labor of its own, and indeed, as illustrated in the curves, at an unstoppable and ever increasing pace, endowed with a terrifying power to drain and consume. All human creations, indeed all earthly things, are subject to the eternal universal law of becoming and perishing. Every thing wears itself out. Everything ages and eventually decays into dust; only loan capital is supposed to be eternal, and not only eternally immutable but eternally growing into infinity!

Uncoupled from the rise and fall of nations, it should reign over nations, untouched by the laws of transience, untouched by the forces of destruction, untouched by the giant creatures of our cannons that crush cities and villages. For even if factories and mansions, railways and bridges are smashed into dust and rubble by grenades: the mortgages remain intact, the railway and state debt certificates are not thereby annihilated; forever must the unfortunate owners of their destroyed dwellings and the suffering populations of countries devastated by war toil to pay the interest on the debts from loan capital. Joyfully, the golden Internationale watches the reckless frenzy of humanity; the insane devastations of war, which have claimed villages, cities, and entire provinces as victims, provide the desired opportunity to issue new debt certificates, until finally the whole of humanity restlessly serves as the interest slave of the golden Internationale. Inevitably, we touch here upon the deeper roots of the World War.

We have risen far above our narrow national perspective with this vision. Therefore, we must also address the question of whether the idea of breaking the bondage of interest, which undoubtedly has international significance, can be implemented within the framework of our fatherland. This question must be unequivocally answered in the affirmative, if only based on the brief considerations we have outlined in these pages, and even more so because of the overwhelming necessity imposed by the circumstances we find ourselves in. Our financial situation is so fantastically bad that only a measure that at first glance appears fantastical can save us; with the planned means of our professional tax policy, we cannot make progress; we will only sink deeper and deeper into debt servitude and stumble into the laid golden snares of the Entente.

It is clear that, as a politically and militarily powerless people, we can do nothing against foreign interest claims at the moment. These interests must simply be paid until the force of our liberating example has shaken the peoples of the world and also prompted them to break the chains of the golden Internationale. I am well aware that the preceding pages do not exhaustively treat the problem; I primarily wanted to introduce the idea into the debate of opinions; nevertheless, I have tried to anchor the thought at least to the extent that it cannot be swept away in times of great upheavals on the basis of inherited views.

The enormous disparity between the fortunes of the billionaires and the incomes of millions of the working population, the knowledge that the damages of our capitalist economic order are much more to be charged to the account of big loan capital than to industrial big capital, the realization that our entire tax policy has been tailored solely to the benefit of loan capital and, given our current enormous indebtedness, must lead to a complete exhaustion of the people's labor force; finally, the realization that our interest, debt, and tax economy is a terrible money fraud, may well encourage serious reflection on breaking the bondage of interest.

Whoever further engages with the proposal should always keep both sides of the picture in mind; what appears as a loss or a deprivation on one side is relief, improvement, betterment on the other. The idea is certainly not conceived out of maudlin sentiments for those who have set up their lives for the comfortable consumption of their annual interest, although even these might always keep in mind that, despite it all, in such a solution to our financial troubles, a much wider protection of the middle and smaller property holdings is possible, while the plan that seems absolutely necessary to us would energetically focus on these property holders. And compared to the senseless upheaval of Russian economic life, the purposeful restructuring proposed here will appear to them as the lesser evil.

The idea is to form a united front of the entire working population, from the property-less worker who, as we have seen, is heavily burdened by the indirect tax burden for the purpose of satisfying the loan capitalists, through the entire bourgeois strata of officials and salaried employees, the peasantry and the small tradesman's middle class, all of whom, in the form of housing misery, land rents, bank interests, etc., feel the relentless dominion of money, right up to the leading minds, inventors, and directors of our great industries, all of whom, more or less, are in the claws of big loan capital, for whom the primary task is always: to generate rents, interest, and dividends for the monetary powers pulling the strings behind the scenes. No less important are all the groups in the intelligentsia: artists, writers, actors, scientists, as well as those in the liberal professions.

Whether big capital, consciously or instinctively, as a natural group of persons or as the personification of the principle of interest, seeks to conceal the fact of its unrestricted domination; whether our entire jurisprudence, derived from Roman law, and thus a law serving the interests of a plutocracy, places the protection of property in the foreground and thus ingrained this in the legal consciousness of our people—the breaking of the bondage of money interest must come as the only way out of the impending economic enslavement of the entire world by the golden Internationale, as one of the ways to expel the poison of mammon along with its stultification and contamination of the mentality of our age.

CHAPTER 3

THE SOCIAL STATE

First published in the weekly journal for education and law *"In Plain German,"* edited by Dietrich Eckart, 1st year, 14th and 15th issues from May 24, 1919.

The old state form has collapsed. What shall take its place? That is the most important problem for the future; for the democratic-parliamentary monstrosity in Weimar, which has no vitality, appears to have reached the end of its limit after the complete, merciless collapse of its international politics. The peace conditions of the Entente are the terrible wake-up call that dispels the socialist illusions and dreams. Where is the reconciliation peace of Mr. Scheidemann? Where is the economic peace of Mr. Erzberger—guaranteed to be ready in half an hour (!)? Where is the League of Nations, where is the world revolution of Mr. Eisner? Where is the workers' state in which production doubles—where is the higher morality—where is any reconstruction to be seen?

Weighed and found wanting—that is already the verdict of one's own people, of one's own contemporaries. History will curse and curse again the German revolutionaries who have betrayed their people, who with shortsighted megalomania first sucked the belief in victory and the will to win from the bones of the brave nation and then, with the cowardly courage of an assassin, stabbed the fleet in the back in its heaviest hour to seize a power they cannot use. For it is one thing to strike down a roaring giant from behind, to uproot a dynasty that has already become alien to the people, and to lift from its hinges a bureaucracy that has lost the living connection with the life of the people—and quite another thing to prove one's revolutionary strength when it comes to infusing new vital force into the mortally wounded people and preparing a new, vibrant state organism. Where is the revolutionary strength of the German revolutionaries? Where is the French, the English, the Italian revolution? Where remains the world revolution?—Nothing of all their promises—nothing have the Messrs. Ebert, Scheidemann, Erzberger, Eisner, Hoffmann, and whatever their names may be, been able to keep. Why? Because no new state idea guides them, because in the best case they imagine a class rule, or worse: a parliamentary compromise rule as the new state form, because they are so far removed from the true socialist state that they lack the courage to confront big capitalism, because they have not yet grasped at all what the deepest issue of the World War was about, namely: the final struggle of the international money powers, for their definitive world dominion.

We ask ourselves at best: What main shortcomings of the old state must we avoid? I list:

The irresponsible divine right of the crown, the fact that the army and navy as well as the higher bureaucracy were oriented towards the sovereign ruler. Furthermore, the utterly inadequate representation of the people in the parliaments, which, entirely entangled in disgusting party strife, had lost every sense of national interests, a Social Democracy that seemed to find its life's mission exclusively in inciting the working class against their employers. These were undoubtedly the most prominent shortcomings in the state life of our people before the collapse. Therefore, the most important task is to avoid these main shortcomings. The revolution has thoroughly cleared away with the misconceptions of the old state form: the irresponsible divine right, the exaggerated and distorted militarism and bureaucratism. But the much deeper flaw, the utterly hopeless parliamentarism, is in full bloom and prepares, unless all signs deceive, to come to terms with the capitalist powers. This would naturally annul the only profound meaning of the revolution, namely: the liberation of productive labor from international economic enslavement by the golden Internationale, and seal the economic subjugation of productive work under the interest slavery of the mammonistic powers.

Therefore, the new state must radically reject all principles of Western democracy. It must in particular fundamentally break with parliamentary party and clique machinations and must above all not mix up the political and economic representations of the people in one parliament, but must provide for the fundamental separation according to a bicameral system. Specifically, the House of the People (as the first chamber) represents the political interests of the entire nation, while the Central Council must represent the economic interests of the working population.

The most important thing for the reorganization is a completely different electoral system, built on new foundations, which shall be developed in the following.

The House of the People

The welfare of the people is the supreme law, the only guiding principle for the people's representation. It cannot be a matter of setting guidelines for the supreme leadership of the state; they are contained in the above principle.

More important is the form of election for the delegates, which must be built pyramidally on the broadest foundation and open the way for the best to rise to the next higher level.

In the new state, every person has the right to representation. The entirely arbitrary minimum age limit of twenty years is unjustified by anything, and therefore it must fall. On the other hand, not every person can act as a voter, although they have the right to representation.

A voter, therefore, is one who can demonstrate the legal or voluntarily assigned representation of at least 5, generally 10, persons. This representation mandate is territorially limited and valid only once at the place of the main residence, and each person can only appoint one other person for their representation. This shall be explained immediately with a practical example:

In a small town of about 6000 inhabitants, the list of voters is to be compiled. Then it is left to each individual person of the population to freely form groups of 5 to 10 persons according to their own judgment. The family will appoint the father, the mother, the grown son, or the eldest daughter as their representative, as a voter. Clerks and maids will form groups of 10 persons, designate the person who appears most suitable to them as a voter, and confirm this with their signatures. The voters thus determined in a municipality— about 600 voters out of 6000 inhabitants—assemble on certain days to elect from their midst the people's councils. This is done in such a way that groups of ten well-acquainted voters form, designating one from their midst as a people's councilor. For this actual election process, in contrast to the previous method of a single election day, an adequate period must be set so that those who come together in groups purely mechanically can get to know each other and discuss, in order to designate the person who appears most suitable to them from their midst. Such an election procedure has, first, the extraordinary advantage over any other general election system that it broadens the basis for the people's representation further than before and includes all natural persons, while significantly reducing the circle of actual voters by substantially restricting the honor of being a voter and excluding from the outset persons who, due to age, personal suitability, personal interest, or personal trustworthiness, do not qualify as actual voters.

The people's councilors designated by the voters are the first political instance. Each one of them represents 100 persons who have entrusted him with their confidence and to whom he is responsible, with whom he remains in close contact through the group of 10 voters.

It appears clear that in this way a very careful selection is made. There is little room for the machinations of ambitious politicians. The trust relationship between voters and elected is too close; this also significantly increases the sense of responsibility of the elected.

These people's councilors then assemble in district assemblies. They get to know each other there, join together again in groups of ten, and elect their district councilors. The district councilors, corresponding to the number of inhabitants of the territorially divided districts, form the local political people's representations. They have the right to control the governing bodies, district offices, etc., as well as the duty to report any found misconduct to the regional or governing councils. Conversely, they have the duty to inform the people's councilors of all politically significant measures and government decisions, in order to awaken political understanding and interest in the political life of the entire people among their voters. This district people's council, which may consist of 60-100 or more district councilors depending on the size of the district, thus represents 1000 persons per individual delegate, hence 60-100,000 or more inhabitants. At these district meetings, the district councilors get to know each other more closely. They again form groups of ten and designate one from their midst as a People's Government Councilor. The People's Government Councilors meet over longer periods in the district capitals. They have the duty to represent the political interests of their district and have analogous control rights over the government and district authorities. In an analogous manner, the People's Government Councilors, each of whom already represents 1000 voters, then elect, again in groups of ten, one delegate to the Council of People's Representatives. Each of these People's Representatives is thus the direct spokesperson and responsible representative of 100,000 individuals. Consequently, the Council of People's Representatives in Bavaria would consist of 67 members, corresponding to a population of 6.7 million. This Council of People's Representatives is the highest political authority. It passes laws and appoints, from its own ranks or at its discretion from outside its ranks, the People's President or Presidents vested with extraordinary powers, who represent the country both externally and internally.

This organic structure of the political representation of the people is by no means cumbersome. On the contrary, it is precisely through its natural, grounded form the true expression of a social community based on mutual trust. However, such an election process cannot be completed in a single day as before, following a dizzying election campaign. Slowly and steadily must the election and the construction of this new political penetration of the people take place. Many months will pass before the People's Councilors, District People's Councilors, and People's Government Councilors are elected. Election processes must nevertheless be timed. Ultimately, the Germans, despite their individualism, will be able to agree on one from their midst as their suitable representative.

It must be left to each individual reader to contemplate the very clear and simple structure of the proposal and to become clear about its advantages for themselves. Especially through comparison with the serious disadvantages of the existing election system. I do not want to claim that this proposal must necessarily lead to a selection of the most politically capable heads, but it certainly eliminates all hollow chatterers and political charlatans.

The Central Council

As the name suggests, it is the body that centrally deliberates on the economic interests of the country. In it, the work of the entire productive population finds its expression. In it sit the appointed expert representatives of employers and employees from all trades and professional groups. In it sit the delegates from the district 21.B.C. councils. It is thus a permanent body, not a political one, but the representation of economic interests.

In the Central Council, all classes must be represented, and indeed for each class, one representative of the employers and one of the employees. It does not come down to the number of votes here, but rather that each class can have its representative speak. The predominance of individual professional groups is to be prevented by the veto right of each individual Central Councilor. It is also not the task of the Central Council to issue fixed regulations for individual professional groups, even though it is authorized to do so. The primary task is a comprehensive consolidation of the entire production, control of this production, determination of the needs, and, based on this, regulation of production and its distribution based on the insights gained. Hand in hand with this, a comprehensive labor organization and labor assignment must be ensured. Collective bargaining agreements as well as decisions in all tariff matters also lie within the purview of the Central Council.

The Central Council has emerged from the district N.B.C. councils, which in turn have emerged from the workers',

1) A collective term for various types of councils. farmers', works', specialist's, etc., councils of the various group operations, classes, etc.

Here too, it is advisable for simplification if not every single individual votes, but the mandate holders of at least five professional groups act as the actual voters.

Numerically, this results approximately in the following picture for Bavaria.

In 1907, there were 3,279,914 gainfully employed persons:

Sector	Men	Women
Agriculture & Forestry	324,918	973,030
Industry including Mining & Construction	804,837	215,366
Trade & Transportation including Hospitality & Related Services	421,281	145,900
Public Services & Freelance Professions	145,047	36,324
Casual & Irregular Wage Labor	10,569	26,642

We would thus initially have approximately 600,000 voters who elect their workers', farmers', civil servants', industrial, craftsmen, trade, etc. councils for their district. These districts are grouped around larger cities and municipalities, insofar as they are economic centers of the respective regions. If we assume approximately 60 such economic centers in Bavaria, there would be about 6000 district 21.B.C. councils to be elected. In individual districts, for example in rural districts, fewer occupational groups are present, which naturally reduces this number. These district councils meet in the district cities. There, they do not unite numerically but according to their professions and each designate one representative to the district 2.B.C. council. The district 2.B.C. councils in turn convene in the state capital to elect the Central Council, in which each profession, each class groups itself professionally and appoints one representative to the Central Council. Thus, the Central Council is elected on a similar basis as proposed for the People's Representatives.

The central council is, as should be repeatedly emphasized, the expression of the working community of the entire people. Only the best should have a seat and voice in it. Every profession, every class should be represented. The closest cooperation should have an educational effect in the best sense, in a social sense, meaning that it is not about representing special interests for individual occupational groups, but rather about the best integration into the whole. These are the general principles for the structure of this council system and its anchoring in the constitution.

I believe that these general guidelines for the new state constitution leave no doubt that the proposed bicameral system has nothing to do with the parliamentarian-ism of Western democracies, which I consider our greatest misfortune. The house of the people is the image of political life; the central council is the public expression of the work of the entire people. In both chambers, only the best of the various population groups, only the most proven of the individual professional classes, should have a voice.

I would like to conclude with an image that particularly should show that in every state structure, it is not actually about a building, but about a tree, about a lively organic entity. The usual comparisons from the realm of trees, which have become customary in our way of expressing ourselves when we concern ourselves with the reconstruction of our state, are quite misleading; for although ultimately all comparisons are more or less imperfect, the usual comparison of a people's constitution with a building overlooks the most essential point of comparison, namely, that a people is an organism and a building is a dead construction.

This consideration becomes very clear when one compares the popular image of the field of ruins that we must now rebuild with the collapsed house that one is supposed to rebuild. 2015 from demolition materials one cannot rebuild the house from scratch. On the other hand, even a severely damaged tree, even if large parts have been taken from it, even if some roots have been cut off, can come back to life. But it must renew itself from its own internal life force, both in the case of the tree and in the case of a people. Not from the outside and not with artificial constructions can a sick organism be healed; the healing must come from within. The task of the new statecraft must be to find the conditions for an organic renewal in a new constitution that guarantees every individual member of the people the fullest development of their personality within the framework of the national community, based on the clear recognition that this fullest development of personality in the aristocratic sense finds its natural organic limit in the higher interests of the social national community.

CHAPTER 4

THE MANIFESTO FOR THE BREAKING OF INTEREST SLAVERY OF MONEY

First printed in 1919, Joseph C. Huber Verlag, Diessen near Munich.

Mammonism is the severe, all-encompassing and overwhelming disease from which our modern world of culture, indeed all of humanity, suffers. It is like a devastating plague, like a consuming poison that has seized the peoples of the world.

Mammonism can be understood as:

Firstly, the international money powers, the supranational financial authority that reigns above all selfdetermination rights of the peoples, international big capital, the so-called golden International; Secondly, a state of mind that has taken hold of vast sections of the people; the insatiable greed for profit, the purely materialistic outlook on life, which has already led to a frightening decay of all moral concepts and must continue to lead there.

This state of mind is embodied and driven to its peak in the international plutocracy.

The main source of power of Mammonism is the effortless and endless inflow of goods created by interest. From the thoroughly immoral idea of loan interest, the golden International was born. The spiritual and moral condition born from the greed for interest and profit of every kind has led to the alarming degeneration of a portion of the bourgeoisie.

Loan interest is the devilish invention of big loan capital. Loan interest alone makes possible the idle drone-like existence of a minority of moneyed elites at the expense of the productive peoples and their labor power. It has led to the deep, insurmountable contradictions, to class hatred, from which civil war and fratricidal war are born.

There is only one universal remedy. The radical remedy for the healing of suffering humanity is the breaking of the interest-slavery of money.

The breaking of the interest-slavery of money means the only possible and definitive liberation of productive labor from the secret supranational money powers.

The breaking of interest-slavery means the restoration of free personality, the redemption of man from enslavement, from the spell under which his soul has been entangled by Mammonism. Whoever wants to fight capitalism must break the interest-slavery.

Where must the breaking of interest-slavery begin? With loan capital!

Why?

Because loan capital is so overwhelmingly powerful compared to all industrial big capital that the big money powers can only be effectively combated by breaking the interest-slavery of loan capital. The ratio of loan capital to industrial big capital is 20:1. Over 12 billion in interest for loan capital must be paid annually by the German people in the form of direct and indirect taxes, rent, and cost of living increases, while even in the high-conjuncture years of the war the total sum of all dividends paid out by German joint-stock companies amounted to only 1 billion.

Beyond all human comprehension is the avalanche-like growth of loan capital through the effortless and endless inflow of goods from interest and compound interest.

What blessings then does the breaking of interest-slavery bring to the working people of Germany, to the proletarians of all countries of the earth?

The breaking of interest-slavery gives us the possibility to pursue the abolition of all direct and indirect taxes. It concerns you, the value-creating people of all countries, all states and continents. All state revenues flowing from direct and indirect sources flow relentlessly into the pockets of big loan capital.

The revenues of the productive state enterprises, such as the postal service, telegraph, telephone, railways, mines, forests, etc., are completely sufficient to cover all necessary state tasks for education, justice, administration, and social welfare.

As long as: all true socialism will bring its blessings to humanity only as long as the revenues from communal enterprises remain tributary to big loan capital.

Therefore, we first demand as a basic state law for the German people, and then as a basic law for all those brother peoples who wish to join us in the cultural community of a league of nations, the following:

§ 1. The war bonds as well as all other debt instruments of the German Reich and all other debt instruments of the German federal states, especially railway bonds, as well as the debt securities of all self-governing bodies, shall be declared legal tender at their nominal value by abolishing the obligation to pay interest. They shall be converted into bank deposits.

§ 2. For all other fixed-interest securities, mortgage bonds, industrial bonds, mortgages, etc., the obligation to pay interest shall be replaced by the obligation to repay; after 20 or 25 years, depending on the level of interest, the borrowed capital shall be repaid and the debt extinguished.

§ 3. All real estate debts, mortgages, etc., shall be repaid in installments according to the encumbrances entered in the land register as before. The real estate thus freed from debt shall become partly the property of the state or the self-governing body. In this way, the state will be in a position to determine and reduce rent prices.

§ 4. The entire monetary system shall be under the control of the central state administration. All private banks, as well as the postal savings banks, savings banks, and credit cooperatives, shall be incorporated as branch operations.

§ 5. All real estate credit shall only be granted by the state bank. Personal and petty credit shall be left to private bankers by state concession. This concession shall be granted with consideration of needs and with prohibition of establishing branches in certain districts. The fee structure shall be set by the state.

§ 6. The dividend-bearing securities shall be amortized in annual installments of 5%, similar to the fixed-interest securities. The surplus profits shall be partly distributed as compensation for *"risky"* capital (in contrast to the fixed-interest and safe securities) to the shareholders, while the remaining surplus shall either be socially distributed or used to reduce the prices of products.

§ 7. For all persons who, due to physical reasons (old age, sickness, physical or mental incapacity to work, extreme youth), are unable to earn their living, the current, and possibly even increased, interest incomes from existing capital assets shall continue to be paid as annuities against the surrender of the securities.

§ 8. In the interest of reducing the existing inflation of means of payment, a general, strongly graduated property levy shall be imposed, which shall be paid in war bonds or other debt instruments of the Reich or the states. These securities shall be stamped out.

§ 9. Through intensive popular education, the people must be made aware that money is and must be nothing other than a token of performed labor: that while a highly developed economy needs money as a means of exchange, this also fulfills the function of money, and that money must not be given any supernatural power to grow by itself at the expense of productive labor.

Why then have we not yet achieved all this, which is so self-evident, which one must call the egg of Columbus for the social question?

Because in our mammonistic blindness, we have lost the ability to see clearly that the doctrine of the sanctity of interest is a monstrous self-deception, that the gospel of the all-saving loan interest has entangled our entire thinking in the golden nets of the international plutocracy. Because we have forgotten and are deliberately kept in the dark by the all-powerful money powers (with the exception of a few money magnates) that the so-called beautiful and beloved interest is completely consumed by taxes. Our entire tax legislation is and remains, as long as we do not have the liberation from the bondage of interest, only a tributary obligation to big capital, and not, as we sometimes imagine, a voluntary sacrifice for the realization of communal work.

Therefore, the liberation from the interest bondage of money is the flat solution for the true world revolution: for the liberation of the working labor from the shackles of the supranational money dictatorship.

§ 1. It is absolutely indispensable that all state and municipal debt securities are treated in the same manner, as only in this way can a unified and comprehensive regulation of our entire monetary system be carried out in conjunction with the breaking of the interest bondage.

§ 2. That the breaking of the interest bondage must simultaneously be applied to all other fixed-interest securities is already clear because an absurd rush into the void of these securities must not be brought about; this would, of course, occur if only state securities were declared interest-free. The transfer of the debt as such would be accomplished through annual repayments, thereby bringing about a steady and uniform reduction of debt for all encumbered objects.

§ 3. This paragraph is in the closest connection with the preceding ones, just as with the nationalization of real estate credit demanded in § 5. The farmer or homeowner encumbered with mortgages continues to pay the same amount he previously had to pay to the creditor, but no longer as eternal interest, but as repayment. After 20, 25, or 30 years, depending on the level of the previous interest rate, the property and house holdings will be debt-free in this manner. During this time, the mortgage bank, of course, can similarly continue to pay the corresponding mortgage bond interest to the bondholders. Concurrently with this debt reduction, a community property right to the freed real estate holdings will arise.

A general building and real estate register would have to be prepared in advance, because even debt-free real estate holdings naturally have the right to repay the invested capital as well as a lasting claim to the portion of the rent used to cover all costs associated with real estate holdings, expenses, etc., and to corresponding compensation for personal exertion.

§ 4 and §5. These paragraphs demand the socialization of the entire monetary system. Money is a unit exclusively issued by a state community, representing performed labor. Issuing currency is one of the sovereign fundamental rights of the state. The forgery of state currency is subject to the severest penalties. Therefore, it is an absolutely compelling social demand to place the monetary system under the control of the community. The labor performed by the community is the only substrate of the currency, and only the neglect of this fundamental fact has led to the mismanagement of our public finances and to the complete anarchy of the monetary system.

With the proposed transfer of personal and small credit to private bankers in § 5, a deep incision into the entire credit system is made. For the state credit system as well as for the communal one, and also for real estate credit, the breaking of the interest bondage must be upheld with utmost determination and consistency, because it is the indispensable prerequisite for the social state as a whole.

The situation is different with personal credit. In and of itself, we also demand interest-free conditions for personal credit, but this demand does not carry the same immense and principled significance. We are reminded of the 250 billion in fixed-interest loan capital compared to only 12 billion in dividend-bearing securities. All such credits, shares, participation certificates, stakes, participations, etc., are risk-bearing capital. The income from this capital depends on the diligence and capability of the persons to whom the money has been entrusted. Here, therefore, the element of risk, the possibility of loss, as well as personal trust, comes into question. For this reason, a certain compensation of a special nature remains indispensable. The owner of shares, etc., receives no compensation or profit if the enterprise to which they have entrusted their money earns nothing. They lose their money entirely if the enterprise collapses. This is different, for example, with the holder of debt securities of the Reich railways. The Reich railways of Alsace-Lorraine are completely lost with their loss. Nevertheless, the holder of railway bonds continues to receive their interest. From whom? From the taxes of the community. The railways may operate with even greater deficits, as in Prussia and Bavaria last year, yet the bondholders still receive their interest. From whom? From the tribute of labor power and the consumption of the working population.

One should only thoroughly grasp this fundamental difference—in order to finally recognize where the vampire sucks at the labor power of the people. Thus, personal credit should be left to the personal handling of private banks or again be directed towards them. The personal competence of the credit seeker, which the banker personally knows, should once again become decisive for personal credit. The fees set by the state will naturally regulate themselves through the liquidity that will inevitably arise from the breaking of the interest bondage.

On § 6. What is said in principle in § 5 also applies to dividend-bearing securities in particular. In the interest of the social state community, it must be demanded, however, that even for large industrial enterprises, a repayment of the once-loaned capital is aimed for—in order to also bring about a reduction of indebtedness of individual industrial assets compared to those who are merely money providers. For in fact, this repeats on a smaller scale what we could observe with large loan capital in relation to entire nations. Here too, the capitalist exploits the worker, the master craftsman, the engineer, the entrepreneur, all equally, because first comes the compulsion to have to earn dividends. But if we look at the state of industrial and commercial enterprises liberated from the eternal interest sucker, then and only then is the way open to the reduction of prices, the products, the production, and the distribution of the surplus value, partly to the community, partly to the workers and officials, and to the directorate of the individual enterprises—thus to those who truly alone produce and distribute goods.

On § 7. In this paragraph, the entire field of insurance naturally also comes into play, which can be analogously built on an interest-free basis. The premiums paid cannot grow through the accrual of interest, but insurance companies become savings banks, meaning the insurance risk and the insurance benefit remain. For this, the state community must step in.

Never has an idea been able to prevail without contradiction, least of all an idea that breaks so radically with the traditional views of the sanctity and inviolability of interest. In the objections raised and to be expected, one must always observe three things. First, one must examine: What is deliberate distortion of the idea of breaking the interest bondage in the objections made? Second: what is to be answered to all honest and professional concerns?

The most frequent objection is the claim: No one will lend their money without interest.

We no longer want anyone to lend their money. Credit was the trick, the trap into which our economy fell, and in which it is now helplessly entangled.—If the people truly urgently need more capital, they take, interest-free, only against repayment from the central state treasury the needed funds, possibly issuing new banknotes.—Why then should they issue interest-bearing certificates?! Whether interest-bearing or non-interest-bearing paper—it makes no difference! Behind it stands solely and exclusively the labor power, the tax power of the people. Why burden every state expenditure from the outset with the lead weight of eternal interest?!

Yes, but how is the state to fulfill its cultural tasks for the general public? It must have money and can only fulfill this task by borrowing against interest compensation.

This assertion is based on an exclusively mammonistic line of thought. It is, upon thorough reading of the manifesto, deliberately calculated to mislead. For, firstly, we have proven that all cultural and social tasks of the state can be entirely covered by the proceeds from postal services, railways, mining, forestry, etc., after the breaking of the interest bondage. Secondly, the sovereign state has always had the means, by issuing non-interest-bearing securities in place of the interest-bearing securities declared the standard in the mammonistic state, to provide for special cultural tasks. There is absolutely no reason to understand why the state should unnecessarily burden itself with specific cultural tasks, for instance, railway, canal, and water power constructions, through a perpetual promise of interest. If it cannot pay the construction costs, etc., from the current funds of its profit-making state enterprises, then there is no reason to see why the state should not create the money; the sovereign people must indeed step up for it by recognizing this money as a means of payment.—But why should the people, with their entire labor and tax power, stand behind another piece of paper (the interest-bearing bond), which imposes an eternal interest obligation on the people as a whole in favor of the capitalist?! So away with this coercive notion from the mammonistic state!

Then, the capitalists will simply absorb the issued paper certificates and hoard paper money.

Against this, two things speak. First, the demand that mere possession of money should be unproductive would already be fulfilled voluntarily by the capitalists themselves by breaking the bondage of interest; for if the capitalist hoards his paper certificates at home, he voluntarily renounces interest. Second, there is the capitalist's anxiety about his money. One only needs to imagine the sleepless nights of the paper-money hoarder, who holds large sums of money at home and must constantly see his property threatened by thieves, robbers, burglars, house infestations, fire, and water damage. I am convinced that the honest man would not long withstand these torments and would soon find his way to the state bank. The state bank issues a deposit slip and now guarantees the existence of the money, but not for any interest. Furthermore, every individual always has a third option open to them: namely, to work with their money, create values and goods, participate in industrial enterprises, shape their life ever richer and more beautiful, support art and science, in short, to turn away from the cult of mammon and put their money to productive use.

However, it is possible that for certain purposes, a pressing private capital need may arise, for example, for testing inventions, founding businesses by young, skilled craftsmen, businesspeople, etc.

First of all, this has nothing at all to do with the breaking of the bondage of interest! For first, one must logically assume that the capitalist, who after the breaking of the interest bondage no longer has the opportunity to invest his money bombproof and speculate on lazy interest gains, will be much more inclined than before to invest his money for such purposes, so that a lack or need in this direction will occur much less than before. Or have we not heard exactly the opposite complaint from the most capable businesspeople, the cleverest inventors, about how hard it is to obtain money in the mammonistic state for such purposes if a *"profit"* cannot be guaranteed? Second, it must be the task of the coming state to support every capable force with generous assistance. For this too, in the old civil service state, initial approaches existed, but so narrow minded that in most cases, through the chicanous conditions associated with the granting of state assistance, instead of a promotion, a hindrance and frustration resulted. Third, it should be noted that with the provision of several millions, an enormous amount could be achieved. The work enthusiasm, diligence, and ability of the German inventor, engineer, craftsman, etc. are so great that by the state's participation rights in the results of successful inventions, the expenditures made would most likely be abundantly recovered. (England as an example.)

The breaking of the interest bondage leads necessarily to the consumption of wealth.

Whoever has set up his life on the consumption of his capital gains and cannot decide to work, in his case, this is certainly true; he will in 20 years, with an annual consumption of 5%, be completely finished with his wealth. This, however, is entirely in order! We precisely want the breaking of the bondage of interest, we want the renter to cease to be the highest ideal for the state citizen.—We want to end with this mammonistic decay, we no longer want to tolerate that one, that many live permanently comfortably only from their loan interest, that means: at the expense of others.

But it is not true that the breaking of the bondage of interest necessarily leads to the dissolving and consumption of wealth. On the contrary. The breaking of the bondage of interest promotes wealth formation on the basis of creative, goods-producing work, freed and unburdened by eternal interest payments. The breaking of the bondage of interest leads to a thorough reduction in the cost of living, it relieves us of the excessive tax pressure, so that for every working person in the future, the possibility of making savings must be greater than before. The value—and goods creating national economic work of industry, trade, and commerce will in no way be hindered by the breaking of the bondage of interest, but rather will indeed be promoted.

What does the worker gain if the capitalists no longer receive interest?

This question should not have even been asked! Firstly, it was indeed the constant battle cry of the working class that the capitalists exploit the workers; secondly, it is precisely the worker who, through indirect taxes, is burdened in a significant way to pay the loan interest.

Family bonds are weakened and torn apart when one cannot leave any wealth to their children.

Generally, I believe that money has little or nothing to do with family ties. Who has heard that the children of wealthy people are more attached to their parents than those of the poor? Or that rich parents love their children more than the less affluent? What is more important for the children: that their parents provide them with the best possible education, teach them useful skills, and raise them to be diligent, healthy, and courageous individuals, or that they leave them the largest possible inheritance? In particular, there will undoubtedly be a justified desire to secure the children's future financially.

This desire, namely the parents' inclination to save for their children, will in no way be adversely affected by the breaking of the interest bondage. On the contrary. The possibility of savings will increase once our national economy is freed from the all-encompassing pressure of the interest-bondage. I cannot repeat it often enough: The loan interest of small and medium-sized assets is a fraud, a self-deception, a spinning in circles, because all medium and small assets are actually robbed of any benefit through direct and indirect taxes, mortgage interest, etc. Through its subservient press, big loan capital has devilishly spread and corrupted the belief in the sanctity and inviolability of interest throughout the world. It allows everyone to seemingly participate in the beautiful, intoxicating enjoyment of interest, in order to lull the bad conscience that is inevitably connected with idle, laborless interest enjoyment, in order to gain comrades in arms when it comes to defending this supreme good of Mammonism.

The civil servant, the statesman, will say: The state cannot release itself from the obligations it has once entered into towards its creditors.

What does that mean: obligations? Is it perhaps moral to enter into obligations of which the state must know in advance that it can only fulfill these obligations if it takes the interest back from the creditors through taxes, directly and indirectly? Where does morality remain in this?! Or is it not perhaps more honest to admit: I can only pay the interest if I collect just as many taxes—But I had to have the money during the war at any cost, and that's why I made the fraud with the war bonds. Sorry, dear people, it was ultimately for you, and now we want to no longer pretend, I, the state, pay no interest, and you, the taxpayer, need not pay taxes for the interest, which simplifies our business significantly. We save the enormous tax apparatus and also the extraordinary interest service apparatus. Agreed? And you, Mr. Scheidemann, next time do not sign your name as state secretary of the old compromised government under the silly declarations regarding the safety and inviolability of war bonds on every pillar. You only compromise yourselves. The responsibility for the whole fraud lies solely with big loan capital.

The financial politician and banking expert will declare the breaking of the interest bondage of war bonds and state debts as impossible, as it would be equivalent to state bankruptcy.

Forgive me—state bankruptcy we are already heading towards or must become according to your speeches. An official declaration of state bankruptcy, however, would be the greatest stupidity we could commit; it would not only confirm the actual incapability of the current rulers but also hasten the historical confirmation of this incapability.

Why declare bankruptcy when I just shifted three marks from my right pocket to the left? I have no cause to declare my right pocket bankrupt!

And indeed, it was not so with the war bonds! The Reich initially took the first real billions from the people's pockets; then the funds flowed back; thereupon came the new loans, and again the money poured back; once more the drum was beaten, and the billions were sucked in, and they ebbed back, until fortunately, after repeating this game nine times, the state had amassed 100 billion in debts. For that, the Reich had 100 billion beautifully printed pieces of paper in circulation. The public fooled itself into believing it had become so much richer, then the state came and said: *"It's terrible, I have 100 billion in debts and am facing bankruptcy."*—But why? That's just a deception with money! I myself can never go bankrupt, no matter how often I shift my money from one pocket to the other. So we can rest assured about state bankruptcy concerning our internal war debt. Therefore, we really don't need to declare state bankruptcy, and we can spare ourselves the gigantic effort with the stupid interest payments and the large, but even more foolish taxes. Let us finally free ourselves from worrying about the business of big loan capital! Only big loan capital benefits from this interest-tax fraud, as it keeps a handsome surplus, and this surplus is paid by the working people in the form of indirect taxes; the small and medium capitalists, however, simply spin around in circles.

The global economic politician says: The breaking of the interest bondage cannot be carried out in Germany alone; it must be done internationally, otherwise we will lose all credit, the capital will flow abroad, and we will have to meet our interest obligations to foreign countries.

This question is the most difficult because it places us in a reciprocal relationship with the rest of the world. However, the issue has two sides. On the one hand, the idea of breaking the interest bondage is the battle cry of all working peoples against the international interest bondage of money, and on the other hand, it is the radical solution for our internal financial misery. But there is actually no reason to refrain from using a remedy just because the equally sick neighbor does not apply it simultaneously. It would indeed be the epitome of stupidity if we in Germany continued to spin in the same insane circle and pay taxes and interest where we have clearly recognized that this absurd activity benefits solely the big capitalists. Let us take the lead with our liberating example, let us free ourselves from the interest bondage of money, and we will soon see that the power of this victorious, liberating idea will prompt the peoples of the world to follow us. I am even convinced that our beginning if this beginning is not suppressed by the German Mammonists—will irresistibly sweep the other peoples along with it.

The Spartakist says: The whole idea only amounts to sparing capital; it remains as it was: the poor have nothing, and the rich stay rich.

Yes, my friend, it is indeed very difficult to debate with you if you are truly a communist at heart, meaning you genuinely desire that *"everything should belong to everyone,"* and if you even understand and approve of the ideas of the great Bolshevik leaders in Russia, especially Lenin, thus considering what Lenin identified as the immediate tasks of the Soviet republic as *"universal accounting and control of the entire production and distribution"* to be humanly possible. If you are also entirely clear that this task, if possible at all, can only be carried out in the most appalling police state, and you still remain in your deepest heart a convinced communist, then we won't argue further, then we simply don't understand each other, we speak different languages, and the future will decide where salvation lies, whether in the coercive labor state, which can ultimately only emerge from the Bolshevik chaos, or in the new state I hope for, with an economy freed from the interest bondage. But if, at the core of your communist soul—if you are honest—you still harbor thoughts and longings for a wife and child, for a human soul closer to you than an Eskimo or a Buddha water seller, if, when carrying out factory work ordered by the Soviet leader, you think it would be nice to own your own little house, a piece of garden land, if, in the deepest depths of your soul, it gives you no real satisfaction that you are entitled to use any woman who happens to cross your path, like a dog on the street; if you only think of saving part of your wages to belong solely to you: then you are no longer a communist, then you have already broken in your heart with your loudly proclaimed slogan: *"Everything belongs to everyone,"* then you don't want everything to belong to everyone, you want what you desire—a wife, a child, a house, a garden, savings, whether you already have it or hope to get it—to belong solely to you. And you see, my friend, if deep down you doubt that it wouldn't be entirely indifferent to you if the next person came and simply took away your savings in the name of *"everything,"* brought you a different child and took yours with them, because all children *"belong to everyone"*: then, my friend, we are no longer talking past each other completely, then I may well ask you to consider the thought: whether the communist message that *"everything should belong to everyone"* must not signify the end of all culture, whether the absence of any concept of property must not, with compelling logic, reduce humanity to the level of animals.

For if everything belongs to everyone, if in the best case a control and accounting of the entire public production and distribution in the sense of Lenin could be enforced, then at best a massive state emerges. Then we can also dispense with language, surrender our soul, our thoughts, and perform our factory work silently and instinctively. The end of man is here.

But now enough, friend Spartacus. Let this fundamental consideration pass thoroughly through your head and heart! A more precise answer to your question will emerge during the conversation with the other parties.

And now, comrades of the two socialist factions, Moderates and Independents!

I cannot imagine that from your side any serious contradictions or objections to the breaking of the interest bondage could arise, and yet I must fundamentally engage with you, with the entire socialist intellectual world, from Marx onwards up to the current leaders Ebert, Scheidemann, Kautsky, etc.

1. The socialist will: the elevation of the working class is an absolutely victorious idea; so far we are in agreement.
2. The paths taken to achieve this great goal are almost entirely wrong because they
3. are built on false premises.
4. The socialist state idea inevitably leads to communism, and thus to decline.
5. But if Social Democracy has a different goal, namely the elevation of the working class and the entire working people, then it now stands before a frightful internal contradiction: the logical consequences of Marxism lead directly to the opposite of what the practical goal of the labor movement is.
6. From this internal confusion arises the public uncertainty in the leadership of the government.
7. Against Spartacus and Bolshevik communism, a sharp line must be drawn due to the great practical goal(the elevation of the working class), and their methods must be combated with all force. However, the labor organized Social Democracy feels weak in facing these radical groups today because it has adopted Marxist ways of thinking as its educational principle, and because logically all Marxist thought leads to communism.

Now, the proof by example shows that the paths taken by Social Democracy are almost entirely wrong.

The generally carried-out movement has led to a deep division of the population within our own nation; the constant slanders against employers of all kinds, indeed against every bourgeois profession as exploiters and bloodsuckers of the supposedly sole working proletarian have led to an unjustified embitterment and also to the arrogance of the working class, which logically finds its expression in the demand for the *"Dictatorship of the Proletariat"* (Communist Manifesto). The most essential demand of the Erfurt Program—the transfer of the means of production from private ownership into the ownership and operation of the community—has today condensed into the cry for "*Socialization.*"

That full socialization means our economic downfall, complete state bankruptcy, is completely clear to every honest politician. But one does not dare to confess this openly and freely to the people.

Not Socialization, but de-socialization should now be the solution. Thus, one tries to compensate for the obvious failures of every socialization through fantastic tax projects and on this path to expropriate the expropriators a second time. All this, however, means nothing other than abandoning the entire national economy to inevitable ruin. Instead of an increase (a doubling of production, as promised by all socialist literature for the post-revolution period, is completely out of the question), the exact opposite has occurred. The situation would become even worse if the current socialist-labor government were to consider taking up large foreign loans. Not only would that seal our economic decline, but we would also be completely helplessly delivered into the interest-based bondage of the Entente, from which there would be no return.

The fundamental error, the basic fallacy upon which this whole series of conclusions, demands, and promises to the people is built, is the false attitude toward industrial and loan capital. The Communist Manifesto, the Erfurt Program, Marx, Engels, Lassalle, Kautsky—they all failed to recognize the profound difference between industrial capital and loan capital.

On this point, the entire Social Democracy must re-educate itself; this basic error must be clearly recognized and openly admitted without euphemisms. Then, however, the only possible conclusions must be drawn relentlessly. These conclusions mean a radical departure from the senseless, since utterly wrong, struggles against industry, against the employer class; workers and employers belong together, they share the same goal: work, production, for without production, without work, there is no life, no culture, no progress, and no ascent. The obvious, because among humans—precisely because they are humans—inevitable conflicts are far less important than the common great interest of employer and employee. These conflicts can and could be resolved within the framework of collective agreements and workplace organization to the mutual satisfaction of both parties.

Yet these issues, which are incidental within the scope of our consideration of the major political power dynamics, we shall not pursue further, and only reiterate that the interest of the entire workforce is precisely aligned with our national industry, with our national economy.

Anyone who teaches otherwise and places the conflicts between employer and employee in the foreground commits an irresponsible offense precisely against the workers, for with this attitude they strike at the very roots of the tree that nourishes and supports the working class.

This is what Social Democracy has done, and with this it has incurred guilt toward the German working class, with this it has brought nameless misery upon our people, because it cannot keep its promises, because it cannot bring us the peace of understanding, because it cannot create work for us, because it must once again build up an armed force, because it cannot do without the civil service, because it must demand compulsory labor, because no human being can live on the general, equal, and direct right to vote for men and women over 20 years of age, because without a state-guaranteed security of person and property, chaotic conditions would inevitably arise, because without the integration and subordination of the individual into society, no state life is possible.

Thus, a deep, desperate wave of disillusionment sweeps through the entire nation, and while individuals may not yet be fully aware of it, ministers, delegates, and people's representatives continue to lie to each other with apparent joviality, claiming that the *"achievements of the revolution"* must be protected from the *"reaction"*; both concepts about which no honest statesman could clearly tell the people what exactly they are supposed to mean.

The negative activities of the revolution—the removal of a series of outdated monarchies, the dismissal of officers, the abolition of titles, the dissolution of the navy—until now, the great *"breakthrough"* is no *"achievement."* And reaction?! The moribund divine right removed nowhere in the entire people has enough moral backing to lead to any forceful action; the bourgeoisie, insofar as it concerns the real bourgeois, is far too cowardly, far too morally decayed, to rouse itself against the self-conscious working class; thus, neither a monarchist nor a bourgeois reaction should trouble the ruling class of workers.

But the deep disappointment of the people regarding the so-called achievements of the revolution, that is, the absence of any real improvement in the situation of the people, is the great danger; this disappointment leads to the shifting of large masses increasingly to the left, where promises of what has already been offered seem modest by comparison.

Ultimately, one cannot promise more than *"everything to all."* And that is pure madness; but every thought, every phenomenon, every activity, when overstretched and exaggerated to the extreme, eventually becomes madness and then turns into its opposite. So it goes also with the communist idea that *"everything should belong to all,"* for this idea ends and finally leads to the point where all—have nothing. Misery, despair, poverty, madness, and need have taken hold in Russia; people have lost the last remnants of courage and joy for life.

I repeat: The enormous fundamental error in socialist thought ultimately stems from the failure to recognize the profound difference between industrial capital and loan capital. The interest-bearing loan capital is the scourge of humanity; the eternal, painstaking, and endless growth of large loan capital leads to the exploitation of nations, not the productive, goods-generating industrial capital.

I cannot bypass the investigation of why this fundamental difference has not been recognized: whether it truly has not been recognized, or whether it might have been obscured in favor of big capital; whether the leaders and advocates in the struggle against capitalism, the authors of the Communist Manifesto and the Erfurt Program, the leaders of all time, have always proceeded with the necessary integrity.

It is the most serious and painful thing to cast doubt on the absolute honesty and conviction of another; it becomes even more difficult the more carefully one examines the phenomena of life in search of reasons and connections. I therefore do not wish to provide an answer to these questions myself, but merely point to the great, obscure connections, referring to a statement by Disraeli, the great English Prime Minister Lord Beaconsfield.

In his novel *"Endymion,"* he writes:

"No one may treat the principle of race, the question of race, indifferently. It is the key to world history. And it is precisely for this reason that history is often so confused, because it has been written by people who were unaware of the racial question and its associated elements."

The Citizen: Breaking the bondage of interest destroys the spirit of saving, and man ends up in the poorhouse.

That breaking the bondage of interest would have a general influence on the spirit of saving must be decisively denied. The spirit of saving, just like wastefulness, has nothing to do with prevailing economic views. The spirit of saving and the tendency to waste are human traits that either exist or are absent, regardless of whether an era preaches the concept of interest or condemns it.

During periods of transition, an increase or decrease in the spirit of saving may indeed be observed. However, in this specific case, I tend to believe that a sensible, economically inclined person will say to themselves: In the future, I can no longer count on living solely from my interest. Yet, I want to live in my later years and still leave something for my children; therefore, I must save more now. This effect, in my opinion, is what breaking the bondage of interest will have on the majority of people, as otherwise, they would be dependent on public support in their old age. I must also emphasize once again that under the current burden of property through direct taxes and the cost of living through indirect taxes, nothing remains of the fine interest earnings—except when, and this is the unjust and reprehensible part, the entire income flows solely from perpetual capital returns. Consequently, a decline in the spirit of saving is not to be feared. Is (the detestable) big capital really so entirely unproductive? Has it not also provided the means for magnificent progress, yielding greater fruits for humanity than the interest from loan capital?

The question itself proves only that mammonist phraseology has clouded the clear vision here.

Big capital has not provided the means for magnificent progress; rather, big capital has grown out of labor. All capital is stored-up labor. Big capital is inherently unproductive, as money itself is a completely sterile thing. It is through intellect, labor, and existing and already produced raw materials or mineral resources that values are created, goods are produced, through labor and only through labor.

No matter how much money one pours into the most fertile soil or the richest coal mine, the soil does not yield grain, nor does the mine spontaneously spew out coal.

If human beings invented money, it is very meaningful and sensible; for in any complex economy, this (universally recognized) *"token of performed labor"* is needed. But that such an *"abstract symbol of value"* should possess the power to eternally grow into the colossal—and this is what money does when it bears interest—that is what our inner being revolts against, that is what elevates money far above all other earthly phenomena, that is what transforms money into an idol. And all of this is nothing but the most monstrous financial fraud of humanity! Money itself is utterly powerless. A table, a cabinet, clothing, a house, tools— everything around us has some value; even the oldest table can eventually be burned for warmth, but with a twenty-mark note, I can do nothing, not even wrap a piece of bread in it. Only after people have sensibly agreed to facilitate the exchange of goods by issuing acknowledgments for performed labor does this piece of paper gain meaning and purpose, and it is very reasonable that the farmer does not receive a coal cart for his barley but money instead, that is, a claim to other performed labor, such as plows, utensils, seed, and geese. But with that, the power of money should be at an end.

So it is not money that has brought about the magnificent progress of humanity; rather, it is the people themselves who have done it, their bold spirit, their proud courage, their clever ingenuity, the strength of their hands, their collective, thus social, diligent labor. This we must see clearly and proudly. It was the people themselves, not the pitiful little pieces of paper that humans invented to simplify the economy.

The breaking of the bondage of interest, however, is not the ultimate goal of the new statecraft; it is indeed the most decisive act, the only act that can unite all peoples into a true alliance against the all-encompassing tyranny of mammonism. But it is not the final goal. Instead, the breaking of the interest-based economy must precede all further steps, because it strikes at the root of the world's evil, indeed at its main root.

Only when the fundamental demand for the breaking of the interest economy is fulfilled will the path to a social state truly open. This must be clearly recognized and enforced against all mammonistic powers. A socialist state on a mammonistic foundation—the cry for socialization is nothing more than the attempt to bring about the monopoly of industries and everywhere form giant conglomerates, over which, despite all property taxes, big capital will continue to have the decisive influence—is an absurdity and inevitably leads to a compromise between the already heavily mammonistic social democracy and big capital.

We, on the other hand, demand a radical departure from the mammonistic state and the construction of a state in the true spirit of socialism, in which the guiding principle is the duty to nurture, in which a fundamental communist demand can find its reasonable and meaningful satisfaction—in the form that every citizen is granted his right to the homeland's soil through the state-mediated provision of the most essential means of sustenance.

We further demand, as the framework for the new state, a popular representation through the chamber of people's delegates, to be elected on the broadest possible basis, alongside a professional chamber of labor, the central council, in which the working people, organized by profession and economic structure, have their say. Finally, we demand the highest responsibility for the leaders of the state. But the prerequisite for all of this construction remains the breaking of the interest economy.

My unshakable belief, nay, more, my knowledge allows me to clearly recognize that the breaking of the interest economy is not only enforceable but will and must be met with indescribable jubilation everywhere, for, mind you: Contrary to all other well-meaning thoughts and movements and efforts that aim to improve humanity, my proposal does not attempt to improve human nature but instead targets a poisonous concoction, an invention that is utterly opposed to the innermost feelings of man, nay, a devilish invention designed to make humanity sick, to deeply ensnare it in materialism, to rob it of its best possession: the soul. Alongside this, the terrible, merciless torture of the money powers continues, for whom people are merely interest slaves, existing only to work for rent, for interest.

Deeply shaken, we recognize the terrible clarity and truth of the ancient biblical prophecies, in which Yahwey, the eternal God, promises his chosen people: *"I will give to you all the treasures of the world. At your feet shall all the peoples of the earth lie, and you shall rule over them."*

This world question is now unveiled before you all. World problems are not solved in the blink of an eye, but the idea is as clear as day. And the deed must be carefully prepared; we must be clear that we are facing the mightiest enemy, the globally encompassing money powers. All violence on the opposing side, on our side only the law, the eternal law of creative labor.

Give me your hands, worthy workers of all lands, unite!

CHAPTER 5

THE STATE'S RESCUE BANKRUPTCY

First Edition 1919, Josef C. Huber Verlag, Dießen near Munich

"I am wrestling with the specter of state bankruptcy," declared State Secretary Schiffer in 1919 during one of his financial speeches in Weimar.

Indeed, the *"specter"* of state bankruptcy, that is what our Weimar rulers have succumbed to, a specter that hides nothing but the fear of an imagined, unreal apparition. It seems almost ironic to me that Herr Schiffer refers to state bankruptcy as a *"specter,"* since he wants to designate something terribly frightening, something dreadful, yet the very concept of the word *"specter"* implies that it is about something that does not truly exist. The *"specter"* of state bankruptcy is the *"bogeyman"* of the capitalists, with which they frighten statesmen and deceived peoples. The *"specter"* of state bankruptcy is the thunder and horror story, with which fearful natures can be reliably taught to shiver, so that they do not dare to face things with clear, open eyes in the light of day.

It brings an indescribable feeling of happiness when one wakes from a heavy dream, when the specters dissolve into nothing and bright daylight shines through the window. The dreadful figures that the evening twilight has formed from the objects around us have disappeared, the stove has no glowing eyes, it stands calmly in its place, the wardrobe does not grow to an enormous size, the cloak thrown over the chair is no eerie ghost that has crouched at the foot of the bed and threatens to rise up mightily; it is all nothing, it was only our own overheated imagination that conjured specters before us, while a small, brave act of will would have sufficed—to make light—to banish all specters.

But how then does it stand with state bankruptcy (this spectral appearance)?

In a widely read book *"What Everyone Must Know About State Bankruptcy"* by Fr. Rost (Th. D. Weber, Hanover), the author defines state bankruptcy as *"the complete or partial non-fulfillment of contractually assumed debt obligations by a state towards its creditors, regardless of whether this is due to insolvency or a lack of willingness to pay or both causes simultaneously."*

This legal definition is undoubtedly correct within the framework of traditional thinking, and if one cannot break free from the well-worn grooves of thought based on Roman law, one will be able to label any sovereign alteration of debt obligations assumed by a state as state bankruptcy.

However, it is entirely different if one delves deeper into the nature of state financial economy; there, an alteration of debt obligations does not always appear as *"bankruptcy."*

"Banca rotta," the broken counting table, has taken on a nefarious connotation; the concept of *"bankruptcy"* is always associated with the idea that creditors are harmed in their entirety. So: the presence of a harm to creditors is, in my opinion, the criterion for the justified use of the word *"bankruptcy."* If no harm has been caused, if no harm has arisen for the mass of creditors, then one cannot speak of a *"bankruptcy"* in the usual sense of the word.

If a *"partial non-fulfillment of contractually assumed debt obligations by a state"* means for the overwhelming majority of citizens a release from a terrible and unbearable pressure, a liberation of the entire national economy from outrageous taxes: who would then dare to label such a state action as state bankruptcy?

Such an act of liberation is the suspension of interest payments on our war bonds as well as on all other debt securities of the Reich and the federal states, accompanied by the declaration of these debt securities as legal means of payment or, better yet: the conversion of these debt titles into interest-free bank deposits.

At first glance, the suspension of interest payments on war bonds may appear to be a harm to the holders of securities and thus indicate the occurrence of a state bankruptcy. However, upon closer examination, this is by no means the case, as the following explanations will demonstrate.

Precisely the exaggeration and overextension of our state loan economy make the absurdity, the madness of our entire state financial system, glaringly clear.

For the sake of a mammonistic dogma, a swindle, we entangled ourselves in a debt economy. This dogma states: *"When the state needs money, it must borrow it from the capitalists and then dutifully pay interest."*

This equation of the state community as a whole with the individual in terms of raising money through credit and interest has led to the hopeless confusion of our state finances, which are now so far removed from any healthy economy that one must speak of an imposed national fraud in favor of a small group of big capitalists.

First, let us consider the origin of our war bonds. 100 billion in war burdens were raised through loans, our state financial artists proclaimed triumphantly against the hostile foreign nations; 100 billion in war bonds, the German soul rejoiced, demonstrated the unbroken economic strength of the German people, despite four hard years of war; with a war effort of 100 billion, the homeland felt itself equal to the front-line army, and one did not hesitate to boast about it everywhere.

The issuance of war profits at 5% interest! It was a sacrifice, a patriotic deed of such heroic magnitude that the bank directors shed tears of joy over the German people's spirit of sacrifice with every new issue by General-Geldmarschall von Savenstein.

But the people were also told everything else that would make them willing to pay! Each time, a true flood of war bond propaganda poured from the bank counters; lectures, meetings, posters designed by first-class artists ensured that understanding of the necessity of war bond subscriptions spread everywhere. During those weeks, it was even permissible to think *"pan-German,"* i.e., to wish that Germany might win.

In short, it was a disgusting hullabaloo around the golden calf (a calf, because the German people truly became one), such a nauseating Mammon cult, such a degrading speculation on the profit greed of the masses, that one cannot be surprised that the war bond propaganda contributed in the worst way to the moral decay of the German people, thereby primarily preparing the collapse.

And yet, all of it was pure swindle; whether deliberate or not, it was the greatest national fraud of all time.

The German people thus burdened itself with 100 billion in debt, and that in the form of interest-bearing debt. Therefore, the German people must raise 5 billion in taxes if it wants to pay its interest, meaning it must give with one hand and take with the other; that is the immediate effect of this noble war bond issue. However, the folly of the war bonds does not end there.

For this is not a mere social game, but an enormous apparatus for tax collection and, equally, an apparatus for interest service, thus a colossal waste of labor when viewed on a grand scale, involving thousands upon thousands of bureaucrats, millions of tax declarations, paperwork, bank transactions, and all of this—merely for the sake of a grand monetary deception.

Yet, this might still be bearable, though every somewhat national-economic heart rebels against it, but the worst is yet to come: the whole farce—whether consciously or unconsciously, we leave that open—amounts to a colossal national fraud. Because the majority of all small and middle-class savers and capitalists not only gain nothing from their so-called interest, as demonstrated above, but because the entire working people must bear the taxes in the form of downright grotesque indirect taxes!

The matter stands as follows. Officially, they do not want to admit to the entire war bond swindle and declare that the interest on war bonds could naturally only be paid if taxes were collected in the same amount. That would at least be the act of an honest finance minister. Instead, they collect taxes in an indirect manner on a massive scale. Taxes are levied on coal, beer, mineral water, spirits, wine, tobacco, transportation, etc., in a cunning manner, all for the sake of interest. For the sake of interest alone, every person in Germany must freeze or pay double the price for coal, drink less or expensive beer, wine, or mineral water. And that's not all; the income from work is subjected to a massive tax increase—all for the sake of interest. And in reality, it turns out: it's not enough! Because in addition to the fixed-interest war bonds amounting to 100 billion, there are still around 50 billion in treasury bills or other short-term credits to be interest-bearing. In total, therefore, 150 billion, which devours 7 to 8 billion annually for the unforeseeable future.

It is deeply saddening to see and read how hopelessly our financial politicians have fallen prey to interest madness—I quote in the following one of our most outstanding financial experts, the former Finance Minister of Baden, Dr. J. Rheinholdt, who, in his otherwise very readable and clear work *"The German Financial Economy During the War and the Possibility of Its Order,"* writes, after discussing the various new extensive war taxes: *"Through the legislative acts in the field of finance in the years 1916, 1917, 1918, which brought the budget for 1918 additional revenues amounting to 4 billion compared to the years 1914 and 1915, it has at least been possible to meet the interest on the war debt thus far from the available income."*— There we have it—thank God, it has at least been possible to cover the interest on the war debt, since 1916, with the law of June 12 (R.G.B.BI. G. p. 507), tobacco was taxed with an increase of 130 million, freight costs were taxed with the law of June 17, 1916 (R.G.B.BI. G. p. 555), with 570 million, post and telegraph fees were increased by the law of June 21, 1916 (R.G.B.Bl. G. p. 561) by 200 million, the turnover of goods was taxed with the law of June 21, 1916 (R.G.B.Bl. G. p. 577) with 250 million.

The year 1917 then brought:

The taxation of passenger and goods transport, law of April 8, 1917 (R.G.B.BI. p. 329), with 315 million, the coal tax, law of April 8, 1917 (R.G.B.Bl. p. 340), with 500 million.

1918 then further increased the taxation of the turnover of goods with the law of July 26, 1918 (R.G.B.BI. p. 779), whose additional yield is even estimated at 1000 million.

The amendment to the Reich Stamp Tax Law, law of July 26, 1918 (R.G.B.Bl. p. 779), is estimated to yield 210 million.

- The wine tax, law of July 26, 1918 (R.G.B.BI. p. 831), is expected to bring in 103.5 million.
- Sparkling wine, law of July 26, 1918 (R.G.B.BI. p. 847), is expected to bring in 12.6 million.
- Mineral water, law of July 26, 1918 (R.G.B.BI. p. 849), is expected to bring in 52.5 million.
- Beer, law of July 26, 1918 (R.G.B.BI. p. 863), is taxed further with 339.5 million.
- Spirits, as the first financial monopoly according to the law of July 26, 1918 (R.G.B.Bl. p. 887), is even expected to yield an additional 800 million.

These monstrous taxes, which, as can be seen, almost exclusively burden the consumption of the broad masses of the people, resulted in just over 4 billion in taxes, which, with great effort and strain, sufficed to cover the interest on the war bonds. However, as Dr. Rheinholdt continues, *"the budgets for 1916 and 1917 showed significant shortfalls of around 2.5 billion..."* So even that!—And the other actual tasks of the Reich, cultural and economic in nature, etc.? ? ?

But undeterred, Mr. Finance Minister then states on the same page: "To the 150 billion of today's state of the

Reich debt, many more billions must be added, the interest for which must be provided."—*A few pages later, Dr. Rheinholdt declares again (p. 69):* "The war bonds and their interest must absolutely remain secure according to the lending conditions. If this were not done, the credit of the Reich would be irrevocably lost, both domestically and abroad."—There we have it again: the interest—that is the be-all and end-all of our financial misery.

That must not be shaken; before the sanctity of interest, all finance ministers, all tax politicians, all—and here comes the deeply saddening part—

socialists, as if on command, come to a halt!—Mr. Scheidemann proclaims on every advertising pillar to the frightened people for their *"reassurance,"* that the security of the war bonds will by no means be tampered with.

So, you big capital, you can rest assured!! Your interest remains yours; the people are stupid enough, bribed by the promised interest to the small bondholders, and allow the most outrageous taxes to be imposed on them, directly and indirectly. But who benefits from this? Only the benefit of big loan capital!! The powerful financiers certainly don't consume more beer and schnapps, tobacco, wine, or mineral water, salt and sugar, matches, and coal than the little man from the Volk, than the worker, the civil servant, the employee! And so, every man in the great mass of the people pays just as much as the multiple millionaire, only so that the multimillionaire can receive his war bond interest.—The most disgraceful, most vile fraud, the most infamous swindle is the entire war bond economy. Crafted to benefit the big capitalists. For the sake of this goal, not only is the labor force of the entire people exploited to the utmost, but much more: through the shameful bribes called war bond interest, the little man has also been harnessed to the triumphal chariot of the golden International, and his heart and mind have been corrupted by mammonism!!

This is how it stands, this is the truth! Who dares to say anything against it?! Like scales, it falls from our eyes, and we recognize clearly where this abysmal disgust, this indescribable rage of the awakened Volk instinctively comes from, even if the Volk itself is not fully aware of it, but only feels the general pressure of it, to which I have given clear, numerical expression in the preceding explanations.

Poor Volk! Poor and deceived Volk!

You will go bankrupt if you stop paying the interest on the war bonds! Has it now become clear to you why state bankruptcy is a specter?! Has it now become clear to you why the state bankruptcy, in the form I proposed of suspending interest payments, is not a bankruptcy at all, but a joyful liberation, a redemption from the claws of mammonism?!

Let us break the interest-based power of money, and all of us, the entire hard-working Volk, will be free.

From the war bonds, we have come to recognize that the war bond economy is nothing more than a capitalist deception of the people; with the other state loans, it is fundamentally the same, of course, only that it was easier to disguise. Here I am primarily speaking of the railway loans as by far the most important state loans by volume. The entirety of the German state railways represents an invested capital of 20,795 million by the end of 1916. All these state railways were built from borrowed funds or acquired through purchase. All these capital funds, thus roughly 20 billion, must be annually subjected to interest payments to the capitalists. Year after year, our state railways must yield roughly 800 million marks in revenue just to cover the interest for the esteemed railway bondholders.

I do not want to dwell too long on details, but it is nevertheless interesting to observe that the magnificent surpluses of the railways, which in Prussia, for example, were always praised as the *"backbone of the state budget,"* were just enough to cover the perpetual fixed interest payments on the railway loans. Sometimes there was indeed a bit more, and a few million remained as net surplus, but the essential thing was the famous 7% interest on the Prussian-Hessian state railways, thus an over-return of about 3% beyond the obligatory interest payments to the capitalists.—This picture has now catastrophically deteriorated in recent years; the railway budget for 1918, according to the statements of Prussian Finance Minister Simon, shows a deficit of 1,300 million—thus a shortfall equal to the revenue of two good peacetime years. —But that doesn't matter at all, because the railway bonds are fixed-interest securities, so the interest must bepaid no matter what, regardless of where the money comes from. Very simple, so one will simply tighten the tax screw —for what else is the working Volk there? Blessed is only the interest, even if the state perishes over it, that is: Woe if the state were to stop paying the interest, that would be state bankruptcy, thus in the mammonistic phraseology the most serious crime one could imagine, because it would hit the little pensioners who have invested their money in *"safe and secure"* securities. Now, the little pensioners were of utter indifference to the big capitalists, unless they themselves held large amounts of these state securities. So it is very good that the little capitalists possess these *"exceptionally safe and secure investments,"* because one cannot *"disappoint the trust of the people"* who have *"trustingly"* and *"confidently"* entrusted their *"penny savings"* to the fatherly state. How beautiful and noble that sounds, and yet it is a thoroughly cunning, mammonistic swindle—just like with the war bonds.

If almost the entire net revenue from the income of the railways were not used for the interest payments on the railway loans, the net income from the state railway operation would suffice to cover the largest part of the state expenditures for the entire internal administration, and thus much fewer direct and indirect taxes would need to be levied. Again, the same picture: the small and medium capital holders do not benefit in the slightest from the interest on their loan securities from the state railways, as these interests are taken away from them directly or indirectly; for the citizen who is not fortunate enough to possess such *"ultra-secure"* government bonds, the interest on the railway loans represents an exorbitant taxation of his labor for the benefit of the major bondholders. Only big loan capital profits.

In Bavaria, the situation is exactly the same, in fact even worse, because the net income was negatively affected from the outset by the Kleinbahn railway policy and the more challenging terrain conditions. With a railway debt of around 2000 million, the interest payments amount to approximately 75 million, while the contributions to the state treasury averaged 70 million before the war. A notable exception was the year 1911, with 93.7 million, while the year 1918 ended with a significant loss.

The financial results of the Bavarian railway operations are shown in the following table for the decade 1902-1911.

All figures in millions of Marks unless otherwise noted Millions Total= expenses incl.

Year	Total Revenue	Total Expen-ditures (incl. Pensions)	Gross Surplus	Interest Payments	Net Yield	Loss
1901	166.7	136.4	30.3	37.4	-	7.1
1902	169.7	131.6	38.1	40.4	-	2.3
1903	176.1	133.5	43.6	41	2.5	-
1904	181.7	141.6	43.1	44.2	-	1.1
1905	198.4	148.6	49.8	46.5	3.3	-
1906	208	155.1	52.9	47.3	5.6	-
1907	213.1	161	52	48.9	3.1	-
1908	219.7	170	49.7	51.5	-	1.8
1909	266.41	208.9	57.5	63.8 (Of which 2.4 was repayment)	-	8.7
1910	281.6	199.5	82.1	65.5 (Of which 2.9 was repayment)	16.7	-
1911	297.4	203.6	93.7	68.2 (Of which 2.6 was repayment)	22.9	-

And so here we see the same picture again. The net earnings barely suffice to cover the interest on the loans: the *"backbone of our finances"* has done its duty if it covers these interest payments.

The situation is exactly the same in the other federal states, and not much different is the case with the *"general state debt,"* which was not even raised for so-called renter purposes, but rather for the state's cultural tasks, etc. B. Railroad construction, torrent control, Sochmaffer dams, bridge construction, drainage systems, etc. All such enterprises serve social purposes; they have in and of themselves no objective value.

I have long heard the impatient question: But how else should the state build its railways, its roads, bridges, and other improvements, if not through borrowed funds? To build requires money, so the state must borrow, and no one would lend money to the state without interest!

In this question, in this belief that the state, like any penniless person starting a business, must absolutely borrow the money for it, lies the tragedy of our entire modern state financial economy, and more: the assertion that no one would lend their money without interest, that the state must therefore issue interest bearing notes to obtain money for social enterprises, has contributed significantly to the mammonistic decay of our entire age. Here lie the roots of the emerging renter ideal, here lie the seeds of the unprecedented growth of big capital, here lie the causes of the economic enslavement of the working population.

Thus, out of an erroneous state conception, the disastrous debt economy has arisen. From the idea that the state, just like an individual, would need to take credit for every economic undertaking. This notion must be rejected as entirely false and directed against the interests of the community.—There is no way to understand or justify why the state, that is, the entirety of its citizens, would need to borrow money from wealthy individuals and issue interest-bearing notes to these people; it is entirely unclear why the state, as the sovereign embodiment of the entire people, should not just as well issue non-interest-bearing notes to contractors and suppliers, behind which—and here is the crucial point—just as with the interest-bearing notes, ultimately stands only the labor power of the entire people as security.

This clear realization is the key to the entire present circumstances.

It may be particularly difficult for the expert who feels competent in these matters to recognize and admit this fundamental error, as it concerns deeply ingrained prejudices. However, it will not be so difficult for the simple man from the people and for common sense to understand that, for the community as a whole, which ultimately always has to bear the taxes or interest in some form, there is no difference whether the state prints interest-bearing notes or non-interest-bearing notes to fulfill its social tasks. In fact, the difference would immediately speak in favor of the non-interest-bearing notes—the so—called banknotes—since the state would thereby be freed from the tremendous burden of perpetual interest.

But the mammonist is not at a loss and hurls the terrible word *"inflation"* at me.

What is inflation? The flooding of the money market with paper payment means. The payment of state enterprises with paper payment means is supposed to adversely affect the economy. Well, I am so bold as to claim that this too is a mammonistic swindle. Again, we must keep the original creation in mind. Let us say the Bavarian state wants to build a railway that costs 100 million; this sum must be approved by the state parliament, then a loan is issued. In the meantime, however, the railway is already being built, and the construction contractor must be paid. With what? With banknotes. So notes are printed. But then the interest-bearing notes must also be printed, the loan bonds, and along with them the coupons, and these coupons must in turn be redeemed with banknotes. Here we see a paper economy—an inflation—that is significantly larger than if the entire amount had been printed directly in banknotes. So why not print 10,000-mark notes? These would in any case no longer be a means of payment in the sense of small change; they would simply be held as a cash reserve in the vault or used for larger transfers—quite apart from the possibility of much simpler cashless transactions. I have deliberately chosen the somewhat more cumbersome method of proof through ordinary notes to show that *"inflation"* could again only be spoken of as a *"specter"* to frighten superstitious statesmen.

In reality, inflation through the loan route is much worse than if the state, based on the credits once approved by the legislative body, had simply printed that money. We would not have fallen into the absurd and self deceptive interest-based economy from which we must now escape under any circumstances.

It is entirely clear that with the presence of ample payment means, these notes would have been credited to the state banks—insofar as they had not found other investments—and very soon it would have even come to the point where no new notes would have had to be printed for the approved state credits, since the state banks had enough notes lying in their deposits and the so-called *"loan titles"* no longer needed to be printed at all.

However, this would have resulted in—in stark contrast to the inflation claimed by the mammonistic side—no inflation at all, and the continual erosion of the purchasing power of money would have been avoided.

The devaluation of money has kept precisely the same pace with the swelling of our loan titles, and in fact, this fact can again be observed by any layperson in the developments during the war. We have already adequately illuminated the war bond swindle, but it shows us even more: namely, that the devaluation of money has progressed exactly in proportion to the swelling of the war loans—on average, we can now observe, with an approximate tripling of the sum of fixed-interest securities compared to before the war, a tripling of all prices.

We can now observe a tripling of all prices, i.e., a decline in the value of money to one-third. In contrast, the concurrent flooding with notes has by no means had such devastating effects. For the insane printing of notes, which has nearly decoupled our paper payment means, only began in the past year (1918), by which time prices had already risen to 2.5 times their previous level; furthermore, the price increase since last year has by no means grown in proportion to the mass of paper payment means, and finally, it must be admitted that the vast majority of these notes have been stored away, meaning they are kept interest-free.

Let us now imagine how the entire war financing would have proceeded if we had dared to print, based on the granted war credits, say, 5 billion notes and used them to pay for war supplies. Interest-bearing investments would not have been found for these amounts anywhere, so they would have been deposited as cash reserves at the banks; a mere notification, or perhaps even penalties against hoarding paper money with only a tenth of the effort spent on the war loan, would have redirected the money back to public financial institutions, i.e., the Reichsbank, from which, based on new credits approved by the Reichstag, payments could have been made without new note printing. I believe it is not an overstatement to say that the Reich could have managed the entire financial war effort with 5-10 billion new notes, and otherwise through account credits.

For example, a law stating that all war deliveries should only be paid to suppliers through account transfer, and that cash withdrawals from the—despite the war—interest-free credits should only be allowed for pure wage payments, would have avoided all the catastrophic consequences of our war loan economy.

We would thereby have arrived at the ultimately sound path of state financial management.

To round off the picture, let us imagine the further course of events: The war industry, the war-supplying farmers, and artisans receive their payments for deliveries through a credit note from a Reichsbank office. Wages, etc., can be withdrawn in cash (under control), supplier payments are settled via check or transfer, and the rest, the profit, remains as an interest-free credit. The credits, i.e., the debts of the Reich to the individual credit holders, would admittedly have also swelled to a similar degree, but without the additional interest. The internal indebtedness, i.e., the indebtedness of the whole to the individual credit holders, could in no way have burdened the economy as much as the interest economy.

We touched on the connection between the loan economy and the devaluation of money in the last section, but it may still not be entirely clear why this internal connection exists.

This internal reason lies in the original nature of money.

In its innermost nature, money is nothing other than *"a claim on performed labor."*

The completely false and accidental conception and valuation of money as capital that, by its mere existence, works and thus bears interest, is simply nothing more than a thoroughly deceitful mammonistic swindle.

The correctness of the above definition of money as *"a claim on performed labor"* can best be understood through a very simple example: For the grain he delivered, the farmer did not receive, in exchange from the coal mining company, 1 cartload of coal, but rather money, that is, *"a claim on performed labor."* This means he can use this money to purchase performed labor, such as plowing, harrowing, or a scythe; the plow and harrow maker, in turn, can use the received *"claim on performed labor"* (money) to purchase performed labor, such as coal or iron from the mining company. In this short cycle, we recognize the absolute correctness of this definition of money as *"a claim on performed labor."* Money is thus an entirely ingenious and necessary facilitation of trade and exchange in any complex national economy. This property of money is not affected as long as it is stored away, so long as it is not bestowed with the supernatural ability to bear interest by itself. It is only with the idea of interest that money has become an independent demonic force, a terrifying power that exploits and drains people, and it is the principle of interest that has led to the economic enslavement of nations.

Money, in its original meaning and invention, is *"a claim on performed labor,"* nothing more!—With the concept of interest, money has been turned into an earthly god.

According to this definition of money, it is clear that the presence of many such *"claims on performed labor"* must drive up the prices of goods (goods being performed labor) when there are few goods available, that is, when the supply of money is greater than the supply of goods. The supply of goods, production, in a national community, remains relatively stable as long as the population—and thus the labor force—does not significantly increase or decrease. On the other hand, the monetary tokens, these *"claims on performed labor,"* can of course be arbitrarily multiplied; this is most simply done with the help of the printing press.

The result is naturally that the prices of all *"performed labor"* rise accordingly, or the purchasing power of money falls. Here we have the direct connection between the devaluation of money and its original concept. —The mere existence of paper notes devalues the purchasing power of these notes, for only the commodity has intrinsic value, not money.

We can now quite precisely trace how the swelling of our paper *"values,"* our *"securities,"* since the year 1870, has led to an exactly parallel devaluation of our money, and it was precisely the mass of *"interest-bearing" "securities"* that contributed to this devaluation; for the mass of non-interest-bearing notes is much less an expression of the paper economy—(before the war we had only about 4 billion banknotes in circulation)—than the flood of self-interest-bearing securities of all kinds born from the insanity of interest and credit.

Incidentally, it should be noted here that the rise in prices has always followed the issuance of paper values, like a wave; herein lies the secret of the terrible redistribution of wealth in our nation.

The development of the over saturation of the market with paper payment instruments of all kinds during the war and the resulting devaluation of money have already been discussed in the last chapter, and together with the explanations just given, full clarity should now exist about the hopelessly tangled nature of our state's money and credit economy.

But something else must be discussed, where it is again very painful not to question the good faith (*"bona fides"*) of the capitalist circles: it is the fact that all small, medium, and even quite respectable fortunes, say up to even half a million, are completely devalued by the insane inflation. The gap between the world domineering plutocrats and the entire productive population grows ever larger. The entire middle class, even the propertied upper class, sinks into the proletariat, while the golden International, seated on its billion-dollar throne—which is propped up only by the madness of interest—is positioned to take control of world dominion.

And it becomes clear to us once again that only the breaking of the interest-based economy can save us from complete economic enslavement by the powerful international money powers.

CHAPTER 6

LEAFLET FROM APRIL 5TH, 1919

Written by Dietrich Edartt based on the *"Manifesto for the Breaking of the Interest-Based Economy."*

To all productive individuals!

To all who work, no matter what or where, as long as they work!

To all reasonable people!

Nowadays, there's hardly any topic that isn't criticized. Industry, agriculture, the church, the bourgeoisie— whoever has money, or at least seems to have it, gets their share of reproach. But one thing is never spoken of. You never hear a word or a hint about it; and yet, there is nothing in the world that is such a curse on humanity as this. I mean **Loan capital!**

Do you know it? Surely everyone has heard of it, but to truly know it, to really understand it—I don't think you do. Otherwise, you would forget all quarrels today, stand shoulder to shoulder, and strangle this monster before morning comes.

I will describe it to you in broad strokes. Listen carefully! Because if anything can transform you into what you aspire to be—free and happy individuals—it is this. Nothing else but this!

Loan capital earns money without labor, earning it through interest. I repeat: without lifting a finger, the capitalist increases his wealth by lending his money. It grows by itself. No matter how lazy someone is—if he has enough money and invests it for interest, he lives the most comfortable life; even his children never need to work, his grandchildren, his great-grandchildren, for eternity! How unjust it is, how shameless, doesn't everyone feel that?

Loan capital grows to immeasurable heights through compound interest. Just one example: In 1806, the lending business of the House of Rothschild began with the millions entrusted to it by the exiled Elector of Hesse. It must have been something over 10 million, certainly no more than 20. Today, after roughly 110 years, the Rothschild fortune amounts to 40 billion!

40 billion is what the House of Rothschild possesses!

Not millions, but billions! And if this continues, it will be 80 billion by 1935, 160 billion by 1950, and 320 billion by 1965. Billions! It sounds like the delusion of a madman, but it is true! The Rothschilds only need to manage their wealth, simply ensure it is always well invested; they don't need to work, at least not in the sense of what we understand as work.

But who expands their money in such colossal quantities? Where does the interest come from? Who must earn these new billions, or rather endless billions, through hard labor? It is you, no one else but you! Indeed, it is your money, painfully earned through hardship and worry, that is drawn like a magnet into the coffers of those insatiable people!

Once again: The single House of Rothschild owns 40 billion. But you hear nothing of it, not a single word! Always only about the agrarians, the heavy industry, and industry in general; and it is exclusively on these sectors that the nationalization plan of our leading revolutionaries focuses, with deafening clamor! *"There's nothing else to socialize!"* They drum and whistle this into your ears daily until you believe it and are happy that such generosity is being shown toward you. Cleverly thought, I must say, and cleverly executed. Do you know how much the capital of our entire industry amounts to?

The capital of the entire German industry amounts to less than 12 billion!

Let that sink in! *"In all areas, in our industry for iron and coal, for clothing and textiles, for stone and metal mines, shipbuilding and chemicals, glass and wood, in our construction sector, in the vast chemical factories, in our once world-dominating electrical industry, in our machinery and automotive factories, shipyards and paper factories, in the transport and food industries—in short, in the infinitely vast field of all industries, there is less than 12 billion!"* Calculated based on the shining pre-war standards! Even back then 40 billion was what the single House of Rothschild owned!

It likely owns even more today, after the enormous interest the war brought it! You could combine all the agrarians of the entire world, and their combined cash assets still wouldn't come close to the 40 billion of the single Rothschild family!

There are countless such *"Rothschilds"* among us: the Mendelssohns, the Bleichröders, the Friedländers, the Warburgs, to name just a few of the most prominent ones. And even if none of them matches the gigantic model, yet each likely has more capital rents to consume than all our pronounced agrarians combined! Yet, it is precisely the landowners whom we hear repeatedly branded by the *"saviors of the people"* as the worst, indeed the sole exploiters, while the true bloodsuckers never receive a word of reprimand, not even the slightest! We are consistently distracted by the far lesser evil so that we do not see the main evil, the all-consuming loan capital; and so it has been handled since Marx and Lassalle up to Leviné, Landauer, and Mühsam! Are your eyes not yet opening to this?

More than 200 billion marks of loan capital weigh down on the German people!

In which forms most of it exists, do I still need to tell you? Not 100 billion marks in the form of war bonds, but 100 billion in debts, for which the people must pay the loan interest through taxes! In addition, there are 30 billion in unsecured debts that must also be repaid with interest! Similarly, 25 billion in unfunded debts of the state and imperial railways, not a penny less! Furthermore, 12 billion in debt securities of the land credit institutions and 11 billion in mortgage bonds of the mortgage banks, for which the people must pay the interest in the form of high rents! And finally, there are 6 billion in debt securities of German cities and municipalities to be repaid with interest, and who knows what else!

But it's not just us, it's the same all over the world! Wherever we look, the working people groan under the slavery of interest. Like a polyp, loan capital stretches across the globe and sucks at the lifeblood of peoples.

Internationally, it hangs together, must hang together, so that it finds new nourishment wherever opportunity arises. In alliance with the Mendelssohns, the Bleichröders, the Friedländers, the Warburgs are invisibly the Dabs, the Schiffs, the Cahns, the Spires, the Morgan Americas! As to how many there are, Rathenau's brilliance once betrayed it to us. "*300 men who among themselves,*" he triumphantly declared years ago, "*guide the destiny of Europe.*"

300 stock exchange men rule the world!

Through their immense loan capital! Everything is subservient and obedient to them: the press, the theaters, the cinemas, everything by which public opinion can be influenced! Even our princes were, even our kaiser was, because multiplied a thousandfold with these "*chosen ones*"! But gold does not rest or rust; it wants to devour unceasingly and grow fat! From the earth it rises, in Africa, in Asia, always anew and knows only one drive: to be invested, to yield interest. "*May war long live!*"

Let palaces and towns, railways and bridges be shattered into dust and ashes by grenades: the mortgages remain intact. The railway and government debt securities are not thereby canceled; forever must the unfortunate owners of their destroyed dwellings, forever the unfortunate populations of the countries ravaged by the war toil for the interest payments on the loan capital! Jubilantly, the golden International watches the mad antics of mankind; the intoxicating upheavals of war, to which villages and cities, entire provinces have fallen victim, provide the desired opportunity to draw up new debt securities, until finally all mankind serves restlessly as interest slaves to the golden International!

That is the curse of the world war!

That alone! Others have long recognized this, but—nothing changed. *"For twenty-two dynasties,"* wrote the Berlin Spartacist paper *"Freiheit"* at the onset of the revolution, *"have fallen or still cling desperately to the crumbling foundations. They were but the puppets! Now the puppeteers must be brought to light! They are the bearers of the capitalist yoke, the uncrowned kings of the stock exchange and the bureau, the real authors of our misfortune, of the criminal policies that conjured up the world war!"*

Thus it sounded once, clear enough, but since then nothing more has been heard. Now one hears only that the kings, the military were behind it. Why the reversal? Because capitalism has in the meantime also taken hold of this new movement, by means of its agents, who act so wondrously people-friendly! *"He comes,"* as the *"Bormärts"* timidly suggests, *"towards the masses, to deceive them. He feels secure—that's why socialization is only half as bad to him. For he knows that he will find ways and means to assert himself."*

There you have it! We are to be deceived once again, and this time through the stock exchange game! There's only one remedy against this:

Break the bondage of interest on loan capital!

Let us no longer trust those who have turned a blind eye to this oppression of humanity! Such leaders are suspect from the start, and they would be doubly so if they suddenly started speaking out now, after we have become aware!

We Germans, and especially we Bavarians, must take the lead in this!

We, the peasants, must take the lead in this!

It began with us in the upheaval! It is also up to us to steer the revolution towards its true goal, not the false one, where it would inevitably end up if we continue to rely on foreign spirits! Did they not say there was nothing to socialize for the time being? Now you know better!

Honest people from our midst must come together and deliberate on how the bondage of interest can be broken! However difficult it may seem, it is not impossible! After all, the German people lived without interest for 600 years! Only we must will it and not relent! Away with the liars who only serve the stock exchange!

Only this revolution is the genuine one!

Onward to action! It will sweep all peoples along! No other can do it! Liberated humanity will thank us in a brotherly way! Us, the betrayed Germans!

CHAPTER 7

CHEAP BREAD OR NEW TAXES?

Letter to the Bavarian Minister-President

215 Flyer of the *"German Combat League for Breaking the Bondage of Interest,"* printed by Josef C. Huber, Dießen near Munich

Murnau, December 26, 1920.

Dear Herr von Kahr!

If I may take the liberty of addressing Your Excellency directly, it is because there seems to me to be urgent danger.

Reports are circulating through the press that the government intends to transform the Bavarian large water projects *"Walchensee and Mittlere Isar"* into share companies.

I raise a vigorous and passionate protest against this surrender of important parts of the Bavarian people's wealth to capital. The Bavarian people are quite capable, under all circumstances, of developing the Bavarian water resources for the benefit of all, interest-free. It has sufficient labor, sufficient skilled intelligence, sufficient building materials, etc., within its own borders to carry out all the necessary construction work from its own right and from its own labor, and it has sufficient surplus products to trade for the parts of electrical equipment that cannot be produced within the country.

It is therefore completely incomprehensible why the Bavarian state should make itself the collector of interest for capital greedy for interest, while it could create the necessary funds interest-free from its own right, without once again placing itself in the unnecessary and unworthy dependence on capital.

If the state government dares to assume the task, through its financial sovereignty, of collecting taxes for the interest payments to capital—if it thereby has usurer interest of 8%, and in approximately 12 years it has to collect the total construction sum already in the form of interest and hand it over to capital!—Or if it allows, as indirect taxes, that the Bavarian people pay their own electrical energy derived from their own water resources perpetually, burdened with this interest tribute,—then the state would also be just as able, sovereignly, from its own right, to provide the required amounts for the expansion of water power over the years in the form of taxes, by temporarily issuing unsecured non-interest-bearing checks on the state bank from its own right and not as a lackey of big capital.

The issue of non-interest-bearing checks by the Bavarian State Bank is nothing new, as we had for approximately 120 million marks last year for quite unproductive purposes. If, however, such an issue of state money were made explicitly for the purpose of productive work, then even from the strictest concept of financing, there could be no objection raised. The state would initially—during construction—give paper for performed work but subsequently exchange electric energy, air power, etc., for the paper. A completely flawless process that the state can confidently carry out through its economic sovereignty.

This financing of major state and social construction activities is only a small excerpt from the general interest problem. Your Excellency knows that for several years now I have made the interest problem the subject of in-depth investigations in both word and writing. Members of all political parties are united in the *"Combat League for Breaking the Bondage of Interest"* that I founded; large German economic associations, various political parties, a number of prominent politicians, economists, and banking experts see in my demands the only way out of our financial misery. There is also no doubt that the interest question is the core issue of our public monetary system and thus also for the management of the state budget; the interest question is, moreover, the focal point of the social question, insofar as the poisoning of our domestic political life stems from the justified indignation of all those who work with head and hand against the free riders of pure loan capital. And the interest problem goes even further, as it is a question of fundamental importance for the entire Western cultural sphere, insofar as the peoples belonging to it will have to choose between downfall in Bolshevik chaos or sinking into the slavery of the interest-based economy in the face of the usurious capital of the Franco-Anglo-American high finance. The breaking of the interest-based economy is the slogan, it is the tangible expression of the worldwide struggle of work and achievement against the overpowering and exploitative tendencies of supranational financial power.

"It is about securing the interest on the German war debt," declared Lord George before Spa. And anyone who can see beyond the superficial causes of the war knows that the inexorable law of interest gave birth to the world war. The threat to the secure profits of world capital posed by German labor, by a Germany of work and achievement, by the land in which values such as loyalty to duty, military honor, diligence, and honesty had not yet succumbed to money, demanded the annihilation of this *"German Socialism"* —not militarism or Kaiserism, etc.—in the interests of establishing a world money dictatorship. The German sword was feared, but the ethical assets were hated. That is why the demoralization of the German people, the denationalization of the German soul, was pursued by every means and crowned by the Treaty of Versailles. For me, the Treaty of Versailles is nothing other than the manifestation of the interest principle against an entire people, it is the formal legal cloak covering the colossal injustice of the enslavement of the labor power of an entire people in the face of supranational financial tyranny.

The same is true of the interest concept in general, a legal notion that has little to do with the concept of money—as a medium of exchange, a reference to performed work. That interest is a property of money, as some economists attempt to make us believe, is of course completely misguided; interest has as much to do with money as a tumor does with the bloodstream. The legal safeguarding of interest claims has led to a distortion of the interest concept, the moral untenability of which has been recognized by all great lawmakers throughout history and across cultures as soon as the virus of interest threatened to stifle any creative public work. I refer to usury laws, Solon, the *"lex Gemicia"*, Justinian, Pope Leo I, Luther, I point to the interest ban in the Islamic world, in the Chinese world. It already contradicts our deepest sense of justice that one can, through money, acquire debt instruments of all kinds, giving the owners of these securities a practically eternal right to the work of others. Then this legal concept becomes a crime if the state itself abandons its interest sovereignty to the interest principle. Instead of defending the interest in its most fundamental rights one of its most important sovereign prerogatives—it has placed itself and thus its people in dependency on money-holders. Even more, it has necessarily become an adversary of the people, enmeshed in the tentacles of a monetary power that has increasingly subordinated the state.

It has, so to speak, become the trustee of big capital interests in opposition to its natural and most essential task: to be the trustee of the whole community.

Who could deny it: today, with its means of power, the state is the collector of interest for capital; it is not free—and as long as this anti-social condition persists, the accusation of the capitalist state will be rightly made, and a calming of internal political tensions will not be achievable.

In direct contrast to the exploitative idea of interest stands the concept of property. When Proudhon says, *"Property is theft,"* he commits a crime against cultural humanity, because property, possession, wealth of all kinds is never theft in its essence, since the possession of gold and silver objects, beautiful paintings, land and house-ownership, a beautiful library, etc., never exploits the labor of others, as loan capital does. Rather, property is the foundation of all culture, and the protection of property is one of the most important tasks of the cultural state.

I have made this brief insertion because my efforts are often defamed by interested parties as communist. They certainly are not; on the contrary, they are the breaker against Bolshevik chaos, because through the implementation of my demands to break the interest-based economy, the only legitimate demand of the Marxist-socialist thought world—the elimination of unearned income—is fulfilled and thus a detoxification of internal political relations is brought about, which alone can unite the population, torn apart by parties, into a national community, a true community of fate, which will first enable a prosperous social-political life. Interest, however, is theft, and the surrender of important native natural resources to capital appears, according to what has been said, as state aid to organized robbery of the people in a case where the social, state development of peasant water resources could and should place the peasant people in a position to open up an inexhaustible source of value and free themselves from the obligation to pay tribute to capital.

With this, I have returned to the starting point of my remarks. My letter has become longer than I thought. I am nonetheless unable to offer the usual phrases of apology, as this would be doing injustice to the importance of the matter.

I am driven not by personal ambition or the desire to speak of myself and my work, but only by the concern that irreparable decisions might be made through which the Bavarian people could lose values that in their unavoidable struggle for personal freedom, in their historical mission to recover their national personality from their own right, could strongly support them.

I have also felt compelled to make this personal appeal to Your Excellency because various resolutions from national assemblies that dealt with the interest problem and were submitted to the state government, the Reich government, and the relevant ministries have altogether remained without any response. The public does not understand that the government does not take a position on this important issue, but at best obtains private information and expert opinions from circles and people who must inevitably be opponents of the demands of the *"German Combat League for Breaking the Bondage of Interest."* For the general assessment of my demands, no special expertise in national economy or financial technology is necessary, as the solution to the interest problem is a question of general moral and social ethical nature.

— Gottfried Feder.

CHAPTER

8

GUIDLINE OF THE "GERMAN COMBAT LEAGUE FOR BREAKING THE BONDAGE OF INTEREST"

(Founded September 1919)

For the public speech on April 4th and 11th, 1921 in the Wagner Hall in Munich

The German Combat League for Breaking the Bondage of Interest demands the cessation of public interest service, which is essentially only organized plunder of the people in favor of pure money assets, demands in particular the recovery of the note privilege (the right to create money) surrendered to a share company (Reichsbank) into the power sphere of the state through the nationalization of the Reichsbank demands the nationalization of banks, which no longer fulfill their actual social task of mediating money transactions, but violently dominate economic life and ruthlessly extort tribute from all labor in the form of high interest, demands adequate compensation for small renters for the devaluation of savings due to an all-corrupting financial and tax policy, demands in particular that the economic freedom and future of Bavaria not be jeopardized by surrendering our most valuable natural resource, water power, to interest-bearing capital demands that the state, by organizing the labor forces at its disposal, undertake the development of water power from its own resources, by creating the necessary circulating credit through its sovereign right of minting and issuing, which will be fully covered by the resulting values and their yields, demands that the people's wealth and tax power be directly utilized to create productive assets, rather than merely guaranteeing wholly unnecessary loan capital, demands a limitation on capital raising by joint-stock companies.

The joint-stock companies should use their profits to strengthen their operations; they should not distribute excessive profits only to have to raise new funds again later. New funds mean new debts, incur new interest, and lead to price increases! The German Combat League for Breaking the Bondage of Interest protests against the insinuation that its demands are *"utopian"* or *"likely to unsettle the people."*

The financial health of our national economy through the eradication of state interest service is highly desirable for the whole community and not *"utopian."* Concern can only be stirred by those opposed to economic recovery. Even if certain selfish interests may suffer somewhere, the saving action must not be neglected any more than a life-saving operation can be postponed because of the pain involved. The German Combat League for Breaking the Bondage of Interest declares that the state's interest economy is in the most urgent need of a solution, because the damage from the failed state financial policy affects the entire people. Here, it is a matter of general social concerns. Meeting private credit needs cannot be managed by state measures (e.g., a complete ban on interest following historical precedent), which must remain determined by individuals' individual will. All that can and must be sought is that money is only paid against a risk of loss or if it shares in potential profits, ensuring that a lender is not, in addition to full security and compensation of all costs, further guaranteed a permanent and effortless increase in wealth through fixed interest.

The German Combat League for Breaking the Bondage of Interest;

sees in the resolution of the interest problem not only the prerequisite for remedying our German financial distress but also the liberation of all nations of the western cultural sphere from their enormous indebtedness.

Breaking the dominance of interest;

is the means to end a colossal struggle that rages around the world between labor and capital, for the benefit of the freedom of labor, without dissolving or undermining property, the acquisition of wealth through dedicated productivity, diligence, and outstanding intellectual achievement.

A reconciliation of the people, now divided along class lines, can only be achieved through dismantling the dominance of interest, as idleness that yields unearned returns from mere possession of finance is then prohibited.

Dismantling the dominance of interest is the most important moral claim from a social standpoint; it stands above all everyday issues in its overall importance, it resolves the social question, and it is the only way out of the terrifying tangle our world is caught in.

Our way out from the financial-capitalist form and the avoidance of the communist form of alienation and the mechanization of labor, via dissolving the dominance of interest, leads us to a genuinely social economic realm; to the state of accomplishment and achievement.

CHAPTER 9

THE COMING TAX STRUGGLE

Written by Gottfried Feder, Dipl. Ing., and Dr. W. Budele g (1921, Josef C. Huber Press, Dießen bei München).

1. The Current Situation

With the London Ultimatum, the Versailles Peace Treaty has found new form in the light of public international law and for the moment ends a fight between the global hegemony of mammon and German industry's workers' toilers' struggles that has raged unabated.

The financial oligarchy of the City of London, Paris and Wall Street have finally gained possessorship of interest-bearing legal claims in the shape of

"Restoration Funds," classes a, b and c, which under a mantle of internationally formalized agreement, have secured the perpetual exploitation by high finance of the working might of the German people forevermore. Thus, the veil has been lifted from the final connections, which provide the explanation for the causes, course, and goals of the World War.

France's idea of revenge was certainly one of the active driving causes of the war, as was the policy of the Grand Dukes in Russia, but France alone would never have dared to take the step; even in Russia, there were very strong reservations against going to war with Germany. None of these active warmongers could have pursued their policy—indeed, one might say, been allowed to pursue it—without the tacit approval of the financial powers in the press and parliament, if the subjugation of Germany had not been part of the overall plan for establishing world domination through supranational financial power.

It is extraordinarily difficult, indeed nearly impossible, to provide documentary evidence for the ultimate connections. Such documentary evidence can be much more easily provided for specific actions, for the existence of orders, decrees, concerning mobilization, etc., as in the Suchomlinov trial or the trial against Princip. However, such evidence always remains at the surface and never reveals the deepest driving forces, which are what truly matter.

Only the actual final results of the World War are truly conclusive evidence.

What, then, is the final result of the World War—the one that truly matters? The subjugation of Germany? The victory of the Entente? The German Revolution? The expulsion of the German princes? The Bolshevization of Russia? The moral and economic impoverishment of all peoples of the Western cultural sphere?

All these are merely preconditions, necessary steps, accompanying circumstances, and negative, destructive phenomena—but not goals. All this would have no meaning if it did not benefit someone. So, who benefits from war and revolution, death and hardship, collapse and decay, class struggle and fratricide?

Does the French farmer gain anything from the Entente's victory? Does he get to see any of the German war reparations? Does the English worker benefit from the economic exploitation of Germany? On the contrary, is not the English coal industry, and thus the English miner, severely threatened by the forced German coal deliveries? What does the German people gain from its revolutionary freedom except the prospect of slowly being strangled to death? Does the worker benefit from the dictatorship of his—let us say it correctly— betrayers?

If we set aside the parasites on every sick body of the people, the profiteers and black marketeers; who truly benefits from the war and the revolution? Perhaps the revolutionary governments or their leaders? Not even them. The revolution devours its own children: Eisner executed, Jaffé in an asylum, Landauer executed, Leviné executed, Liebknecht executed, Luxemburg beaten to death, Graber executed, the rest of the compromisers inevitably getting stuck in their own or inherited debt.

Do the civil servants benefit? With 5-6 times their salaries and up to 10 times prices. The soldiers? In return for their sacrifice of life, they harvest mistrust and contempt from their fellow citizens and suffer bitter hardship.

Artists and freelance professions? How they all suffer under inflation! The entire middle class stands in danger of being crushed. The renter class, a dying class.

Over all labor, over all income, over every yield, over every profession, over almost every single economic transaction hovers the tax. Like an enormous threat, the tax stifles even the seed of any successful economic activity. If, nevertheless, someone decides boldly to cover their needs, the tax devours like a greedy fire the largest part of their earnings. Every form of wealth accumulation is prevented, every morsel of bread is taxed, every journey carries multiple tax burdens; the foundation of our national economy, coal, is loaded with taxes that amount to many times its production costs. Every exchange of goods—the purpose and content of the national economy—is burdened with huge turnover taxes; beyond that, most goods and luxury items are burdened with special taxes: tobacco, sugar, salt, spirits, beer, lemonade, matches, light bulbs. Thus, the tax lies like a gray, life-killing veil over all economy.

Taxes and inflation: these are the two most essential characteristics of our economic life today, taxes and inflation, each dependent on the other, each drawing the other after it.

2. The Emergence and Consequences of a General Tax Struggle

These are the inevitable consequences of such unbearable burdens and constraints? Initially, the cabinet of fulfillment will find itself in ever greater difficulties—difficulties that lie precisely in the impossibility of fulfilling the task. These difficulties could, in themselves, be of little concern to the German people, as long as they merely pertain to personnel issues, but they cannot remain indifferent when the changing of personnel is accompanied by an ever-increasing tax burden. For the government and the people must finally become fully aware that the arithmetic of interest payments to world capital—that is the purpose, means, and content of the Treaty of Versailles—remains unsolvable with the current methods of taxation, because these eternal interest payments represent the most sophisticated method of exploitation in history. If this deception can now be based on legal titles, the responsibility for it lies with the Reich government.

The people themselves, and particularly the German people in their endless patience and endurance, will eventually demand a full accounting from their government when it becomes clear to every individual that the unbearable tax burden serves solely the purpose of paying interest to world capital. Only when they realize that with every piece of bread, every warm room, every achievement, they are paying interest to the enemy—not the wartime enemy, the Frenchman or Englishman who stood opposite them in the trenches, but the global enemy, the supranational money power, for which the governments of the enemy alliance are merely executors—only then will the protest, the outrage, and the will for liberation arise. Only when everyone sees that their own government considers its foremost task to be the fulfillment of the unfulfillable, and thus degrades itself from being the steward of national tasks, of national reconstruction, about which so much is eloquently spoken—to being the steward and tax collector of the enemy alliance, will the will to refuse payments emerge, the only thing that promises liberation from such an unprecedented interest slavery.

One should not imagine the outbreak of a general tax struggle as though a slogan were issued from some quarter and suddenly, on command, from the next day forward, the entire people ceased to pay taxes. Such a spontaneous initiation of a general tax struggle would only be conceivable under the assumption that the tax struggle was systematically prepared for a long time by some organization working toward this goal, and that this organization, upon issuing the slogan, would find a well-prepared ground due to some fortunate development of circumstances. It is, however, unlikely that such circumstances will arise, circumstances that would, so to speak, instantly make the necessity of a tax struggle clear to the entire people. For given the indifference and lack of judgment among the broadest circles of the people, and given the entanglement in party, class, and other oppositions, even, for example, the occupation of the Ruhr would not be enough today to rally the people to the cause. The probable and presumed outbreak of the tax struggle will instead unfold in the manner indicated above: some political or economic group issues the slogan for the tax struggle; if this group is strong enough that the state's means of defense and its organs fail to counter it, then this will naturally lead to a general tax struggle.

Like any systematically initiated battle and like any other struggle, the tax struggle has a specific goal. Once this goal is reached, there would, in itself, be no reason to continue the tax struggle.

The goal of a general tax struggle will be: resistance against an unhealthy, excessive, overreaching, and paralyzing tax policy, caused by the general financial mismanagement in the country and caused by the unbearable and un-affordable payments to the enemy. The opponent that should be defeated through the tax struggle is thus the misguided tax, financial, and economic policy. Perhaps even more clearly, specific cabinets, specific governments, or specific parliamentary situations may appear as opponents. As a distant and final opponent to be vanquished through the tax struggle appear the unhealthy and unfulfillable demands of the enemy, especially when the additional consideration is made that this enemy, although it once imposed on us the so-called Peace Treaty of Versailles and declared it the legal basis for our payments, itself never adheres to this treaty but repeatedly and continuously seizes opportunities to impose new burdens on us under various pretexts.

The tax struggle thus serves both the fight against domestic conditions perceived as untenable and the fight against the external enemy in place of a conflict with weapons; the tax struggle is therefore more than mere passive resistance; in its effect, it is an attack on the state's function as a tax collector and henchman of the enemy.

The question, therefore, is when and from which moment the goal of the tax struggle is considered achieved, and what is then to be done to return to normal conditions, or whether it is even possible to find a way out of such conditions brought about by a tax struggle.

Here, it must be emphasized in advance that the phrase *"conditions brought about by a tax struggle"* is misleading; for the conditions that have triggered the tax struggle are the causes of the destruction of the national economy and the ruin of the state, not the tax struggle itself!

The conditions resulting from a prolonged general tax struggle can be summarized into the following groups:

a) Effects on the workings of the state

As already described, the state will direct all its defensive measures against the tax struggle toward maintaining its grip, that is, keeping its organs and functionaries in power—in other words, preserving and sustaining the bureaucratic apparatus and the authority of the administration. How far this succeeds will depend on the impact, extent, and duration of the tax struggle. Since the state administrative apparatus represents, for the people, the embodiment of misguided state measures, and since this state apparatus must primarily be funded from tax revenues, a tax struggle will inevitably create a strong rift between everything that constitutes authority on one side and the people on the other, or it will deepen an already existing rift to monstrous proportions. It can be assumed with considerable certainty that the likely consequence will be the disappearance of any authority of the authorities. The best chance of maintaining authority remains for the outlying offices, but only where a prudent, reasonable, and popular personality stands at the head of an office. It might go as it did during the dissolution of the naval units brought about by the revolution: wherever an unpopular officer stood at the head of a smaller troop unit, the soldiers' councils took command; but wherever officers managed to earn the internal respect of the men, they could lead their company or detachment back to the homeland in an orderly manner. Thus, where at an administrative post an official manages to retain his authority even in such times based on his previous activities, he will still exert some influence within his district and be able to maintain somewhat orderly conditions there; but wherever an unpopular, overbearing, intolerant, or bureaucratic official holds a position that constantly puts him in contact with the people, the authority of the office will very soon be nullified in such times. The central authorities will continue to issue orders to the subordinate offices, but they will soon hear from the outside that their orders can no longer be enforced.

b) Economic consequences

Since it was among the first defensive measures of the state to sustain itself through the continuous use of the printing press, an immense deterioration of the currency would already occur simply due to the flooding with paper payment instruments. But even the fact of the tax struggle as such alone would, theoretically, shake the credit of the state. The currency would thus continue to plummet rapidly in the shortest time, making any import that is not barter trade impossible once again. For domestic business activity as such, there would be no inherent necessity to restrict production. On the contrary, given the poor currency, the entire people would have to be nourished from the domestic products of the country, making it necessary to push domestic production to the highest level, to focus the production of goods on so-called essentials, and to limit the production of non-essential goods or luxury items.

As far as productive activity is concerned, it would, by and large, continue in an orderly fashion. Since the struggle is explicitly directed against the state's paper money policy, the people would reduce the acceptance of paper payment instruments and conduct business primarily through barter.

This would largely paralyze the activity of the banks. Indeed, the asset-backed securities would still have the same underlying assets as before; in fact, these assets would have even greater significance, as the pure paper money, as part of the national wealth, would have lost its value. However, the liquidity of the shares, the ability to trade, and speculation in stocks and foreign exchange would become difficult, indeed, it would cease on its own.

From the moment the tax struggle has advanced to such an extent that the state's paper notes are no longer accepted as a means of payment by the people, and are instead considered worthless, the tax struggle has achieved its goal in this regard: combating the state's financial policy.

c) Domestic political effects

One of the most severe tests for the political maturity of the Germans is when they are called upon to take a stance on the question of German unity.

The phrase: *"The last thing we have left after the collapse is the unity of the German Reich,"* dominates and confuses the minds of almost all political parties, so much so that it seems to unite right and left-wing parties on this ground. It seems so, because in reality each side understands something different by it.

The *"loyal to the Reich"* right-wing party member thinks of the commanding power of the Bismarckian Reich when hearing the term *"unity of the Reich,"* whose restoration he longs for; in doing so, he completely forgets that the present Reich is fundamentally different from what he envisions when he advocates for the preservation of the unity of the Reich.

The *"loyal to the Reich"* Social Democracy thinks of the *"unity of the Reich"* as the maintenance, indeed, the expansion, of its holdings of ministerial posts, the position of the Reich President, and the defense of everything that could endanger the *"unity of the Reich"* as *"reactionary," "backward," "federalist," "local narrow-mindedness,"* etc.

The *"loyal to the Reich"* Democrats are the trusting and credulous Germans who believe they can reconcile today's democracy with patriotism. The *"Democrat"* associates the *"unity of the Reich"* with the ideals of 1848, with the longed-for liberation from pre-March petty-state rule and police despotism, and overlooks, just like the right-wing party member, that today's democracy of the Weimar Constitution is only the disguised form of the rule of the elite following the model of Western democracies.

For the calm observer, the present unity of the Reich consists solely of a ruthless centralism in Berlin, which serves only the interests of financially powerful and plutocratic circles. This *"unity of the Reich"* has absolutely nothing to do with the people of Germany.

If we have made these fundamental preliminary remarks here, it is because we feel obliged, in our investigation of the coming tax struggle, not to bypass the burning question: whether, and when, and what influences a general tax struggle could have on the existence of the Reich.

That this question will arise is clear, and indeed it will be posed in the form of assertions or accusations: that a tax struggle would destroy the existence of the Reich. Precisely because we anticipate these reservations and accusations, we must emphatically point out that the consequences of any causes cannot be blamed for further consequences. It is not the farmer's *"fault"* for the bruises the caught railway thief bears, but rather the perpetrated or intended theft that caused the bruises. Just as little is the tax struggle to blame if the existence of the Reich is endangered or destroyed, but rather the unbearable tax system is the cause, which must invite the tax struggle, because otherwise, the people and the economy will perish under the taxes, not under the tax struggle!

Admittedly, the tax struggle is directed against the Reich government—but this Reich government is by no means to be equated with the *"German Reich,"* let alone the German people. But it is the German people that matter, not the so-called *"unity of the Reich,"* which today must not be understood retrospectively as the old, lost powerful Bismarckian Reich, nor as the ideal of the struggle for German unity from the years of 1848, but rather must be understood as: the unity scrap of party concentration and the convenient exploitation headquarters in Berlin for the supra-statal money powers. Herein lies the unity of the Reich today.

If this realization were held fast to in political decisions, all difficulties regarding the feasibility of *"holding on to the idea of the Reich"* and *"sacrifices for the Reich"* would resolve themselves. The salvation of the Fatherland stands far above all constitutional questions, far above the *"unity idea,"* far above economic viewpoints, and above all else, far, far above mercantile and financial interests.

Does the unity of tax collection and administration even have anything to do with the unity of the German *"people"*?

Do not our German-Austrian brothers belong a thousand times more intimately to the German people than German citizens of Jewish faith? Are the speculators and moneylenders, even if they are Germans by birth and Christians by their childhood faith, more important for Germanness through their daily visits to the German great banks and stock exchanges than the Germans in the Sudetenland in Czechoslovakia, in Poland, and in other foreign territories, who are heavily persecuted because of their Germanness? Does the unity of a people not consist far more in the unity of its language, its customs, its culture, its tradition, in the unity of its worldview, its race?

Whether the so-called unity of the Reich is torn apart or endangered by a tax struggle thus stands and falls with the answer to the question: whether one considers the existing, and after the enactment of the new taxes, fully enforced plundering of the German people by the Berlin central government to be useful or harmful.

Even if a general tax struggle truly meant the collapse of Berlin's unity (even if we ourselves regard this as a falsely posed question), it is by no means certain that the German people would suffer harm in its internal national unity.

A genuine reconstruction of the German Reich certainly requires, as an absolute and indispensable precondition, the radical liberation from a downright deadly form of state finance and tax management.

d) Foreign political consequences

The effect of a general tax struggle on foreign countries must also be examined in a theoretical discussion of the possibility and likelihood of such a tax struggle.

Unfortunately, we are today in Germany so far along that no issue of importance can be raised without raising the shameful question: What will the enemy and foreign countries say about this?

The enemy has two conflicting interests in the tax struggle: Firstly, the enemy must fear that due to the tax struggle he will not receive the expected payments from Germany. This view will spur him to do his utmost to prevent the spread of the tax struggle. But the enemy will not fail to receive the expected payments from Germany because the people are rebelling against the taxes, but rather he will not receive them due to internal necessities, because the demands placed on Germany exceed human capabilities, and because neither the enemies nor the German people have the power to make the impossible possible. It will therefore depend solely on whether, at the outbreak of the German tax struggle, the hostile governments come to recognize the unreasonableness and impossibility of the demands placed on Germany or not. Unfortunately, there are still no signs that such insight will take hold among our enemies.

A formal declaration of war by France against Germany is not to be expected. It would also be nonsense and superfluous. For we are already still living in a continued state of war with France, only with the difference that we can no longer defend ourselves with military weapons. The people themselves, however, know and feel that all the continued legal violations by the enemy are nothing other than acts of war. The support of the Polish intrigues in Upper Silesia, the sanctions, the concentration of troops in the Ruhr area, with the readiness to march in at any moment, the occupation with its unheard-of demands, finally the division of Upper Silesia, which is not only in contempt of the Versailles Treaty, but even more so of the principle of the *"right of self-determination of peoples,"* aiming at the economic strangulation of Germany:—all this is continued war, only war not with weapons, but war with humiliations and economic exploitation. This type of war will then be continued with all means that have already been suggested.

3. The way out

It is therefore not the tax struggle, but the financial policy of the Reich that must trigger all the consequences that have been described in the preceding sections. Financial policy is indeed too narrowly conceived; for the different types of policy cannot be separated from one another. Thus, the inadequate policy during the war undermined and transformed the successes of military warfare into the opposite, the fragility and irresoluteness of internal policy has sapped the internal cohesiveness of the German people and led in foreign affairs to catastrophic consequences. The document and the certificate of incompetence, that is, the proof of incapacity for our entire policy, is called: Treaty of Versailles.

That dilettantism in state leadership has further expanded in the post-war period is obvious to all eyes. However, the most palpable expression of this entire policy of the German government is found in the tax burdens that are imposed on the German people as a whole.

With these observations, however, as already noted, we have by no means exhausted the ultimate reasons that have led to the seemingly insoluble confusion of today. Only the following realization will lead us there: the extent to which the entire disastrous policy has unfolded.

The subjugation of all the peoples of the world was the goal and purpose of the World War. How close the power of big money has come to this goal is shown by a brief overview that encompasses the indebtedness of the most important states of the Western cultural sphere. I base this on the data from the well-known large English statistical yearbook for the year 1921.

The Statesman Year-Book gives the indebtedness of England—that is, of the English people to capital—as of March 31, 1921, at £7,537,200,000 with an annual interest of £349.6 million.

The United States of America, according to the same statistical source, owed as of March 31, 1920, $24,297,918,411 (24 billion 297 million 918,411 dollars), a colossal sum that the victorious American people must pay in interest as the fruit of victory to the all-dominating power of money.

France owes to domestic and foreign state creditors 285 billion-883 million francs, which the people must pay in interest—to the same supranational financial power to which we and the other peoples have become indebted through a fundamentally flawed financial policy.

Italy pays for its *"sacred egoism"* with a public debt of around 72 billion lire.

Canada, with its population of 7,206,643 people—roughly equivalent to Bavaria—is indebted to capital at $3,014,483,774.

Australia must extract the interest for a public debt of £381,415,317 from its 5.2 million inhabitants!

The victors are therefore no better off. Everywhere we see the same phenomenon of boundless indebtedness of the peoples to international finance capital, which has everywhere placed the governments of the peoples in the service of interest for its own interests.

We need not even imagine that all the finance ministers, on the basis of bribes, followed the dictates of the big capitalists. Rather, their behavior is based on a deeply and firmly rooted legal notion that has become almost common property of the Western world, the legal notion that any kind of ownership of money implies a right to a continuous flow from the labor of others—interest.

Herein lies the enormous significance of the interest problem—and therefore the solution of the interest problem is the first and most important task for the entire world. With national economic scholastic notions one comes nowhere near understanding the global problem of interest. The economic justifications for taking interest are in no way explanations for interest itself, but only the repetition of often very superficial attempts at justification by the interested parties. Furthermore, and this is the more important point for our entire consideration, economics in its presentations on interest on capital deals almost exclusively with private credit and the resulting relationships between creditors and debtors, but not with the modern form of state credit.

There is no room here for a longer discussion with academic economics. For us, it is a question of economic survival for all the peoples of the Western cultural sphere, among whom the notion of interest has precisely led to the so-called highly capitalist credit and interest economy, the consequences of which we now see before us. That these consequences are disastrous and untenable should, after the figures presented above on the international indebtedness of all the peoples involved in the war, need no further proof. This insight alone justifies the conclusion that the pursued financial policy—the covering of the monetary needs of the states through borrowing—was wrong. Just as wrong, moreover, is the equation of the state with the private beggar of money, which the defenders of state financial policy repeatedly rely upon, fundamentally wrong as it is. If the parallel were correct: private individual equals state, then the private individual should conversely also be in a position to levy taxes for himself—perhaps in his neighborhood—to cover his financial needs, or to enact laws for himself and condemn his inconvenient neighbor to death or expropriation—all functions that undoubtedly belong to the sovereign state but never to the private individual.

Precisely the idea of the state's sovereign power in collecting taxes shows that the state indeed has very different means to cover its financial needs than the private individual, that the state is by no means dependent on the borrowing route like the private individual. Moreover, the state possesses in its minting authority and in its right to create money based on legal provisions by the people's representatives a further possibility to cover its financial needs without incurring interest.

Recalling the already often demonstrated sovereignty of states in cases of declared partial or complete state bankruptcy teaches us that the state also has this possibility, to liberate itself from its debts through its own sovereign power and without any obligation of damages.

From these insights, naturally challenging proposals arise that are suitable to solve the chaos and to show new paths for the future.

A two-fold task must be fulfilled by any truly incisive reform= proposal: firstly, the abolition and dissolution of the existing interest liability with the utmost preservation of economic life, and secondly, funding new major state tasks on a non-interest-bearing basis.

The *"first"* and *"second"* must not be understood such that in temporal sequence, first the elimination or dissolution of today's interest obligations must occur, so that then the funding of state tasks without interest basis can happen. Quite the contrary, indications suggest. That our proposals for the funding of major works on an interest-free basis will have been implemented for some time, yet the states still struggle in fulfilling their interest obligations through more and more insane increases in taxation.

For today—as Lord Churchill put it in his last major speech in Dundee —the collection of interest has become *"the state's main industry"*, so we are thereby only confirmed by a voice that is respected by everyone that we have always pointed correctly to this condition in our affirmations.

Since all peoples have been ensnared into the interest servitude through fundamentally flawed financial policies, the natural and simple demand is consequently: elimination of this interest servitude through the termination of the usury-interest-services of the state.

Therefore, our first demand is: cessation of the usury services on all interest-based debt obligations of the Empire, the federal states and all funds specially administrated by counties, particularly in war bonds, Imperial promissory notes etc. All debt titles are to be continued to the owners as deposits without interest.

The second basic demand is: the government budgets expenditures for public utility establishments (building of water facilities, canal constructions etc.), insofar the money for them is not being generated immediately from tax revenues, through issuing non-interest treasury notes. The funds are being recauppled from the earnings of the new facilities.

How individual financial and banking technical, the transformation of different bond instruments into deposit balances should be carried out, can not be the task of this document. That such proposals are entirely not dilettantish or Utopian emerges from the demand by one of the respected banking experts, the deceased director of Hamburg's mortgage bank, Bendixen, who drafted such actions for war bonds and for this purpose proceeded an already worked up legislative blueprint in the *"Bank Archive"* of December 1, 1919.

These two demands are consistent with the fundamental insights obtained. Without trickery, without twisting these two proposals emerge through correct analysis as the best methods for convalescence from the root sickness problem—usury-interest.

The veritable fact that the peoples of the western cultural era have have been engulfed by interest-based obligations cannot now be disputed, given the figures divulged about public debts—from friends and foes alike. Equally irrefutable, the obligation to service this immense debt has become the supreme concern even before taxation, as now most of parliaments efforts center on the process of inventing new taxes and implementing their collections. Against these monstrous present-day facts, there exists but one remedy for curing them: liberation from the usury-interest serfdom!

Clausewitz once said: In war everything is simple, but the simple is extremely difficult. In this most difficult war that humanity must wage for the freedom and burden of labor, the foregoing answer is likewise extremely simple, but its implementation is extremely difficult. Difficult not because of the measures to be taken, but because of the unlimited means of power of the opponent.

The interest-free declaration of fixed-interest government securities, along with their simultaneous conversion into interest-free bank deposits, is as simple and easy as the enactment of any other law. In any case, much easier than the enforcement of any tax law. Difficult is only the overcoming of the resistance of those who have an interest in maintaining the current state of affairs.

The number of those who are truly interested in the current state of affairs is in itself vanishingly small; large is only the number of followers who supposedly benefit from the state's interest service.

The clear recognition of the real conditions is obscured by the fact that alongside the few large loan capitalists, who proportionally hold by far the largest mass of securities in their possession, many millions of middle and small capitalists (the term *"capitalists"* is actually not quite the right expression for these people, as it involves the owners of savings) have also invested their savings in interest-bearing securities. These people expect small amounts of interest from their securities: before this pleasant fact they forget that they themselves must pay these interests—because the state can only give what it takes back from its citizens in some form—through direct or, more concealed, indirect taxes. Moreover, not only must the small interest recipients pay their own interests, but they must also pay, together, a good part of the interests that are to be paid to the large loan capital owners.

The distress of these small renters and pensioners exceeds any measure in today's already occurring and still progressing devaluation of money. It must plainly be said that the renter class economically has no justification. And under today's economic form the renter class has indeed become a dying class, and thousands of parents have had to give up the idea of leaving their babies a well-filled money box from which the children could live without work and effort from the interests—that is, from the labor of others. This is as it should be. It was high time that the renter ideal was thoroughly done away with. One should be industrious and learn to save as much as one can, and no one has anything against it if one in later life enjoys the fruits of diligence in peace.

However, the conversion of savings into interest-bearing paper had become a cancerous lesion of our national economy. The idea of interest had crept so deep into our legal conscience that it was considered just as careless to *"attack the capital"* and spend more than the yield of the interest. Usually, no one gave thought to where these interests came from. The ever present opportunity, offered by government securities, of turning each spare bank note into an interest-bearing paper, let the mysterious property of money *"to bear interest"* seem quite natural, as a property ascribed to money almost self-grown from.

Opposite as this *"self-growing"* of money was to all earthly experience, so there became the bearing of interest to an infallible dogma of the last decades. We say not too much when we assert that this matter, in this matter-of-fact unquestioned phenomenon of interest-bearing money, must be sought as something like a kernel in the modern capitalist system.

The infecting of our economic view by the interest and renter idealism has in every way affected disadvantageously the social instincts of men. Who collected a heap of money, enough to live comfortably on the interest thereof, desisted from effort, was emancipated from all effort to maintain their fortune—the state became their rent collector. To such men was no longer of interest the poet's admonition, *"Our heritage by elder time won, procure it, make it your own."* With the renter idea, the gentleman of unearned ease graduated from the ranks of his laboring citizen classmates. This is basically what distinguishes the owner of loan capital from any other form of ownership. Neither the farmer, the landed proprietor, the merchant, the industrialist can sit idly and have others work for him; all must be active, be industrious, cultivate the soil, labor, provide for raw materials and for an outlet, and the greater the enterprise—the greater the ownership becomes the more does the man of property become the highly responsible administrator of his in the interest of the whole society again in this own. In another case, the yield falls effortlessly into the lap of the owner, like the interest for the holder of fixed-interest securities.

Like a terrible punishment for the beneficiaries of the renter ideal, they are now struck by the complete devaluation of their interest and their capital. Not as punishment in the bourgeois sense, but rather metaphysically as a punishment for a perverse anti-social mental disposition, the millions of small and middle-class renters are deceived of their capital and interest.

However, the aid for those defrauded of their savings must not occur as an equally undignified and hopeless beggary, but as a thorough state aid measure. This aid can only occur in such a way that the small renters and those who have been defrauded of their income by the existing concealed state bankruptcy—for that is what the state-induced devaluation of money must be called—deliver their debt securities to the state, and the state in return establishes a sufficient life annuity corresponding to the healthy money value. Through such aid, the small renters could be effectively helped, immense misery alleviated, and at the same time the state could be freed from a perpetual interest payment. For with the death of the renter, the debt would also be extinguished for the state. Such aid for the small renters and the citizens in similar positions would be nothing other than an act of social justice as a matter of course. There can be no doubt about its feasibility when one considers the enormous sums that our government has committed to pay to the enemy. And the moral duty not to let our own fellow countrymen starve stands far above the fidelity to treaties towards insatiable and vengeful enemies, regardless of all signed and extorted agreements. Taking into account the aforementioned social aid measures for those most severely affected, victims of a perverse financial policy as well as a fundamentally false conception of saving for the sake of the renter ideal, the only rescue, the only way out of the otherwise irredeemable financial, economic, and moral chaos is the abolition of the interest service on all fixed-interest securities of the states and similar papers.

For Germany, the refusal of interest payment on the reparation securities is a condition for survival. It does not even need to be associated with a refusal of reparations, as such a refusal is entirely within the legal consciousness of the victor, who by virtue of his victory has the right to demand atonement and compensation for actual damage caused. A reconstruction of Northern France, however, lies within the capacity of Germany: a solidaristic reconstruction effort by the nations involved in the war would even mean a blessed and welcome employment opportunity for all of Europe; but an interest payment that is far greater than the reconstruction costs is equally disastrous for all involved. For no matter how much interest the world-dominating money powers pocket, not a single expelled Northern Frenchman gets his destroyed home rebuilt, and the enormous interest burden on the French taxpayer is not reduced by a single centime. But everyone is equally struck by the same misfortune of the devaluation of their savings through a general devaluation of money, with the increase in income nowhere keeping pace. Only the power of supra-national capital rises mightily and all-dominantly to world-ruling size.

Liberation from the world domination of Mammonistic powers is not only a national, economic, and financial necessity, it is also a necessity of the highest moral significance.

Whether with the insightful cooperation of the current beneficiaries of the high-capitalist system or against them, the breaking of the interest-based economy will occur by the force of nature. For the Mammonistic world rulers have long been unable to master the world economic crisis. A rule based on fundamentally false legal conceptions cannot be maintained in the long run; it must collapse.

The illusion that the state, in order to satisfy its need for money, must inevitably turn to big capital, for which it would have to pay interest, is a deliberate misguidance with the intended and almost successful end goal of subjecting the power of government exclusively to the service of the money powers. It is precisely at this unnaturalness of such a condition that the rule of the money powers over the states and peoples will break.

This bondage will break all the sooner, the sooner a bold decision dares to finance a great project on an interest-free basis.

This brings us to the second proposal, which shows the way in which future abuses of state financial policy can be avoided.

The state covers the costs for new creations (development of water power, railway and canal construction, etc.), to the extent that the funds for this cannot be raised through direct taxes, by the issuance of interest-free state treasury notes.

We feel obliged to explain this proposal with a particularly illustrative example.

The example closest to us Bavarians—the harnessing of our water resources—is especially suitable because the case at hand, *mutatis mutandis,* is applicable to any major new creation.

We contrast: how it was done and how it should have been done.

The development of Bavarian water resources incurs a cost of approximately 800 million marks in today's currency. For this purpose, a share company was founded. This share company, however, consists only of some state officials and commissioners, so that we are essentially dealing with a sham foundation by the state. The capital of this share company was almost entirely provided by the state. Naturally, the so-called "D" banks are also involved. The share capital amounts to DM 75 million marks.

This joint-stock company is now issuing a massive loan of 800 million Marks under state guarantee. The loan is to be issued at 98% of face value, bears 4½% interest, and is to be repaid over approximately 63 years at 1½% annually, starting in 1926, the year operations are expected to begin. This was resolved and implemented despite timely counter proposals.

We must now ask ourselves: What do our Bavarian hydroelectric plants cost us?

1. Estimated construction costs to be raised:

- 800,000,000 Marks

2. Interest on the borrowed 800 million Marks until the year 1926, during the construction period at 4½%:

- 180,000,000 Marks

3. Interest during the designated repayment period:

- 712,000,000 Marks

Subtotal: 1,692,000,000 Marks

4. Now add just a 6% dividend on the paid-in share capital of 50 + 75 = 125 million Marks, over the repayment period of 37 years:

- 277,500,000 Marks

Total Estimated Cost

1,969,500,000 Marks

Note: This is described as the most favorable (i.e. optimistic) estimate.

We do not even want to argue about a more or less of a few hundred million, since the Bavarian state, with the chosen financing through loans, will in any case far exceed one billion. Paid to the big capitalists, who are so friendly as to pump their surplus millions—for otherwise they could not lend these millions—to the poor Bavarian state at 4 1/2% interest.

If, as is absolutely to be expected, the projected construction costs are far from sufficient, new loans will naturally have to be taken out, and no amortization can be considered; then the Bavarian water resources will cost the Bavarian people year after year so much that one could build a new Walchensee plant every five years. The expansion of Bavarian water resources through highly capitalist financing method is not actually an increase in wealth for the Bavarian people but merely a convenient opportunity for the placement of 800 million in liquid funds at good and unconditionally secure interest for big capital. This is why the Bavarian state—meaning in this case the Bavarian taxpayer—must assume the unlimited liability for capital and interest (see the issuance conditions). Therefore, it makes no difference whether the plants can truly deliver electricity, or whether a natural event, such as an earthquake, destroys the plants, or if they remain half-finished: the capitalists receive their interest, even if it comes from taxes specifically levied for this purpose.

We must also particularly point out that with the issuance of the 800 million in new securities, the Bavarian state is effectively bringing 800 million in freshly printed paper into circulation, which, due to its special security features, is at least as good as ordinary new paper money. The fortunate owner of a few million water power bonds can purchase whatever he wants with them. Whether he directly uses these water power bonds as payment or conducts a small banking transaction in between makes no difference for the free exercise of his purchasing power based on his possession of water power bonds.

In summary, what we have in the expansion of Bavarian water resources is as follows: The Bavarian state borrows 800 million, which it must pay interest on and intends to amortize. This will cost at least 2 billion. Therefore, the expansion of the water resources does not cost 800 million, as the patient taxpayer assumes, but rather, through expensive electricity prices or even through taxes, the taxpayer must cover over 2 billion for the expansion of Bavarian water resources. Additionally, the taxpayer must assume the full guarantee towards the capitalists; the water resources are not the free property of the Bavarian people but are explicitly pledged to the *"money lender."* The Bavarians do not receive cheap electricity from their Bavarian water resources; instead, due to the interest obligations, electrical power costs about 3-4 times more than the actual production costs of the electricity; meaning that the salaries and wages of all workers, lock-keepers, engineers, technicians, merchants, administrative officials, electrical technicians, office personnel, etc., employed at the *"state water power plants,"* as well as the expenses for all necessary lubricants, packing wool, fuses, repair work, etc., amount to only a third or a quarter of the annual interest payments! Moreover, the state issues a few more train carloads of new securities to address an urgent need.

In the jargon of high capitalism, this is called: *"a particularly fortunate financing on the broad basis of a common foundation."*

Now, to our proposal:

Clear, logical reasoning must conclude: The plants are indeed designed by our Bavarian engineers, they are built by these engineers, Bavarian workers and Bavarian contractors carry out the work over many years of difficult and diligent labor, Bavarian administrative officials or merchants will manage the plants later, and the entire Bavarian people, through the approval of their parliamentary representatives, have given their consent to expand Bavarian water resources. Moreover: the Bavarian people in their entirety have already declared themselves ready to approve the necessary credits for the construction. Why then—we ask—does the state not provide the necessary funds from its own authority and based on the approved credits? If the state is already liable for 800 million— towards the capitalists—then why does it not issue non-interest-bearing vouchers from the Bavarian State Bank instead of the *"interest-bearing"* 800 million in new securities (the water power bonds)? Of course, there can be no question of simultaneously issuing 800 million in new government bonds, as it does not need them immediately. For the payment of workers and contractors, it might need 40-50 million in the first year, an amount that the entire Bavarian economy would barely sense as inflation. In the following year, a large portion of these millions would already have returned to state coffers through the channels of monetary circulation, and, if needed, only a much smaller additional amount would have to be introduced in the second and subsequent years. This does not even consider the monetary transfer system that would eliminate any inflationary effect from the outset. In reality, one cannot even speak of inflation in this case because the issued notes are backed by newly created values, unlike our current government financing, which is—nothing !

In recent years, people have truly not shied away from making money out of paper. The *"backing"* of this paper money may have been considered—with horror—but nothing was done about it. And now, when an outstanding economic resource is to be developed, the issuance of a few million new vouchers, fully backed by tangible assets, should be called *"inflationary"*? Such objections may be made to the poor, frightened taxpayer, but not to someone who clearly sees through the outrageous swindle of high-capitalist debt policies.

When the Bavarian revolutionary state urgently needed money in November 1918, it was suddenly able to print money on its own authority;

approximately 120 million completely unbacked paper money was issued, and various municipalities in Bavaria issued their emergency war currency: a total of 138 million, all *"unbacked"* money for entirely unproductive purposes. That was inflationary monetary policy. Such fiscal policy has certainly not been held up as an ideal, but it was implemented.

Covering the entire state's needs with the help of the printing press is pure financial alchemy. Bolshevik Russia, with this supposedly anti-capitalist monetary policy, has fallen into complete and irreversible dependence on big capital. Nowhere is it easier for big capital to obtain economic concessions of all kinds.

Austria has conducted its financial alchemy with great success, and there too, all state needs are covered by the *"printing press."* The result is an unprecedented impoverishment of the middle class, rapid currency devaluation, and the surrender of all national assets to foreign big capital. The fact that Austria's financial subjugation to foreign powers through the channel of foreign loans has not progressed further is due to the lack of a state authority that could guarantee the proper inflow of interest to international capital.

It is also highly noteworthy that in Austria, too, the financial Bolshevism of printing money has been abandoned for the construction of large power plants, and the creation of major productive assets adheres to the proven methods of Western European high-capitalist debt policies. In Germany, the land of absurdities and compromises, the land where, alongside immense energy and strength, pitiful weakness and spinelessness prevail—in this Germany, which must inevitably appear to foreigners as the European sphinx—financial matters are the most confused of all. In the subconscious, there is still a lingering belief that the state's needs should be covered, as per the old Frederician recipe, by communal contributions to the state: hence, taxation is pursued with such fervor. Yet, to avoid appearing old-fashioned, financial alchemy has been so extensively employed that we now possess around 90,000,000.00 Marks of beautifully printed paper money, practically unbacked by any tangible assets. In addition, we have made over 300,000,000.00 Marks of fixed-interest bearing debt, and, for the sake of preserving long-established principles, we are striving for the complete socialization of German property through boundless tax projects, with the result that Alfred Lansburgh described in the August issue of **Die Bank** as follows: *"The temptation for tax fraud does not only grow in proportion to the severity of taxes, but much faster, as soon as property-owning classes, bound by traditional concepts of ownership, no longer perceive taxes as a fair contribution to national needs but as—intended or unintended—expropriation."*

In passing, we would like to point to Lansburgh's stance on the concept of property, as we noted this statement not because of the accurate remark about healthy tax morality but because of the comment on *"property-owning classes bound by traditional concepts of ownership."* Naturally, we wonder what n e w concepts of property, *"free from the constraints of traditional notions,"* Herr Lansburgh might wish to see in the future. In our view, there is only one unambiguous concept of property, which can be simply expressed in the words:

"What is mine is mine." The Marxist notion, according to which, as Proudhon said, *"property is theft,"* has today transformed in many minds into these words and, unfortunately, also into deeds: *"What is yours is mine."* How far this widespread modern concept of property has been spiritualized and sublimated and adapted to Rathenau's organizational forms by Mr. Lansburgh, we cannot say.

It was necessary to address the repeatedly raised objection that the issuance of new state energy vouchers would mean inflation. We have demonstrated:

First, that there can be no talk of *"inflation"* when new values are simultaneously created;

Second, that through the printing of hydro power bonds, new securities are also created, which have *"purchasing power"* for their holders;

- Third, that in the usual method of raising funds through loans, much more new paper is printed than if the ongoing construction needs were met simply by issuing new notes;
- Fourth, that only a very small fraction of the total demand would actually have to be issued in new notes, as the majority of payments could be made without cash;
- Fifth, how enormous sums are added to the cost of large power plants by financing them through loans;

- Sixth, that the usual form of financing through loans is equivalent to handing over the most valuable national energy sources to loan capital: It is not the community that benefits from the work of their engineers and workers, from the natural resources and water power, but the consumers who must pay a multiple of the cost for the electricity or the products derived from it, such as nitrogen, due to interest obligations;

- Seventh, that the community has explicitly guaranteed all these tributes to big loan capital.

Only when one keeps all these points in mind can one get a picture of the downright unbelievable clumsiness of our financial circumstances.

For this second proposal of ours, it also holds true that its great simplicity and clarity does not make its implementation difficult because it is inherently challenging, but because the resistance arising from interested opposition, mental laziness, and convenience is infinitely hard to overcome.

Precisely because we know this, we have gone into more detail in justifying this proposal, particularly in the direction of exposing the falsehoods in existing ideas.

It is self-evident that only such a state financial administration can be considered sound which draws its ongoing expenditures for administration, justice, art and science, national defense, etc., from ongoing revenue—that is, from the surpluses of profitable state enterprises and from taxes—while the costs for new creations, insofar as they cannot be covered by special levies, are met, on the basis of the approval by the national representation after the most conscientious examination of necessity and expediency, by the interest-free issuance of state vouchers.

The concept of *"money creation from one's own right"* may be briefly explained by an example from everyday life. In a small circle of mutually acquainted businessmen, someone who has received a delivery from another tears a sheet of paper from his notebook and writes on it: Voucher for 100 Marks, and signs this voucher with his name. The recipient will be able to pass this voucher on within the circle of acquaintances as good as cash. In the neighboring town, however, this voucher will not be accepted as money. What has this voucher issuer done? He has *"created money from his own right."* The value token thus created has, of course, only a very limited circulation, it is limited to the *"territory,"* in this case called the circle of acquaintances of the person in question.

When a municipality, in its financial need, prints nice-looking notes with a promise of payment for 50 pfennigs, 1, 5, and 10 Marks, and beneath it puts the names of the mayor and some city or municipal councilors, this money, as we all know from the war period, will be accepted by everyone just like Reich money. What has this municipality done? Money creation from its own right. Here too, the territory is limited to the area of the city or municipality.

When a state like Bavaria—as happened—issues state energy vouchers through its state bank, it has done nothing else but create money from its own right. The territory of this money was in this case the whole land of Bavaria.

Such money creation is permissible in all cases only if behind the promise of payment, behind the voucher, there is the security of conversion into real tangible goods, whether it be that the individual or the municipality redeems their vouchers in some service or delivery. B. The municipality accepts emergency currency as payment for delivered electrical power, gas, or water, or that the state redeems this money from the proceeds of its institutions or plants or accepts it as payment in its treasuries, meaning it takes the hydro power vouchers as payment for the supplied power or fuel or allows railway tickets to be paid with them, thus providing transport services or delivering letters. If such fulfillment stands behind the paper vouchers, and insofar as such fulfillment is carried out, such money creation from one's own right is absolutely permissible and also commercially impeccable, as impeccable as any promissory note, the assumption of a bill of exchange, or a term-based payment method.

Such *"money creation"* cannot be prohibited, as the new decree of the Reich government attempts to do by banning the issuance of emergency currency. This prohibition makes the knowledgeable deeply concerned, for it shows the Reich government in complete subservience to the one-sided interests of big loan capital, whose entire power rests on maintaining the interest delusion. Only when the insight becomes common knowledge that the state does not have the means to ensure the interest payment of the billions of big loan capital will money once again be more aligned with its true purpose as an operating resource of the economy. Money will then be displaced from its dominant role and become the servant of the economy again, as it was originally invented and created to be. At that point, it will also become much easier for every diligent and capable person, every industry, to obtain operating funds for expansions and improvements of their businesses, because the pure money holder cannot simply buy government papers that yield him secure interest, but—like any other economic actor—must seek investments for his money if he does not want to keep it only as un-earmarked savings or deposit money in his safe. He will have to actively offer his money, competing with the enormous sums that will seek investment after the abolition of the state's interest service, undercutting each other in their demands on those who are entrepreneurial and create new value.

Contrary to the often-expressed fear that after the bondage of interest is broken, no one will lend their money anymore, we will experience that fulfilling the demand for money will never be easier and cheaper to achieve than under the pressure of necessity, which the money owner will face once the bulwark of modern capitalism, the state's interest madness, is abolished.

For this reason, it will not be necessary to issue a general interest prohibition for private individuals, as we know it from medieval history. Such general interest prohibitions were too severe intrusions into the individual's right to determine the use of their money, inevitably being circumvented and bypassed time and again. It should remain open to everyone to allow the person who enabled them to set up a business or establish a factory through a loan to share in their profit. This concerns private agreements.

The aim and purpose of the state financial reform we propose cannot be to solve the interest problem through a general interest prohibition, to provide a cheap or interest-free source of money for private money needs, but only to create the preconditions for a market structure beneficial for goods production as a side effect of the main task: the liberation of the state and the people from the bondage of interest vis-à-vis the supranational financial power.

As a supplement to the two major fundamental demands, as a third measure for Germany, the nationalization of the Reichsbank must be pursued. This is not the place to elaborate on this in detail and point out that it is in itself already a bold move and calculated on the ignorance and carelessness of the population, that the "*Reichsbank*" despite its name is not a state bank but a joint-stock company, which, among other special privileges, has been granted the note-issuing right by the state.

It is not yet too late, for it is never too late for a turnaround. But the turnaround must be decided upon and carried out without hesitation, lest a general moral, economic, and political decay seal the doom of Europe.

CHAPTER 10

LONGING AND HOPE

Introduction to the first edition of the pamphlet *"The German State on a National and Social Basis"* 1923, German Nationalist to the others (open Library, just Seft 35 of the 20ationals. Der fogsbuchhandlung, Bibliothet", 43. bis 47. Saufend

With deep concern and strong hope, we look into the future. Germany will live, Germany cannot perish. Shaken by the overwhelming birth pangs of a new era, Germany will shed the terrible burdens of its own guilt as well as the chains of foreign oppressors, and with a mighty jolt, it will cast them off, and Germany will march at the forefront of nations.

If only there were not so much suffering and hardship associated with collapse and ruin, we could participate in the creation of a new era with a certain sense of happiness. For when we lift our gaze above the lowlands of the day, above the confusion of the present, we see everywhere vigorous will, earnest work, and brilliant intuition. The German soul stirs its wings for a new flight.

Today's tasks are immense, greater and more challenging than ever in the sorrowful history of the Germans.

Thus, the dual task must be accomplished: to renew both the state and the economy—not merely to *"rebuild"* them, but to give them a new form. This new shaping will also extend to the cultural and intellectual life of our people.

The old German longing for a united Germany must finally become reality, a new economic law will emerge, and the horrifying interest-capitalist economic system will be replaced.

So comprehensive and overwhelming are the tasks that await us. The spirit of the past stands behind us, earnest and admonishing; with reverence for what has been historically ordained, and rooted firmly in the best German tradition, based on Aryan wisdom, the people and the state, economy and culture, must be recreated anew.

The leaders must be deeply aware of their tremendous responsibility, yet they are carried by the hope of the entire nation—their hope for freedom!

The National Socialist idea, however, is much more than just a return or turn back to old, fatherly customs; it shatters the chains of the Marxist state and economic order, and it fights as the first and most determined conscious force against the mammonic powers, against the world-spanning might of all-Jewish imperialism, and against the spirit of greed, selfishness, and indifference.

Its most powerful, strongest-willed, and most resolute vanguard is found in the National Socialist German Workers' Party. The party has laid out its goals in a short program, summarizing the fundamental demands of the movement in 25 points. Alfred Rosenberg, the chief editor of the *"Völkischer Beobachter,"* the combat newspaper of the National Socialist movement of Greater Germany, has in a commendable manner elucidated each program point in a brief publication. At least in this small pamphlet, it is possible to tell friends and foes alike what the National Socialist German Workers' Party aims for. However, in the literature of National Socialism, there is still a lack of a more comprehensive work that accounts for the political and economic ideas from which National Socialism arises, which paths it intends to take in state policy to reach its ultimate goal: the National Socialist German state, the state of work and achievement. This task is what the present work seeks to fulfill. We will, therefore, illuminate the starting point, the path, and the goal of National Socialism, showing in what essential ways the German National Socialist state will differ from the existing state, which areas will remain largely untouched, in which areas significant reforms will take place, and where fundamentally new paths will need to be forged.

We will have to seek and show new paths for public life, especially for state financial policy, for the treatment of the race question and the related issues. Beyond that, we must fundamentally address the already voiced objections, distortions, and lies of our opponents.

The task we have set for ourselves is overwhelmingly great, yet it is only a small section from the overall scope of Germany's renewal.

All effort would be in vain if not preceded by a death-defying resolve and an unyielding will to lead, creating the prerequisites for the effectiveness of the ideas.

The strongest will would be recklessly squandered if we did not steadfastly carry in our hearts a clear vision of what this German state—what Germany, our father and children's land, should look like according to our will—according to our victory!

Munchen—Murnau, September 1923.

— Gottfried Feder.

CHAPTER 11

ANNOUNCEMENT IN THE "VOLKISCHER BEOBACHTER" OF NOVEMBER 9TH, 1923

Announcement in the "Völkischer Beobachter" of November 9, 1923

Until the legal regulation of the entire monetary and credit system, all banks and other financial institutions will be stripped of their private legal character and placed under state supervision. Any alteration or removal of assets will be punished.

The Finance Committee:

signed, Gottfried Feder.

The coincidental timing, that I was at the Munich bank on the evening of the *"Hitler Putsch,"* where I had my savings, which had been devalued to fractions by inflation, lying dormant, in order to withdraw this long requested deposit, which, however, was not fully prepared and thus I did not take it, led my opponents and the opponents of our movement to accuse me, who had issued the above-mentioned announcement, of *"shifting"* and similar actions. I was compelled to file several lawsuits for this reason and will continue to do so whenever this accusation, which is aimed at discrediting our movement through me, is raised against me.

In one of the latest judgments in these lawsuits, the *"Völkischer Beobachter"* (of September 8, 1932) reported the following statements:

Final dismissal of a persistent lie:

The *"shifted"* bank deposit of Mr. Feder.

Some time ago, Gottfried Feder, despite the Nuremberg District Court, the *"Fränkische Tagespost,"* already having condemned the eternal lie about the *"shifted bank deposit"* of Feder, was slandered once again by the Black Press, which shamelessly repeated this already exposed fraud about the *"set aside"* bank deposit in a pamphlet by the deputy of the Bavarian People's Party, Tröger, published by the Gebhardus Verlag, G.m.b.H., Nuremberg. This publisher did not hesitate to use this lie as a sales pitch for the book in countless prospectuses.

Now, finally, these people have been silenced.

On June 2 of this year, the IV Civil Chamber of the Nuremberg-Fürth District Court in the case of Gottfried Feder, represented by attorney Dr. J. Müller II, Nuremberg, versus

1. Gebhardus Verlag, G.m.b.H., Nuremberg,

2. R. Tröger, M.D.R., Nuremberg, Goethe Street,

issued a final judgment, prohibiting the defendants under penalty of an unlimited fine or imprisonment of up to 6 months from further disseminating the defamatory claims regarding the alleged removal of the bank deposit on

November 8, 1923. Furthermore, the defendants are prohibited, under the same penalties, from disseminating the claims made in the book *"Hitler und Rom"* on pages 142, 143, 144.

With this, an outrageous lie comes to an end, the baseness of which is unprecedented. As is well known,

Gottfried Feder, as the Finance Minister appointed by Adolf Hitler during the coup in November 1923, immediately issued a decree on the night of November 8 to 9, 1923, placing all banks and bank transactions under state supervision to prevent bank and stock exchange profiteering and manipulations. The decree explicitly prohibited the removal of assets. Any interventions or confiscations of property rights were not associated with this.

A pure coincidence led Gottfried Feder, in the course of correspondence with his bank and as a result of the financial meltdown caused by the catastrophic devaluation of money, to attempt to withdraw the meager remainder of his securities, and this withdrawal, which he had been explicitly asked to do by his bank, happened to fall on November 8.

Any decently thinking person must be clear from the outset that there are no causal connections between these two events. This, of course, did not stop the Marxist and Black Press from turning it into a cabinet piece to defame Mr. Feder, repeatedly claiming that he had tried to quickly withdraw his papers from his bank to save his own assets from the confiscation he intended, thereby violating his own principles, which he publicly advocated.

The Nuremberg Court, in a 20-page judgment after thorough deliberation, which was prepared with numerous written submissions, clearly and unambiguously stated that the allegations raised by the Bavarian People's Party deputy Tröger were not true. The court particularly points out that the court records unequivocally show that Feder's visit to his bank was solely a consequence of the correspondence he had been conducting with the bank for weeks. The deposit had been closed with the explicit explanation that Feder did not agree with the calculated fees and commissions, which he deemed outrageous. These facts were confirmed under oath by the owner of the bank as well as the bank employee on duty. The judgment literally states the following:

"The court has convinced itself through the letters of October 10 and 26, 1923, and the notification of October 29, that the plaintiff only wanted to withdraw the securities in accordance with his repeatedly expressed request. Further evidence against an intention to shift the deposit is that Feder did not withdraw even the portion of the securities available to him. Above all, the defendant party overlooks the fact that the announcement of the Finance Committee does not concern the confiscation of securities held in banks; only the alteration and shifting of assets is punishable. The announcement did not interfere with the property rights of the owners of securities. It was merely a measure taken in the context of the upheaval to prevent phenomena such as capital flight, etc. According to the aforementioned program of the National Socialist German Workers' Party, the plaintiff had nothing to fear for his private securities.

The evidence presented by the defendant party, suggesting that Feder wanted to withdraw the papers with the intention of considering the new government's stance on privately held securities, cannot be substantiated in light of these clear findings."

All further speculation, even the question of whether Feder had prior knowledge of the impending coup, is therefore irrelevant to the assessment of the entire case, for regardless of whether the deposit, which once represented a large fortune, still had an residual value of a few thousand Marks or was considered completely devalued amid the horrific inflation; in no case can a connection be constructed between Feder's intended withdrawal of the deposit—which was not even carried out—and his announcement placing banks under state supervision. The measure did not aim at property interventions or confiscations. Gottfried Feder had no knowledge of Adolf Hitler's plans for the evening of November 8, 1923. In the major Hitler trial, it was explicitly established that only a very few of Hitler's military collaborators had knowledge of the coup.

Therefore, no conduct that compromises the personal honor of Gottfried Feder can be inferred in any way.

The lie regarding Feder's deposit withdrawal is definitively settled with this.

CHAPTER 12

ESTABLISHMENT OF SOCIAL BUILDING AND ECONOMIC BANKS TO REMEDY THE HOUSING SHORTAGE

First published in the *"Press Service of the National Socialist Freedom Party"* of June 7, 1924 the faction of the National Socialist Freedom Party submitted the following draft bill in the Reichstag on May 28, 1924:

The Reichstag resolves to grant constitutional approval to the following draft legislation: Draft Law concerning the Foundation for Social Housing and Economic Banks to address the Housing Crisis.

The Reichstag has passed the following law, which is hereby announced with the consent of the Reichstag:

Art. I. The federal states are authorized to grant permission for the establishment of a social housing and economic bank to address the housing crisis.

Art. II. The following fundamental provisions apply to these Housing and Economic Banks (H.E.B.):

§ 1. The Housing and Economic Banks (H.E.B.) are corporations under public law. Legal personality is conferred in accordance with existing laws by the central authorities of the federal states.

§ 2. The purpose of the H.E.B. is to alleviate homelessness and to stimulate construction activity and other objectives valued by the national economy. Loans are to be provided through the issuance of value-stable, secure, and gold-backed bearer instruments (Housing Bank Certificates), or via cashless credit arrangements.

§ 3. Provision of required total funds among H.E.B. requires authorization by the National Supervisory Council of Housing and Economic Banks.

§ 4. The issuance of certificates referred to in Section 3 or the credit facilities can only transpire in such manner and legal form that the total of the certificates issued and currently in circulation, and corresponding credit line claims is fully covered by tangible collateral (priority liens on real property, especially with ground rents, mortgages, material pledges, security transfers, etc. a.). The proceeds from the buildings or other enterprises to be created must ensure the repayment or recall of the granted subsidies within the agreed periods, at the latest within fifty years.

§ 5. As a basis and reserve, funds that have been allocated to combat the housing crisis or are to be allocated for this purpose, particularly the available portions of the rent tax of the H.E.B., shall be made available.

§ 6. The housing certificates issued by the H.E.B., which are denominated in amounts of 1, 2, 3, 5, 10, 20, 50, and 100 gold marks, bear the following inscription:

“The entirety of all housing certificates issued by the ... H.E.B. is fully covered and permanently secured by the total sum of all securities and collateral established in favor of the ... H.E.B. (real burdens, etc.). At least 2%

of the issued certificates are to be recalled annually. To the extent that the recall is not achieved through repayments and payments by the debtors to the H.E.B., the remaining amounts of the certificates to be recalled annually will be called in through publication in .... The holders of the called certificates will receive the face value in gold and gold-based payment means, based on the calculation value of ... grams of fine gold for 20 marks.

The provision of coverage and the recall of all certificates issued by the H.E.B. are subject to ongoing control by the Reich according to the law dated ...

§ 7. The entirety of the securities and collateral established in favor of the ... H.E.B. of a state for the approved subsidies forms a unified coverage association such that all established securities and collateral are jointly liable for the total sum of all housing certificates and credit claims currently in circulation.

A public ledger is maintained by the H.E.B. for all components and rights of the coverage association. Any person with a legitimate legal interest may inspect this ledger or its individual parts.

§ 8. The H.E.B. determines the amount and terms of a loan operation, the securities and collateral to be provided by the debtor, the amount and terms of repayment, and other general conditions with the applicant on a case-by-case basis. It is to be ensured that debtors make repayments in housing certificates of the H.E.B. or in gold-based, stable value payment means that correspond to the sense of the cash redemption obligation mentioned in § 6.

The legal relationship to be agreed with the applicant must comply with the provisions of the law and any other conditions and prerequisites established by the competent authorities.

The H.E.B. is entitled to levy fees or compensation for administrative costs associated with the provision of subsidies and for annual recalls.

The housing certificates of the H.E.B. are accepted and issued at all ... state cash offices of the respective state and the Reich cash offices located there.

§ 9. The forgery of housing certificates of the H.E.B. will be punished with the same penalties as for forgery or misuse of state payment means.

Art. III. The H.E.B. is subject to the ongoing and continuous control and supervision of the Reich. For this purpose, a Reich Supervisory Council for Housing and Economic Banks is established. This council consists of a) the president, appointed by the Reich President, b) two directors, one nominated by the Reich Minister of Finance and the other by the Reich Minister of Economic Affairs, c) 4-8 members, delegated by the Reichstag for its duration.

The Reich Supervisory Council has its seat in Munich.

Justification

1. General

1. Germany currently has more than two million homeless people. The housing crisis prevails predominantly in the cities. In some cases, 10-15% of the urban population is homeless. (Munich has 27,000 homeless families.)

Construction activity has completely collapsed; as a result, brickworks, lime kilns, and other building material production facilities as well as all related trades are unemployed.

All the raw materials required for construction activity are sufficiently available in Germany: wood, clay, stone, lime, glass, sheet iron, etc.

Millions of unemployed people burden the state and municipalities with enormous sums.

The picture is thus: On the one hand, all building materials and construction resources are available to create houses and buildings; on the other hand, thousands of workers are unemployed, and there is an enormous housing crisis. Why is it that one is not in a position to bring the worker to the building material and construct houses from it?

2. The reason given for the halt in construction activity is that the capital for a proper revival of the construction market is lacking because the capital has more profitable and promising investment opportunities elsewhere.

Undeniable facts are: Due to reduced rents in connection with unfairly increased municipal services, such as street cleaning, garbage collection, sewer maintenance wages, and similar, the housing equity has, in fact, been socialized. The former middle-class property owner now holds only formal property rights with the obligation to function as a tax collector, his former capital value has been stripped. Similarly, the former mortgage creditors, especially the wards who have invested their money in guardian-secured mortgage bonds, have been deprived of their asset values through this form of socialization of housing equity; in other words, the capital invested in houses has been destroyed and devalued. Those who today, due to particularly favorable circumstances, can obtain foreign capital through first mortgages from mortgage banks must pay 15-20% per annum for it. Since the current rent is 100-120% per annum, only limited amounts of capital are available for investment in this non-profitable real estate, especially as the funds invested in real estate are visibly apparent to the tax authorities and there is a fear in the capital market that such visible assets may in the future be subject to particular tax burdens and difficulties.

3. In the previous years, attempts were made to alleviate the housing shortage by providing considerable subsidies from public funds for the construction of small residential buildings. Neither the Reich, the states, nor the municipalities are today in a position to allocate significant funds for such non-repayable subsidies.

From a national economic and financial policy standpoint, this subsidy system is and was mistaken. Such subsidies actually represented gifts to a few selected compatriots at the expense of the community, without achieving any noticeable effect in combating the housing shortage.

It has occurred that the owners of such subsidized houses could achieve considerable profits from their property by circumventing the provided restrictions.

In any case, it has been shown that this subsidy economy could not lead to a noticeable revival of the housing market.

4. One of the main reasons for this insufficient relief in the housing emergency was the fact that efforts were solely aimed at constructing owner-occupied homes or own homes, i.e., only such were publicly promoted. It is certainly a desirable thing to resettle workers, employees, or other people from the populace, thereby tying them to the land and making them landowning. It remains as ever a social task to promote these efforts as far as circumstances allow. This, however, lies exclusively in the social domain.

So far as it concerns the combat of housing misery as such, it must be emphasized that the provision of housing is the primary aid, regardless of whether it is an own home or a rental apartment. In connection with the existing economic circumstances, it must be explicitly stressed that the revival of rental housing construction alongside the creation of owner-occupied homes is indispensable if a noticeable remedy to the housing shortage is to be achieved. For hundreds of thousands of workers, employees, civil servants, an own home is unsuitable, as it would only hinder their mobility. Many of those bound by profession to the city and the people active there should be able to change their domicile and residence without difficulty when they can achieve a better livelihood or a better valuation of their labor elsewhere. For thousands, certainly, a small house or an owner-occupied home in a cooperative building is the objective of their dreams; tens of thousands of others find their joy in life in other things. Tens of thousands should not only spend perpetually in saving to pay off an own-home, being it of it. They wish to use their spare small means for excursions into nature, holidays, or other purposes.

The social housing misery as such must be remedied and combated. For this purpose, it is sufficient and necessary to provide an adequate number of houses. If from this viewpoint, a significantly increased number of rental dwellings can be created with the same means, this is to be preferred over a limited quantity of owner-occupied homes.

5. As the starting point for the revival of the housing market, the following must be considered: stimulating private initiative by making the construction of a house once again a promising and profitable endeavor for the small and middle-class individual, one that encourages them to invest their savings or their modest available capital into this cause. In private property, in the prospect of building a house or acquiring a larger housing complex, gradually making it debt-free to secure an asset for the children and family, therein lies, as always, the incentive for providing a sufficient number of rental apartments. Only by reviving these preconditions can the housing shortage be alleviated.

Public funds are fundamentally ill-suited for the construction and maintenance of rental buildings; experience shows that such buildings only too easily fall into disrepair and neglect, because the personal private interest that the individual small and middle-class homeowner has in their property is lacking. The homeowner living in their own house is, as experience shows, an unpaid workforce that daily and continuously ensures the maintenance of the house and remains active.

Cooperative, non-profit construction enterprises are desirable and should continue to be promoted. Where conditions indicate, municipal housing construction should also be encouraged. However, it must be reiterated at this point that private property and private ownership are and must remain the most natural foundation and the most common form of home ownership, unless one wishes to harm the national body through experiments like the misguided socialization of houses during the past period of coercive economic management.

2. The Social Construction Bank

1. In consideration of the economic differences among individuals, it should be left to the discretion of the states whether they wish to establish a social construction and economic bank; only in the event that this occurs, the basic guidelines provided by the Reich for the issuance of construction bank certificates and their backing must be authoritative. For practical reasons, such decentralization is necessary and desirable. The proposed Reich supervisory council, through its composition and activities, shall be the organ that ensures uniform handling of the construction bank system in the individual states and, in public, provides the necessary guarantee that the legal provisions for the construction bank certificates are strictly adhered to.

2. The entities for the individual construction banks should be specially created public-law corporations. This legal form is preferable to that of a stock corporation or cooperative because no private interest of any kind is involved in the public-law corporation. The implementing regulations to be enacted will provide that in the event of the cessation of the legal personality of the B.20.2., its residual assets shall fall to the state. By granting the legal character of a public-law corporation, the B.D.B. is elevated above the societies of private law. This imparts to its certificates a significance beyond simple, customary private law.

3. The certificate of the B.W.B. is a bearer instrument within the meaning of the BBB. Its purpose is to circulate, i.e., to serve as a medium of payment without being a legal tender. The certificate is denominated in gold.

No certificate shall be issued for which there is no prior backing. For instance, if a construction cooperative wishes to build a house with 10 small apartments at a total price of 80,000 gold marks (the apartment at 8,000 DM), the cooperative must have first raised 20,000 gold marks in land and property through member contributions or other communal funds, meaning the B. will, except in particularly exceptional cases, issue certificates only when the applicant already has a corresponding and encumbered asset amounting to approximately 25% of the total construction cost. In the above example, the B.20.23. will issue construction bank certificates for 20,000 M. against the prior encumbrant of the existing property value. With the received funds, construction will continue until a third and finally the fourth installment can be given. The final picture is that for a construction cost of 80,000 M., 60,000 M. B.203.28. certificates were issued, for which a first-priority real encumbrance has been registered on the property. Thus, the certificates are fully backed by tangible assets, and the backing is greater than that which banknotes had during peacetime. (In practice, a significant portion of credit transactions will occur on a cashless basis.)

For the construction period, i.e., until the building is completed, additional temporary safeguards can also be arranged and procured, such as guarantees, deposits of bonds or securities, security assignments, etc. General instructions for this are to be provided in the implementing regulations.

With appropriate management and sufficiently cautious business conduct by the leadership of the B.W.B., it is always possible to ensure that adequate backing remains available during the construction period. For further coverage, particularly for the procurement of initial operating funds and initial securities, and for the future, the states shall, from the outset, equip the B.20.28. with any corresponding values, e.g., by allocating the rent tax revenues designated for construction purposes.

Such funds allocated by the states for this purpose need not be liquefied; they serve initially only as provisions and to enhance the security and endowment of the B.W.B. for the initial period.

4. The circulation of construction bank certificates. The construction bank certificates issued to the builders are used by them to pay the contractors, construction materials, and wages. From there, they flow into the public. The property owner requires from his tenants, and the cooperative from its

members, that the rents are to be paid in construction bank certificates. The tenants obtain these construction bank certificates through transactions. The property owner or the cooperative annually or quarterly returns the agreed installments in construction bank certificates to the B.W.B. (These repayments are amortizations), thus reducing the total debt. With a repayment obligation of 5%, the debts are settled in 20 years. (For the bank's own costs, it deducts a small, one-time fee upon initial issuance and adds a charge of about 0.5% to the annual repayments to cover the associated write-off and accounting costs.)

5. From these repayments received by the B.W.B., the B.W.B. carries out the lawful redemptions of theB.20.28. certificates in accordance with the agreements with the builders. With cashless circulation, the total amount of the issued credits is reduced by the annual repayments, which are then likewise fulfilled cashless or in the form of other means of payment, and the total amount of the registered securities in the books is reduced by the total amounts of the repayments made.

If it is difficult for the debtor to obtain B.20.28. certificates from general circulation, the repayment can be made in conventional payment means converted to the gold standard, whereupon these amounts are then issued to new borrowers in place of construction bank certificates. The effect is the same as if the repayable amounts had been paid in construction bank certificates and an equivalent amount in new securities had been issued in construction bank certificates.

The obligation stipulated on the construction bank certificate to call in construction bank certificates to exchange them for gold or gold-value payment means thus practically does not occur in the case of orderly business operations. In practice, this obligation can only arise if repayments do not come in at the prescribed rate, i.e., if debtors fail to meet their obligations. For such exceptional cases in practice, corresponding redemptions would have to be made from the reserves provided by the states from the outset. It is the task of the implementing regulations and the agreements with the borrowers to include corresponding conditions and clauses through which individual losses can be shifted to the totality of the borrowers and must be compensated by them.

In practice, such instances of default will only be a very small percentage of the total circulation, which can easily be offset by other measures (cooperative purchase of construction materials). The obligation stated in B.W.B. Certificates to redeem called certificates in gold thus practically does not occur or occurs only in very exceptional cases. This formulation of the obligation raises public awareness of the absolute gold value security behind the B.20.28. It appears.

3. The economic value of this institution lies in the fact that through the creation of the B.20.28., it becomes possible to build extensively and affordably.

1. A simple example makes this clear. Let us assume a construction cost of 8000 marks for small apartments.

a) If these 8000 marks are to be raised in the usual manner—whereby 3000 marks are obtained as a first mortgage through mortgage banks, and a second mortgage in the amount of 3000 marks is provided by the state or public funds at a moderate interest rate of 5%—these amounts require an annual interest payment, calculated at only 5% for the construction mortgage, of 450 plus 450 equal 900 marks. In this example, the remaining 2000 marks must, as usual, be provided by the builders or apartment occupants themselves, either through equity in the land or other means. These 900 marks in annual costs are only the capital interest. In addition, an annual amount of 200 marks must be added for municipal facilities, maintenance, repairs, etc. Such a small apartment thus costs the occupant 1100 marks in annual rent, an amount that no one can afford for a small apartment. It is also disregarded that the state or public bodies are, in themselves, in no position to lend mortgage funds at 5% as long as they themselves have deficits in their budgets or must borrow expensive funds for other purposes.

b) If 6000 marks in construction bank certificates are issued, and a repayment of 5% is agreed upon, then 300marks annually must be raised for this. Additionally, 300 marks for maintenance costs. The apartment is thus 33% cheaper than the one financed according to point a).

2. Another economic value lies in the fact that the smaller and middle-class individuals are encouraged to invest small or medium-sized capital for construction purposes through the possibility of obtaining B.W.B. loans.

In this way, money is diverted from useless, unproductive speculation and directed towards productive labor.

All economic strata are thus drawn into stimulating construction activity. In particular, small and medium sized enterprises can be encouraged to make land and initial capital available for the benefit of their workers.

It remains the task of the supervisory council and the control body presented here, elected by Parliament, to provide ongoing instructions and to ensure that the benefits of the B.20.28. loans are made accessible and allocated appropriately to the corresponding population strata.

4. Objections

1. The objection of inflation.

It will be objected that the issuance of these B.20.28. certificates is inflationary. This objection is unfounded. Inflation arises only where additional purchasing power is created in an exceptionally high degree through uncovered money tokens; small, insignificant excesses of coverage have never in themselves created inflation. Only when the issuance of uncovered money tokens occurs in a significant quantity does inflation arise. Here, every money token is fully covered from the outset, and no additional purchasing power is created at all.

2. The B.W.B. certificates would oversaturate the money market and thereby harm the other money tokens of the state.

This objection is unfounded. The amount of B.20.28. certificates to be issued is restricted from the outset by the supervisory body for each country.

Moreover, under the current state of monetary scarcity, it could only be beneficial if greater monetary liquidity were introduced through the B.20.28. certificates and the simultaneous stimulation of the construction market.

Depending on the state of the money market, the B.W.B. can be instructed to issue a larger or smaller portion of its loans in construction bank certificates or cashless credit entries. For the time being, the percentage of construction bank certificates being issued is so small that it is negligible compared to the general money supply.

3. *"The B.20.28. certificates would not be accepted by the public."* Considering that the public accepted the uncovered billion-mark bills despite knowing their lack of coverage, that the public accepted emergency money from cities without hesitation, that it accepted certificates from the Reichsbahn, and even during the money shortage of the previous year accepted all sorts of money surrogates from banks and individual firms, this objection is entirely unjustified from the beginning. Here, we are dealing with fully covered money. It merely requires appropriate clarification by the available institutions and organizations to introduce the money without difficulty. Moreover, authorities and cities have sufficient means at their disposal to ensure that individual firms do not refuse to accept the money. Every construction business will prefer to receive an order for execution and accept payment in construction bank certificates rather than remain idle.

Once the public is informed that these fully covered certificates and their liquidity will alleviate the housing shortage, the public will willingly accept these certificates, especially since they carry the guarantee that they are not subject to inflation or that these certificates will not be affected by any impending wave of inflation, as they are denominated in gold and backed by full real value.

5. Legal Aspects

1. The securities are to be registered as encumbrances on properties. The encumbrance obligation consists in the requirement that a specified sum of construction bank certificates must be delivered annually from the property or its yield. The encumbrance is numerically determined based on the total loan received.

This form frees the B.20.B. from the usual constraints that apply to mortgage banks and similar institutions.

2. The public register of the security association serves as proof that the total amount of circulating construction bank certificates or credit entries is fully covered.

It is the task of the implementing regulations to issue detailed provisions concerning the structure and handling of the public register. The procedure should not be cumbersome or complicated. It is sufficient if the register includes: property and owner, proof of the provided securities, amount of the granted loans, amount of the annual repayments, actual repayments made. Other details should be collected in the annexes to the public register; the annexes should therefore include: corresponding extracts from the land register, notarial instruments, agreement with the borrower, etc.

3. The control has the purpose and is limited to ensuring compliance with the provisions set by the law. It thus, primarily serves to control the securities and the repayments, providing the public with the guarantee that their construction certificates are not issued without coverage and that the collection is carried out in accordance with the law.

The supervisory board naturally utilizes appropriate auxiliary bodies for the execution of the control, such as auditors, controllers, etc.

Concluding Remarks

The housing shortage and the stagnation of the construction market are among the main evils of today's times. These damages cannot be remedied through the usual and former methods of private capital. Therefore, there is no other option but to combat the evil with new, comprehensive measures. No harm can result from the introduction of the B.20.28., as it is always possible to cease the activities of the B.20.8.

Donations and subsidies to individuals from public funds only worsen the general economy and financial situation, as every such measure triggers repercussions on the whole. The B.W.B. does not burden the state in the slightest; instead, it provides the state with the opportunity to build housing on a large scale. Therefore, it is necessary to give the states the opportunity to create the B.20.23.

CHAPTER 13

THE DAWES PLAN

From Part 7 of the *"National Socialist Library"* (1928) and from the *"Stenographic Reports on the Proceedings of the Reichstag"* (II. Legislative Period, 1924)

International law defines in generally valid terms the concept of the sovereignty of a state entity by stipulating the unrestricted sovereign rights that a state must possess if it is to be considered a sovereign state, i.e., a state that is in free, unrestricted control of its sovereign rights.

There are five sovereign rights: territorial sovereignty, military sovereignty, financial sovereignty, administrative sovereignty, and judicial sovereignty.

If even one of these rights is lacking or restricted, one can no longer speak of such a state as completely sovereign. Here we think of the old Ottoman Empire, which, although referred to as the *"Empire of the Ottomans,"* was forced to conclude the well-known *"Capitulations"* with the great powers, which impaired its judicial sovereignty. Consequently, the subjects of foreign states were removed from Turkish jurisdiction and placed under the jurisdiction of the consulates. Nonetheless, Turkey retained the rest of its sovereign rights, as much as one might have debated the issue in the 1880s of the last century. The *"loose man on the Bosporus,"* as Constantinople was whimsically called, had certainly overstepped its limits, but it still had its own military, a completely independent internal administration from foreign powers, was entirely autonomous in its legal proceedings over its own subjects, and, despite its considerable indebtedness to Russia, remained fully in possession of its financial sovereignty.

In terms of constitutional law, however, the *"Empire"* of India was far more restricted before the war than the Ottoman Empire. Despite maintaining the external form of an *"Empire,"* it was, in essence, merely a colony of England. The military was staffed by Englishmen in all key command positions, as were the main administrative offices. Native princes were overseen by English Residents, the title of the Emperor of India was linked to the English royal house, and the so-called Viceroy of India was an Englishman. A state like the Kingdom of Bavaria, as a federal state of the German Empire, enjoyed significantly more political freedom and sovereignty compared to India, and indeed, these were almost entirely intact, save for certain voluntary federal agreements with the Empire. Bavaria had its own military, its own currency, its own railway, postal, and transport administration, its own judicial system, and, as a sovereign state, maintained its own foreign policy representations and a sovereign head of state. Only in the event of war was the supreme command transferred to the German Emperor, and agreements with Prussia and other federal states had been made regarding the unity of the currency, legal system, etc.

The German Empire, proclaimed on January 18, 1871, in the Hall of Mirrors at Versailles by the greatest political genius of the Germans, Prince Bismarck, after a victorious campaign waged with blood and iron, emerged as the youngest and most vigorous great power alongside the eldest sovereign states of Europe: England, Russia, Austria, France, and Italy. (Alongside these six great powers, the press was famously referred to as the seventh, following Napoleon's earlier declaration of it as the fifth great power.)

In full possession of its sovereign rights, Germany, within a few decades of achieving national unity, also developed into an economic powerhouse of the highest order, leaving the older empires far behind and preparing to surpass even England in global trade and world commerce. Truly a shining beacon of the age, as the world had never before witnessed!

The gleaming might of the German fleet, the steel fortresses of our navy, protected Germany's borders and followed its trade flags. A model internal administration, exemplary legal procedures, a perfect railway and transport system, and a sound monetary system were the pride of the Germans, the envy of all neighbors, but also the envy of the malcontents and shadowy figures within.

The entire world looked up to this Nordic-determined empire. World Freemasonry and international Jewry, the global money power, England's trade envy, France's thirst for revenge, and Russia's expansionist ambitions joined forces, bound by intrigue and hatred, to fight against this Germany of labor and achievement, of order and cleanliness, of duty and tireless diligence, against the land where indisputable values still existed: the honor of officials and officers, incorruptibility, a sense of sacrifice, loyalty, pride, and courage.

Twenty-six states waged war, and despite the overwhelming odds, despite all the hardship and deprivation, Germany's victory hung by a thread. The external enemy would not have been able to bring Germany to its knees militarily had it not been for the Marxist revolution within, which aided the enemy.

It was necessary to recall this here, on the one hand, to show that this war was about far more than just any province or purely dynastic interests, and on the other hand, to lay bare the terrible decline in terms of state and international law, the contrast between then and now, and finally, to fill cold and detached legal considerations with the blood and life these events entailed. For we, as Germans, are not to practice *"premise-free"* science, but rather are to view everything from the German perspective.

Viewed thus, the Dawes Plan gains a significance far beyond its economic demands, encompassing state and international law on the largest possible scale. Indeed, for those who truly delve deeper into the matter, the Dawes Plan holds even greater political significance than the Treaty of Versailles itself. The latter was the attempt, but the Dawes Plan represents the culmination of Germany's complete political dis-empowerment and its actual economic plundering.

With the acceptance of the Dawes Plan on August 29, 1924, by a bribed and criminal majority in the Reichstag, Germany ceased to be a sovereign state.

Territorial and military sovereignty had already been shattered by the armistice and the Treaty of Versailles, but Germany still stood as an economic power, almost unshaken; no factory was destroyed, the will to work and diligence remained unbroken. But now, the Dawes Plan ruthlessly stripped the German Empire of its financial sovereignty over currency; the Reichsbank was denationalized and removed from the control of the German government, transportation sovereignty was relinquished, the German state railways were denationalized, removed from state oversight, and degraded into a domain of supranational money powers, internal administrative sovereignty was severely impaired by the appointment of foreign commissioners over customs and the revenues of important taxes. The German government was forced to consent to any act of infringement on all German affairs. Sniffing commissions roamed the entire country, no land, no aircraft, no heavy weapon may Germany possess anymore, while the whole world arms itself relentlessly and prepares for new military buildups. The German judicial sovereignty has also become a hollow concept, as large parts of the country are under foreign military jurisdiction, and disgraceful verdicts against patriotic German men are carried out. The cry of outrage that resonated throughout Germany at the murder of Albert Leo Schlageter was met with nothing but scornful comments in the enemy press. Day after day, the German press reports on the shameful verdicts of enemy courts against German men and women; there is no longer any talk of legal security for life, liberty, and property.

Truly a fall from proud heights and power into the deepest misery and the most wretched impotence. A people of diligent workers of the mind and hand submits to foreign dictates, worn out and tired. A parliament that was once the expression of the most vigorous national will has become a playground for the most pitiful and cowardly instincts.

With false representations and bombastic phrases, the government blinds itself and the parties. The national opposition of the National Socialists is showered with furious scorn and venomous malice. The Dawes Plan is enacted into law in Germany.

The government declarations from Saturday, August 23, 1924, in the 22nd session, lie before me; I take from the stenographic reports, Volume 381 of the 2nd Session Period 1924 (p. 772 ff.), the decisive statements of the leading men of the then Reich government.

Reich Chancellor Dr. Marx (Center Party) read the following in front of a full house:

"The Reich government stands before you to present the outcome of the London Conference and to seek your approval of the London resolutions as well as the laws necessary for their implementation. The resolutions made in London determine the manner in which the experts' report is to be implemented.

The Reich government has accepted the experts' report in its statement to the Reparations Commission as a suitable basis (!) for the solution of the reparations issue."

Marx then continues: Indeed, serious and grave concerns had been raised, that these were deeply impactful changes, but they wanted to account and answer for what had been achieved in London through difficult and responsible work, and literally: "*We do not boast of any* (!) *success that we might have achieved in London.*"

Marx then defends the English Prime Minister and continues: "*I place value on the statement that the accusation raised in the press, that the German delegation in London was presented with an ultimatum or dictated to, is entirely unfounded. (Protests and interjections from the National Socialists: All the worse!) The resolutions of the London Conference are undoubtedly a heavy burden for Germany. Nevertheless, they represent progress compared to the previous state of affairs and serve the goal we all strive for: the revival of the German economy and the restoration of German freedom, especially in the occupied territories.*" (Lively applause and approval from the center. Continued unrest among the National Socialists.)

Marx then made some general remarks on the political situation and even had to admit regarding the point, which had been repeatedly emphasized to the German people as justification for the necessity of accepting the Dawes Plan—the immediate evacuation of the illegally occupied territory—: *"We have not succeeded in achieving the immediate military evacuation of the territories which in our view are occupied in violation of the treaty within a short period expected by the entire people."* Thus declared the Reich Chancellor as a true Locarno follower, *"that at the London Conference, for the first time since the end of the war, a spirit of understanding (loud laughter and continuous uproar among the National Socialists) and the serious will for a peaceful settlement of the tragic war legacy were alive."*

Marx then appeals to the conscience of the representatives of the German people, urging them not to hinder the implementation of the experts' plan, and concludes with the outrageous claim: *"The rejection of the London Treaty would first and foremost mean the destruction of all the hopes cherished by the German people and especially our brothers in the occupied territories. Industry and agriculture will continue to suffer even more than before under the ever-growing credit crisis. Whether our anemic economy, which we have laboriously maintained so far, will not drive our currency into new decline is a troubling question. The increase in unemployment and the general hardship among the broad masses of the people are a certain consequence of rejection* (!)*. In the occupied territories, the terrible military pressure will persist, and the blockade of the population will be maintained... An immense responsibility now rests on the Reichstag. Its decision will, in my innermost conviction, mean either blessing or curse!"*

Thus, *"blessing"* means the acceptance of the Dawes Plan according to the opinion of Herr Marx, the Reich Chancellor by the grace of the Center Party. The German people, the Center Party voters, may thank Herr Marx for the *"blessings"* of the Dawes Plan. After Marx, Finance Minister Dr. Luther spoke. He set out to explain what would happen if the Dawes Plan were not approved; he fully embraced *"fear-mongering"* and elaborated: Unemployment had increased, the trade balance was increasingly in deficit, taxes were too high; yet, the Reich's revenues would decline if the London Treaty were not accepted, and the Reich's expenditures would not decrease but increase. The lack of credit in the German economy urgently demanded the acceptance of the Dawes Plan; without it, the credit crisis would reach its peak, and the farmers would have their overdue loans called in; the overall picture could only be an extraordinary intensification of the credit crisis and rising unemployment.

Luther did not shy away from saying, to also invoke the horrors of inflation as an ally: *"I will only explicitly mention that the path of a new inflation is entirely impossible. We cannot create artificial money a second time in Germany. When we first created artificial money through inflation (shouts from the National Socialists: Were you criminals?), Germany was still rich in comparison to today."*

"...Thus, the entire state of our economy forces us to accept the London Agreements." (Very true! from the DDP, the Center Party, the Democrats, and the Social Democrats; laughter and shouts from the National Socialists.) *"The German delegation fought point by point (!) to make the agreements as bearable as possible for Germany. In this regard, some things have also been achieved that cannot be overlooked in a factual examination."* This claim is a blatant lie; for nothing, absolutely nothing, was achieved in London, as the Reich Chancellor himself admitted with astonishing candor in his speech.

Luther continues: *"On the other hand, it is certain that only by accepting the London Agreements can the relief that our economy rightly demands be provided, namely, the adjustment of our tax system to the economic and social necessities and a tangible reduction in railway tariffs."* (!) Luther goes on and makes a case for the 800-million loan: *"As soon as the London Agreement is accepted, the foundation for the loan is laid."* (In other words: Once the German Reichstag has placed the golden chains around the German people, then the further indebtedness of the German economy will present no difficulties.)

He then concludes with the confession of his beautiful soul: *"I also dare to express the hope that the German people, if they work diligently and save bravely (laughter from the National Socialists and the German Nationals), on the basis of the London Agreement (shouts from the National Socialists: A splendid word!- Continuous laughter).—I also dare to express the hope that the German people, if they work diligently and save bravely (Bravo!)"* in the Center Party, among the Democrats. (Shouts from the National Socialists: *"Once again against them, otherwise no one will believe it!"*), on the basis of the London Agreement, under life-threatening conditions, finally, finally, its recovery will begin."

As the third of the political Graces, our *"much-beloved"* Foreign Minister Dr. Stresemann then takes the floor, to describe in lengthy explanations, but in increasingly meaningless words, the *"advantages"* of acceptance, and mocks the National Socialists: *"For a long time, you said that Poincarism would never give up its rule in France! Now, I must counter by saying that the London program and the London pact are not the product of Poincarist spirits!"* (Shout: Very naive!) Stresemann then concludes: *"I am convinced, London is not the end, London can be the beginning, the beginning of a development, of which Macdonald said that it marks the end of national isolation, the beginning of a joint existence of peoples on an equal basis. Take this foundation, so that you give future German governments the opportunity to lead Germany toward a good future on this foundation."* (Lively applause from the middle parties. Jeers from the National Socialists. – Renewed stormy applause from the middle parties.)

It must also be noted here that the government, namely the gentlemen Reich Chancellor Dr. Marx, Reich Finance Minister Dr. Luther, and Dr. Gustav Stresemann, upon being questioned in the Reichstag, though assured of the approval of the government parties and the approval of the Social Democrats, went to London and, without being able to achieve even the slightest improvements to the Dawes Plan, allowed themselves to be sent home like schoolboys with the order to secure the Reichstag's approval for the Dawes Pact, without the slightest change being made to it. The government, led by Reich President Ebert, was also firmly determined, under any circumstances, to sign the pact on August 30 and, if the Reichstag should cause difficulties, to dissolve it. For all eventualities, Ebert had the decree for dissolution prepared and handed to the Reich Chancellor. And this is what democracy calls *"the will of the people."*

On August 25, the great tragicomedy of the Reichstag discussions on the government declaration began, along with the first reading of the Banking Act, the Private Note Banking Act, the Coinage Act, and the draft laws concerning the liquidation of the circulating Rentenbankscheine, the industrial burden, the German Reichsbahn company, the London Conference, the assessment of the industrial burden, and the personnel relations at the German Reichsbahn company (Stenographic Reports, p. 795 ff.). One can see, an enormous program. In five days, the laws were to be rushed through.

The debate was opened by the then-faction leader of the German Nationals, Dr. Westarp. Among other things, he stated the following:

"We German Nationals believe in eternal justice. We have the gravest doubts; in place of the blood tax comes the treadmill of labor. Nothing of Germany's voluntary signature... Nothing of an enslavement that we ourselves would have brought upon us through our signature... We naturally reject all laws, including the final agreement." He then said: *"Here I stand, I can do no other!"*

But these words were followed by the shameless, despicable betrayal of what was then the largest party: 48 German National deputies voted in favor of the railroad agreement, which required a two-thirds majority, and thus helped secure its passage, along with the other laws. The German Nationals therefore bear full responsibility for the acceptance of the Dawes laws.

From the Social Democrats, represented by C. Severing, we could expect nothing else but thinly veiled joy over the agreement and enthusiastic approval. The *"Vorwärts"* of August 30 wrote: *"The acceptance of the Dawes laws is, in purely factual terms, an enormous success of Social Democratic policy."*

For the Center Party, Chairman Dr. Kaas spoke. The Communists sent one of their renowned representatives of graceful femininity: Mrs. Golke, better known under her former name, Ruth Fischer. She, like many others, has since been expelled from her party as a *"traitor to the working class."* Sic transit gloria mundi! Dr. Curtius declared for the German People's Party: *"We will unanimously adopt the government draft."*

Grtelenz, the speaker for the Democrats, expressed similar views. Dr. Bfleger from the Bavarian People's Party, as usual, voiced the customary hostilities toward the government, albeit in a polished manner. Naturally, everyone then ultimately voted in favor of the laws.

Dr. Bredt, the leader of the Economic Party, prepared the approval of his party with the clever statement: *"We do not regard this Dawes report as a medicine that will make us healthy again; we regard it as the means that gives the patient the strength to survive the serious crisis."* Deputy Runge of the German Socials declared: *"We German Socials consider anyone who signs this report to be a criminal."*

Apart from the Communists, who in the final analysis only opposed the agreement as a counterpoint to the Social Democrats, the National Socialists alone represented the resolute and steadfast opposition. As the speaker for the National Socialists, I myself, the then deputy chairman of our National Socialist faction, spoke on the Banking Act, Deputy Kahl on the Railroad Law, and in the third reading Count Reventlow on the Foreign Loan and Evacuation issue.

In my speech on August 26, 1924, I laid out our position clearly before the world. I will now present this speech as recorded in the Stenographic Reports (p. 895-900).

"A characteristic thread runs through the politics of recent years: the thread of subservience. Our so-called German government has already brought it to the point where it greets every new kick with a polite smile.

To speak about the point of honor, about the war guilt question, is forbidden because it disturbs the smart businessman's show. One wants to be oriented towards the world economy, purely in terms of world politics and monetary theory, and naturally, the unraveling of the guilt question always evokes the most painful sensitivities; one would prefer not to touch these untimely sentimentalities, one would prefer to bypass these unpleasant things, which after all are long past. Unfortunately, one forgets that it would have been essential for our smart business representatives to obtain clarity in London on the important financial issues. I mean the determination of the final sum of German performance, if one is indeed resolved to perform. But one shies away from that as well. Here, too, subservience is the guiding motif of politics. One probably believes there is still a loophole to escape in the golden net that one pulls over the heads of the German people. One has, after all, a salary of 30,000 marks—quite a good wage for a slave driver.

Another point that absolutely should have been raised in London is the accounting of the performance rendered by the German people thus far. I recall that there is a significant discrepancy between the calculations of the German government and those of the Reparations Commission. The German government, as is well known, estimates the German payments at over 40 billion: the Reparations Commission only acknowledges 8 billion. Gentlemen, do you believe that this would serve the resolution at the end of the now 37-year period of suffering of the German people, if we then first had to argue about how great the previous performances actually were? I cannot understand how one could say in the Foreign Affairs Committee that the final sum and the previous performances do not belong together. The prerequisite for the determination of the final sum is surely the preliminary determination of what has been performed thus far.

The situation for Germany was not at all bad before we went to London. The power politics of France had obviously run aground; it had proven that the bayonet cannot be used as a coal shovel. Added to this was the constant concern of world finance that French power politics might yet destroy and possibly completely paralyze the Ruhr region, the greatest interest factory and the greatest object of exploitation in the world. Had a German policy correctly understood how to play off the contradictory interests of French world politics against the creeping overpowering politics of world finance, the London Conference could certainly have taken quite different turns.

In the post-war development, we can clearly distinguish three stages: the Versailles Dictate, the London Ultimatum, and now—the Dawes Plan. The Versailles Dictate was proclaimed by all governments as unfulfillable in its unscrupulous exploitative ambition and nevertheless was fulfilled to the best of their abilities from Scheidemann to Stresemann—(protest from the German People's Party: Incorrect!)—to prove its unfulfillable, no?

"This is a completely characteristic sign of this New German mental illness, the fulfillment paralysis. The Versailles Dictate was built on the lie of German war guilt. One does not like to stir this up now, and therefore in London one avoids unrolling this question. However, the rest of the world knows full well that Germany was by no means actively guilty of the war. But the neo-Marxist governments are content to leave it at that, because otherwise the eyes of the German public would open to the fact that much more could be said about the guilt of the neo-Marxists for this peace. During the war, the policy of fulfillment was called the policy of understanding, and now it seems that one must move from pure fulfillment policy to an understanding of fulfillment.

On the other hand, the situation had been clear for a long time, and attempts were made at various conferences in Genoa, Paris, Spa, and The Hague to find a more harmless form, and this was achieved in the second stage with the London Ultimatum. There, German war guilt was transformed into fixed-interest war debts. This was the second stage of Germany's misery. Germany had to commit to taking on a world loan in three tranches: a) 12 billion, b) 35 billion, c) 85 billion, totaling 132 billion. I note that this was already a deterioration compared to the provisions of the Versailles Dictate, which only foresaw 120 billion. The German people were also told that the London Ultimatum was a step forward, just as one believes one can construct a setback through the Dawes Plan.

But even this second stage did not seem secure enough for the lords of world finance. It was still about debt instruments between states. The war booty was not yet sufficiently secured in private capitalist terms for the lords of world finance. There followed the French interlude, in which the greedy French pounced on German land, and now the question for world finance was: How can we snatch this booty, these spoils, from the hands of French Imperialism? This had to be done very carefully, of course, and it required tremendous pressure from Wall Street on France to make France compliant. I recall the frontal attack of world finance against the French franc, I recall how in this incredibly interesting struggle between Poincaré and Wall Street, Poincaré had to kneel and step down. And now the way was clear to take the third step, the step of mobilization and the technical implementation of Germany's war burdens exclusively for the benefit of world finance. Now the path was clear for the great turning point and shifting.

Herr Stresemann, with his usual bombastic rhetoric, began a notable public speech in Dessau with the declaration: "*I firmly stand on the primacy of state political necessities over economic political demands.*" And five minutes later, in the same speech, he added: "*When Hughes, the American, first proposed in New York that the fate of the world should be taken from the hands of statesmen and placed in the hands of bankers, we immediately agreed to this plan.*" So you see, our characteristic Foreign Minister can also act differently. From the turning point of world history has emerged the largest swindle in world history, a swindle that is a testament to the complete helplessness, defenselessness, and servility of the German government.

The German people are not the only ones who have been deceived. The so-called victor nations are also equally burdened, as stated on page 1 of the Dawes Plan: "*They must be relatively burdened just as heavily as any of the powers represented in the Commission.*" Gentlemen, there is only one lord in the world today: Big loan capital. It was to beg for its favor that our delegation traveled to London. Fulfillment in their hearts, but no national pride, no strength, no will, no burden, and no ideas. They are willing to unconditionally accept the expert report, approaching this task without any tactical skill. It would certainly have been possible to create resonance in the German people against the Dawes Plan, to at least establish a basis for negotiation. But when someone immediately says: *"I am ready to accept everything,"* then it is absolutely impossible for them to get anything out of it. One really wants to grab one's head: Is it stupidity or crime, or perhaps even a certain weariness of responsibility?

Perhaps it is weariness of responsibility, which longs for the strong men from abroad, for the Commissars, before whom the average German is said to always have such enormous respect.

How beautiful and convenient it is now that one has finally found a *"Bible for the Economy"* (as Stresemann called the Dawes Plan), the Dawes Plan, which promises to solve all the difficult questions: the stabilization of the currency, the supervision of taxes, the operation of the German Railway, the control of customs, the issuance of German banknotes, the introduction of the gold standard, the purchase and payment of deliveries. All these things are presented most beautifully in this *"Talmud of the Economy,"* in the interest of loan capital. However, this solution has one flaw: the productive German people are forced into heavy wage slavery, Germany is transformed into a debt state, and the German Reich ceases to be a sovereign state.

I have already mentioned that the bankers have taken the fate of the world into their hands. It is entirely natural that the first and most important instrument of exploitation for Germany must be a banking institution. I must unfortunately refrain from delving into these matters in detail due to the time available for this important question, and can only touch on the essential points in passing.

The Banking Act stipulates in Article I: *"The Reichsbank is to be converted into a private limited company."* Gentlemen, what moral obligations does the private capitalist of foreign origin have toward the interests of the German people? None! Then Article II: *"The capital of the Deutsche Reichsbank shall be fixed at 400 million, which is to be raised through an issue."* It is noteworthy that the justification for this law states that the experts found the financial situation of the Reichsbank to be sound. I do not understand why a restructuring and an increase in its capital to 400 million is needed, since it has been able to manage the monetary policy of the German Reich in a sound state. But one evidently expects enormous profits from this.

The following is particularly characteristic: The capital that the shareholders of the Reichsbank receive for the assets of the Reichsbank is set at only 90 million gold. It is telling how shyly and with an utterly incredible—I can't find a parliamentary term for it at the moment—one has justified the negotiations between the Reichsbank and the Reich. 180 million is the amount for which the German Reich could have taken over all the assets of the Reichsbank under the existing, still valid Banking Act, and in paper millions! It is explicitly stated here: *"The Reich, however, declared that it could not act in an unfair manner in this matter."* But it has indeed been able to act very unfairly, namely by ruthlessly deceiving the war bond subscribers and the holders of government bonds out of their fair money. At that time, one had no feeling for restoring honesty and faith. But when it comes to making a huge gift to foreign capitalists, then of course one cannot act 'in an unfair manner'!

It is also understandable, since the President of the Reichsbank in the Dawes Plan (on page 85) has received a blatant bribe. In the Dawes Plan it states: *"The first President shall be the President of the Reichsbank."* It is therefore not at all surprising that the gentlemen who conducted the negotiations with the German Reich wanted to show themselves favorably to their future employers, the lords of world finance. (Deputy Feder of the German People's Party: What a nadir of discussion! Shame!) I find it outrageous that a German government even accepts such an instrument in which something like this is stated. That is a nadir that a German government dares to offer such a thing to the German people. It is an unsurpassed nadir of German state morality. As you know, in the general council of the so-called German Reichsbank, half of the members are foreigners. The draft budget is reviewed and approved by a financial authority of the foreign country that must be consulted. The commissioner must be a foreigner. The man who will in the future decide how much money shall be made available as circulating funds to the German economy will be a foreigner. He will control the issuance of banknotes. Why? So that the reparations can be consistently collected in full value.

I must now particularly dampen all the illusions, the inflating balloons, that keep rising from the center regarding the anticipated large credits. What does the Dawes Plan say about the tasks of this new bank? On page 87 it states plainly and clearly that the bank shall not grant any loans or advances that are secured by real estate, mines, industrial plants, shares, or government bonds. No credit whatsoever may this bank give to the German public; the German states, the German municipalities, or any other administrative units cannot receive any loans from this bank. How can they keep telling us that the expected credit is what will compel us to finally agree to the Dawes Plan?! Only the Reich receives a short-term credit of 100 million, which, however, must always be covered by the end of the year.

The administration of the Reich's financial assets will be carried out by the new bank, says section X of the experts' report. The Directorate is authorized to grant the Reich, from time to time, advances amounting to 100 million marks. However, all the financial operations of the entire German government must be conducted through this new bank. A gold stream must flow through the coffers of this bank. Nonetheless, it is stated here: "*In consideration of these advantages, the Reich and its financial administration shall conduct all their domestic and international banking business through the mediation of the bank.*" Thus, in addition to the advantages that the bank, not the Reich, enjoys, comes the further advantage for the bank that the Reich must route all its transactions through the bank. Moreover, all funds for the reparation account must be channeled through it. Thus, a new gold stream flows into the coffers of this new bank.

I have already mentioned that the bank is granted the exclusive right of note issue, and that this right represents a clear gift of at least 1 billion marks. For the prescribed coverage is set at only 40 percent, so anything beyond that which is printed in paper bills is a clear gift to the bank. These banknotes will only be issued within the scope of interest-bearing credit to the German economy. This new bank, the bank of the world Jews, is granted an enormous privilege, a privilege for 50 years. Thus, beyond the 37 years to which the burdens are contractually limited, a German government is committing itself to keeping the German people in financial serfdom for a further thirteen years.

It is also interesting to look at the profit distribution. Naturally, one expects fabulous profits from this brilliant financial transaction, profits that are not exhausted by the guaranteed 8 percent for the shareholders. Beyond that, half of the first 50 million achieved will be distributed in favor of the shareholders.

That's an additional 6 percent, or 25 million. Of the next 50 million, the shareholders are to receive a quarter. That's another 3 percent. Thus, they are already counting on at least a 17 percent return for the shareholders of this bank. This is a splendid deal for loan capital. And this deal was not made for the sake of the beautiful eyes of Mr. Marx or any other government ministers.

Unfortunately, I must refrain from addressing the other matters. I only want to point out that it is significant that alongside this Banking Law stands the Railway Law, and that with these two, the most essential sovereignty rights of the German people are being surrendered to world finance. These two things must absolutely remain within the realm of the state; for they are unmistakably sovereign rights of the people. And when the Reich Chancellor repeatedly and helplessly raised the question of other options, other ways, besides those outlined in the Dawes Plan, I would like to attempt a brief response here. The first action arises from the current critique. A basic financial understanding for any German government must be to carry out not the denationalization but the nationalization of the monetary system through the establishment of a truly German state bank, and not to hand over the German note-issue privilege to a private joint-stock company. Do you believe, Mr. Reich Chancellor, that the branches of world finance give you the money because you are you, and not because it is a splendid deal? Thus, rights are granted, even though we are in a position to create something ourselves. After all, everything must be created by ourselves. No one will help us with that. Only the cream is skimmed off by others.

Gentlemen of the government! I warn you against future charges of fiscal and national treason for surrendering German financial sovereignty and German transport sovereignty. What remains of German sovereignty after the adoption of the Dawes Plan? Territorial sovereignty, military sovereignty, financial sovereignty, administrative and transportation sovereignty, and judicial sovereignty define a sovereign state. Territorial sovereignty has been trampled by France for years. Rarely does the German government even dare to label the injustices of the Ruhr occupation as such.

Military sovereignty has been deliberately surrendered. Erzberger once even reduced the figure of 200,000 men to 100,000, presumably to gain favor with world finance. The navy is just strong enough to maintain the threat of order internally.

You now intend to deliver financial sovereignty servilely to the governors of world conscience and thereby rob the German people of one of their most important sovereign rights, without which recovery no longer seems possible.

Furthermore, you are surrendering the German railways and handing over German transportation sovereignty, making any German power politics impossible. You know that a Frenchman is to become the German railway commissioner. By doing this, you are reducing Germany to a slave colony and degrading yourselves to slaveholders in the service of the financial bandits of Wall Street, London, and Paris. Do you not feel the curse that accompanies you if you really go to London to sign the final German agreement? If there were only 1,000 of us Germans—we already have 5 million behind us—then we alone, who see through this diabolical scheme, would have the right and the duty to protest against it. We will not rest until this shame and this bondage are lifted from us. The only possibility with which you can go to London is this.

(The speaker tears up the Dawes Plan.)

I hereby make the following declaration:

1. The National Socialist Freedom Party sees in the intended surrender of German financial sovereignty through the banking laws the cornerstone for the financial enslavement of the German people. It is not foreign bankers, not foreign loans that will help us, but only the establishment of a strong state central bank, free from any private capitalist domination.
2. The National Socialist Freedom Party sees the only possible and viable way to overcome the internal credit crisis in the implementation of a socially just reassessment of old obligations. In this way, we will achieve a restoration of the savings ethic, which has been the foundation of the entire domestic monetary and credit system.

3. The National Socialist Freedom Party fundamentally stands on the recognition of private property insofar as it owes its existence to honest work and achievement. Only Utopians and people's deceivers can advocate the abolition of private property as a means to the welfare of the people. On the contrary, all working citizens must be given the opportunity for real participation in value, which must be earned.

Only by fulfilling these fundamental demands of social justice can a detoxification of internal political relations be initiated, the domestic economy be healed, and thereby the precondition for external stability be created."

Regarding the railway law, our late delegate Dahl (G. 962 ff.) then spoke. He characterized the reasons leading to the corporatization of the Reichsbahn as arising solely from the greedy power consciousness of the French, who seek not only political but also economic dominance over Germany. Where this corporatization leads has already been expressed by Social Democrat Silferdings in 1921. He emphasized: If the railways fall into the hands of a foreign capitalist consortium, this would be a complete surrender of the German economy. It would be the imaginable strongest, most dangerous form of control over the German economy. Dahl then extensively points out the dangers of this control from an economic perspective and draws attention to how mobilization might proceed under the oversight of a foreign commissioner if we were ever forced to take up arms. He sharply criticizes the insolent statements in the Dawes Plan, which claim that railway officials suffer from megalomania and refuse to live within their means. Dahl regrets that Herr Stresemann did not deem it necessary to appropriately counter these outrageous insults to the body of officials, who are diligent and dutiful, enthusiastic in their profession to the utmost, and under whose leadership and management the German railways have operated brilliantly, as it would have been his duty to do. Representative Rahl also touches on tariff policy and remarks: *"The overall impression of this law is so exceptionally bleak that we can only be shocked by it, and we must be particularly alarmed when we examine the personnel provisions."* (How these have played out has indeed been shown in the recent period through the dreadful railway disasters!) Rahl then declares: *"We will reject this law outright,"* and continues: *"If various possibilities are being threatened here to perhaps influence the decision, I say: We are entirely clear about all these possibilities."*

Count Reventlom (1040 ff.) first emphasized that the government, its organs, and its parties have deliberately occupied the public with details in order to obscure the essential points. When the protagonists, the German delegates, traveled to London, they were from the outset given no favorable prognosis by the National Socialists, and in fact, they brought back not even the smallest piece of the Golden Calf. The report was received, so to speak, with a *"ruere in servitium,"* with a precipitous plunge into servitude, joyfully and enthusiastically. But the submission was understood to be anxiously concealed from the people. The main points were not touched upon, nor was mention made of the Rhine and Ruhr occupation, or of the lie of guilt upon which the Treaty of Versailles and then also the Dawes Plan were built. The so-called economic bible is nothing more than the economic bible of the Jews concentrated in America:

It has its perfect analogue in the commandment of the Old Testament: "*You shall devour all peoples!*" The first of these peoples is Germany. The English General Allen says: "*If all Germans were to unite in this feeling (that they are being wronged), then, however disarmed they may be, no power in the world will be able to keep the iron shackle firmly in place and prevent its shattering, if the entire German people resolutely rise up.*" This does not mean war, but the force of the moral will to freedom, the irresistible power of uprising emanating from within. It is downright sacrilegious to designate the Dawes Plan, this document of subjugation, as the path to freedom, as Dr. Marr and Dr. Stresemann have done. The Dawes Report, so politely smooth, sometimes sweetly moral as it speaks, is no document of peace. It is the war by other means: through fear, suggestion, and deception to render us willless, in order to gradually kill any national and German will in the masses of the German people.

On Friday, August 29th, the final votes on the Dawes laws took place.

Seldom has the atmosphere been as tense as on that day. After all, it was about the fate of our people. Groups everywhere stood together discussing the possibilities. The question repeatedly surfaced: "*How will the German Nationals vote?*" For on them, as the strongest party, depended the fate of the Dawes laws, as a two thirds majority was required for the law on the denationalization of the Reichsbahn, being a constitutional amendment. Since they wish to be "*German*" and "*national,*" one could naturally not assume that they would vote for the law of Germany's subjugation, all the more so as the statements of their speakers unmistakably declared that they would reject all legislative proposals. But something seemed to be fermenting, and so the tension was great. Would they hold firm or would they cave in? That was the big question, the pros and cons of which were hotly debated in the corridors of the Reichstag.

Law after law was presented and passed by the simple majority composed of the government parties (German People's Party, Center Party, Bavarian People's Party, Democrats), with the voluntary support of the Social

Democrats and the Economic Party. On the other hand, the Communists and German Nationals voted against, the four eccentrics and of course us National Socialists. The vote was 262 votes for *"Yes"* and 172 votes for *"No."* The German Nationals thus offered the opposition, they were sure that the laws would be adopted even without their votes! But the necessity of the required two-thirds majority for the Reichsbahn law now placed the German Nationals in the most painful predicament. Now they had to *"show their colors"* in the truest sense of the word!

The voting cards are marked with the names of the individual representatives, the Yes-cards are white, the No-cards red, while the blue cards signify abstention.

The vote began. The urns, into which the voting slips are to be placed, are carried around by the attendants. The tension in the entire hall had reached its peak. All eyes turned towards the benches of the German Nationals—but lo and behold, the red slips with *"No"* could be seen in the hands of the delegates everywhere. Several delegates quite conspicuously glanced towards the benches of the Social Democrats and up to the galleries. So, after all—they are rejecting the law—they are standing firm!

But wait, what was that?—Up front, at the very last moment, a white *"Yes"* voting slip falls into the urn! There too! And again—and more and more! Shamefully, these hypocrites had kept the white *"Yes"* slip hidden under the red *"No"* slip until the very last moment, to then, with cunning dexterity, toss it into the urn at the final moment.

Look there!—The grandson of the former Chancellor, young Prince Otto von Bismarck—he too is now submitting the white *"Yes"* slip for the Dawes Plan—and—a pang strikes my heart—even the aged Grand Admiral—Tirpitz—the creator of the German fleet—is voting in favor of this disgraceful law!

The urn is now closed...

The votes are being counted: A total of 441 votes were cast, 314 with *"Yes"* and 127 with *"No"*.

The law is passed!

Forty-nine German Nationals have cast their votes in favor of the disgraceful law.

Their names deserve to be recorded for posterity. They are the delegates: Bachmann, Baeder (Berlin), Dr. Barth, Bazille, Behrens, Biener, Prince Otto von Bismarck, Christ, Döbrich, Domisch (Dresden), Dorfsch (Essen), Dr. von Dryander, Fleischer, Dr. Gerete, Glaeser, Dr. Hannemann, Hense, Hartwig, Hart, Dr. Hoeglich, Hülser, Hülter, von Kömnitz, Dr. von Reudell, Dr. Klönne, Roch (Düsseldorf), KrügerSoppenrade, Lambach, Dr. Lejeune-Jung, Leopold, Lindner, Dr. Matthety, Count Merveldt, O. Mumm, Neuhaus (Düsseldorf), Paul, Dr. Reichert, Baron von Richthofen (Breslau), Rippel, Sachs, Schröter (Liegnitz), Schiller, Dr. Spahn (Cologne), Baron von Stauffenberg, D. Strathmann, Grand Admiral von Tirpitz, Beidt, Bogt und Ballraf.

On behalf of the National Socialist Fraction, Herr von Graefe then made the following declaration:

The Fraction of the N.S.F. considers today, the tenth anniversary of the glorious victory at Tannenberg, on which 314 men and women elected as representatives of the German people have surrendered German sovereignty, the German national economy, and indeed the German people themselves to the grasp of international big capital, with the applause of enemy diplomats, to be the darkest day in German history since November 9, 1918. We state with outrage and sorrow that this hour was only made possible by the fact that approximately half of a faction that calls itself German and national has participated in this act of blindness at the last minute. It bears the primary responsibility for all the terrible consequences. The German people should finally recognize into whose hands it has carelessly and trustingly placed its fate.

One can imagine how extremely unpleasant these courageous words were to the *"Yes-voters."* Through constant noise and persistent heckling, they sought to prevent them and to force Herr von Graefe to stop. Naturally, they did not succeed. Herr von Graefe then introduced a motion of no confidence against the government, which, as one can imagine, was rejected.

The curtain fell on the final act of this unique act of national betrayal in the history of all peoples and times.

CHAPTER 14

BASIC FINANCIAL TECHNICAL QUESTIONS

First published in *"Völkischer Sprechabend,"* edited by Hans Bieberstedt and Otto Lehmann (Sprechabend, October 11, 1924)

The quantity theory of money is still highly regarded by most financial policymakers today. Particularly the current Finance Minister, Dr. Luther, is a staunch defender of the narrow and strict quantity theory. This theory states that the amount of paper money in circulation must stand in a very specific relationship to the quantity of goods in the national economy and must be maintained at this level if inflation is to be avoided.

A doubling of the paper money or currency in circulation would result in prices doubling. In other words: if no new values are created, but the amount of state money tokens is unilaterally increased, one must expect inflationary effects. Therefore, a state that cannot cover its financial needs through tax revenues or other sources of income and resorts to the printing press is pursuing inflationary financial policy—it is driving inflation. It clings stubbornly to the quantity theory of money.

This is approximately the meaning and content of the so-called quantity theory of money.

The events of the past years seem to strongly support this theory. The state covered its money needs through unrestrained printing of banknotes, thereby destroying the currency and the economy. Such a striking practical demonstration is suited to make deceptions appear plausible. Such a deception is the quantity theory of money in the narrow sense. It is false. It is false because the circulating paper money by no means encompasses all claim titles and money surrogates, which must be related to the goods of the economy in exactly the same way as cash, since they enable their holders, just like cash holders, to purchase the products of the economy.

The quantity theory of money therefore only accounts for a portion of purchasing power. Yet this is precisely the point: how much purchasing power stands against the products of the economy.

To better understand these relationships between purchasing power and economic goods, we must first consider the financial technical mechanics of an entire national economy.

On the asset side of a national economy, we must account for all material goods, namely:

I. The state-owned assets, consisting of: railways, postal services, telegraphs, forests, mines, government buildings, etc.

II. The assets of the local administration bodies, consisting of: municipal housing and land holdings,electricity plants, gas and water works, streetcar systems, market halls, hospitals, etc.

III. Private assets, consisting of landed property, factory holdings, urban and rural housing, movable property,and all the countless privately owned items for use and consumption.

Additionally, there are the stocks of economic products from industry, agriculture, etc.

There can be no doubt that these components of wealth, which describe the entire material holdings of a nation, are to be considered as the total assets of the national economy. But against these assets stand very large debt obligations.

Against state-owned assets stand state debts, thus railway bonds, national and state loans, war bonds, etc. Against the assets of administrative bodies stand the debts of cities, districts, and municipalities, thus municipal loans, district loans, and local government loans.

Against the total private assets of industry, trade, and agriculture, as well as against the private population, stand all private debts in the form of mortgages on houses and landed property, in the form of industrial bonds and other types of debt securities. And finally, we must still add to the liabilities the money, that is, the circulating paper money, which is supposed to mediate the exchange and purchase of goods.

There can be no doubt that the above individually listed liabilities of the national economy, the claims against the national economy, just like cash, confer purchasing power on their holders. All such interest-bearing or non-interest-bearing documents of purchasing power must stand in a specific, yet to be examined, relationship to the goods of the economy.

The holder of so many millions of national loan bonds or other securities is just as purchasing powerful as the holder of paper money. Both can equally fulfill their desires when purchasing goods from the economy without further ado. Whether a banking intermediary step is involved through the sale of securities or whether these securities are directly given as payment is naturally irrelevant.

It must be noted here that even the strict quantity theory acknowledges a certain influence of the velocity of money circulation. Even within the framework of the narrow quality theory, it is already clear that by considering this factor a very great uncertainty regarding the strict validity of the quantity theory of money must arise.

Another factor is the diversity or variability of payment customs.

But if we recognize that beyond the cash holdings of a national economy all the above-listed securities and papers in their capacity as purchasing power must and can be related to the goods of the total economy, then it is clear that this narrow quantity theory is fraught with so many sources of error that we may already describe it as false. Let us also consider that the entire payment traffic for almost all larger sums takes place exclusively through the use of bills, checks, and particularly through cashless transfers, then it becomes abundantly clear that the quantity theory described above, which seems plausible at first glance, must be wrong.

Certainly, it cannot be denied that a boundless and senseless multiplication of paper payment instruments to the thousand, or million fold must have the greatest influence on the purchasing power of the currency unit, the Mark. However, in our current, theoretically fundamental consideration, we must not include such an insane period. We must first establish that all the mentioned debt instruments, in addition to cash, in addition to money surrogates, bills, and checks, are available to the national economy for the exchange of goods—and that is, after all, the essence of an economy. A correct quantity theory must, therefore, at least take all these purchasing power factors into account.

Moreover, as mentioned above, it must consider the velocity of circulation and payment customs to gain a reasonably clear picture of the effect of the increase in paper payment instruments on prices.

In any case, it can already be stated as a conclusion that the narrow quantity theory, which only relates the circulating paper money to the goods of the economy, cannot possibly be correct.

For if we numerically follow the data from Steinmann, Bucher, Selfferich, and Ballod and assume the German national wealth before the war to be approximately 250-350 billion, then this total national wealth, which consists of the aforementioned tangible goods, is contrasted by the debt obligations also hinted at above, the approximate numerical sum of which is as follows:

Debt Category	Approximate Amount
Imperial Loans (Reichsanleihen)	5 Billion Marks
State Loans of the Länder (Staatsanleihen der Länder)	15 Billion Marks

Debt Category	Approximate Amount
Railway Debt (Eisenbahnschuld)	18 billion Marks
Debt of Local Government Bodies (Schulden der Selbstverwaltungskörper)	6 billion Marks
Bond Debt of Industry (Obligationsschuld der Industrie)	6 billion Marks
Private Debt Obligations, mostly in the form of mortgage bonds (Hypothekenpfandbriefe)	11 billion Marks

Total: 61 billion Marks

In addition, there are private mortgages, the exact amount of which is difficult to determine.

Furthermore, there are no reliable statistics on the mortgage burden. The figures provided by Damaschke, mentioning 80 billion in mortgages, are certainly vastly exaggerated. If all mortgage burdens mediated through all German land credit institutions, regional banks, mortgage and exchange banks amounted to only about 11 billion, it is highly unlikely that more than 20 billion were additionally invested in private mortgages.

However, for the present investigation, it is not so essential whether this figure is accurate; it is more about the fact that we see in the German public an approximate total sum of around 80 billion in securities, which grant each holder purchasing power to the given extent.

Now, it is undoubtedly the case, and it should be strongly emphasized here, that this purchasing power is only potential, that it is not permanently on the market. But this purchasing power can become effective at any moment, acting as a buyer in the open market.

In any case, the possession of such securities is the basis for almost all larger transactions, for issuing checks as well as for transfers through cashless means.

We refer to these securities as the *"big money"* of the national economy and have thereby found a very appropriate expression for the functions of these securities in the economy.

The entire payment transaction, especially large transactions, takes place almost exclusively on this basis of the *"big money"* of the economy.

In real estate transactions, this is particularly clear. The buyer of a house or a plot of land has certainly never practically paid with 10 or 20-mark coins or paper currency. He has either transferred his holdings in securities entirely or partially in lieu of payment for a house, or he has settled his debt through cashless means using checks or transfers based on such holdings.

Similarly, the entire payment transaction in real estate and industry primarily took place on the basis of bank deposits. Only those with bank accounts or securities in their treasury could issue checks or payment orders based on these credit instruments.

However, it is by no means correct to assume that there is a fixed relationship between the total sum of these purchasing power instruments and these payment substitutes on one side and the total volume of goods in the entire national economy on the other. It can only be said very generally that there are certainly certain relationships between both sides of our national economic balance sheet, but these relationships cannot be precisely quantified in the sense of the quantity theory.

It is only important to recognize that the total sum of securities, which we refer to as *"big money,"* stood in relation to the actual so-called small money of the economy in such a way that the entire big money was incomparably larger than the entire small money. Furthermore, we must recognize that the entire cash flow can be largely replaced by cashless payment transactions. The trend in this direction, especially on the part of postal check offices, is aimed at reducing the use of cash to a minimum.

Practically, it is entirely conceivable to limit the need for circulating payment means to the pure small money transactions, i.e., for daily purchases, tickets, wage payments, etc.

All other payments can practically be handled cashlessly or through money substitutes such as checks or via accounting transfers.

This can also be described as a change in payment habits, where the form of direct payment with cash or paper currency is replaced by cashless payment transactions. In a stable national economy, the value of money as the purchasing power of the currency unit ultimately remains unchanged, regardless of whether more or less paper currency is temporarily in circulation or whether larger financial transactions are conducted. The situation changes drastically, of course, when, as in times of unchecked paper money economy, the amount of paper money is unilaterally increased at an ever-growing rate. In times of peaceful economy, the principle certainly held: A mark is a mark. One could, by offering Munich or Bremen city bonds, railway or imperial bonds, purchase houses, goods, etc., anywhere. The mark was stable.

During the inflation period, a strange shift occurred between securities and paper currency. While in peacetime securities were worth multiple times the amount of paper money, this relationship shifted during increasing inflation to the detriment of interest-bearing and other debt claims denominated in marks, and yet the government clung to the fiction: a mark equals a mark, even though the effects of the extraordinary increase in payment means had long since manifested in insane price increases.

On one side, the circulating paper currency had increased to an extraordinary extent, while on the other side the purchasing power of securities denominated in marks had fallen to zero.

The previously immense block of securities and bonds shrank to nothing in purchasing power relative to the endless mass of paper money.

Inflation celebrated its triumph, and hand in hand with it came the destruction of the currency, the economy, the *"big money"* of the population, and the entire savings of the nation.

A further consequence was the unprecedented credit crisis that followed. As a result of the inflation period came the destruction of the entire savings holdings, the entire securities holdings. During the inflation, it did not yet come to the consciousness of those affected; only the *"stabilization"* made the devastation clearly visible. Suddenly, no one had *"money"* anymore, i.e., the private individuals had all lost their savings, they had suddenly disappeared, nothing was left!

Although agriculture had suddenly been relieved of its mortgages, it was simultaneously defrauded of its entire operational assets invested in war bonds and mortgage bonds and was forced to take on enormous loans.

On one hand, industry had the advantage of the devaluation of its mortgage debt obligations, but on the other hand, it too was stripped of all its credit foundations.

The currency stabilization through the introduction of the Rentenmark was celebrated everywhere as a great achievement.

In reality, there was not the slightest reason for this. For in fact, the so-called stabilization merely made our impoverishment visible.

The equation: One Rentenmark equals one trillion paper marks, it stabilizes the complete loss of all German assets denominated in marks held by mortgage creditors and savers.

As is well known, Finance Minister Dr. Luther takes great pride in this stabilization.

In his brochure *"Feste Mark—Solide Wirtschaft,"* he goes so far as to remark: *"This stabilization and the cessation of the printing press was a great achievement, one rarely found in world history."* Furthermore, Dr. Luther says: *"We have thrown ourselves in front of the speeding car of currency devaluation and after a few more meters, brought it to a halt."*

It would be very nice if Dr. Luther's claim about the cessation of the printing press were true. Unfortunately, it must be stated that this assertion by the Finance Minister is a blatant lie. On November 15, 1923, the circulation of paper payment means amounted to 93 trillion. By mid-1924, this had almost increased tenfold.

In June 1924, the amount of circulating paper money in the form of trillion notes was 810 trillion. And that's not all. In addition, 2,300 million gold marks worth of Rentenmarks were also printed.

Therefore, there can be no talk of a cessation of the printing press since November 1923. On the contrary, a more outrageous inflation has never been conducted than since November 1923.

In a conversation I had with the Reich Finance Minister at the end of June 1924, Dr. Luther himself admitted that the Rentenmark was *"materially"* inflation.

Here, the *"miracle"* of the Rentenmark reveals itself.

In reality, however, neither the enormous new inflation through the issuance of 810 trillion nor the Rentenmark had any inflationary effect.

How can this miracle be explained, which alone is proof of the correctness of my above assertion? The narrow quantity theory of Dr. Luther and official national economics, of course.

Why is it false in this case?

Because the preceding inflationary period had destroyed the entire *"big money"* of the German national economy. Because through this destruction of German savings and capital holdings, an enormous state of emergency had arisen in the entire German economy. Therefore, it was naturally possible to introduce both the 810 trillion and the 2,300 million Rentenmarks into circulation without even the slightest inflationary effect being triggered.

The *"big money"* of the economy had previously been a multiple of this sum, and this multiple, though not fully effective as purchasing power, had nonetheless been continuously present and effective in the German economy as potential purchasing power.

This late and simple realization solves and explains the *"miracle"* of the Rentenmark. It is a logical conclusion, not a miracle, and no one can claim that a significantly larger amount of Rentenmarks could have had any dangerous impact on currency stabilization.

The stubborn adherence to the 2.3 billion Rentenmark was nothing but a consequence of the narrow-minded timidity and financial-political incompetence of our current Finance Minister.

This unfortunate lack of understanding had a double, devastating effect on the German economy. On one hand, it completed the enormous state robbery, of the savings of mortgage creditors and savers, and on the other hand, it deprived the German economy of its *"big money,"* its credit foundations. It plunged millions upon millions of hardworking people into the bitterest misery and at the same time brought our entire agriculture and industry into the worst credit crisis and thus into the clutches of financial capital.

Never before has the supremacy of pure loan capital over productive labor been more complete than today. At no time was the German economy more worn down, more beaten to death than in this period of the glorious currency stabilization by Dr. Luther.

The Third Tax Emergency Ordinance of February 14, 1924, has stabilized and legalized this crime of inflation with all its ensuing consequences.

CHAPTER 15

NATIONAL SOCIALIST LIBRARY

Established in 1927, currently 45 volumes

Foreword to the First Volume:

"The Program of the N.S.D.A.P.". (400.-450. Published in 1932)

The Party Congress in Weimar in 1926 expressed a desire to publish a series of writings that would address all important areas of our entire political life in concise, foundational, and programmatic papers. These volumes aim to present a unified and coherent picture of how National Socialism approaches the various tasks of our public life and how it intends to eliminate deficiencies and errors.

The primary task of these volumes must therefore be to fundamentally examine *"how everything stands,"* then, based on scholarly foundations, to provide an answer to the crucial question: *"What now?"* by showing new paths in state life, monetary affairs, and the economy. In this way, these works must and should distinguish themselves from the otherwise common writings, which, out of sheer scientific caution, do not dare to go beyond the retrospective historiographical work of the *"historian"* or, in the name of *"objectivity"* and *"neutrality,"* allow every opinion to be voiced.

To erect a *"rock of bronze"* in this chaos, to shape clear insights from in-depth studies, and to form a unified political vision—that is the task of this series of writings.

For this reason, it is evident that all writings, while allowing for individual freedom, must unerringly and steadfastly reflect the few great foundational ideas of National Socialism with clarity and precision.

Adolf Hitler has entrusted me with the publication of this series. These volumes are to serve as the official literature of the Party.

To this year's Party Congress, I present as the first volume *"The Program of the N.S.D.A.P."* I extend special thanks to our Führer Adolf Hitler for reviewing the manuscript.

Murnau on Lake Staffelsee, August 1927

From the Foreword to the Fourth Edition:

With sharp emphasis, Adolf Hitler declared at the Reich Leadership Conference on August 31 (1928): *"Programmatic questions are not the concern of the leadership meeting; the program is set, and I will never tolerate any tampering with the foundational programmatic tenets of the entire movement."* I wholeheartedly align myself with this decisive declaration by the Führer, for nothing is more dangerous to the stability and the thrust of a political movement of our nature than when its firm foundation, the program, is subjected to negative criticism or disputes after the fact.

Those who, on the Jewish question, in our struggle against high finance, against the Dawes Plan and the politics of impoverishment, or in other programmatic matters, believe they cannot agree with our immovable, firmly set paths and goals; those who, through adherence to the League of Nations or the Locarno Treaties, believe they can *"secure freedom for the German nation by compromises and cowardice,"* they have no place with us, they stand outside the N.S.D.A.P..; their private conscience, which often manifests itself in tedious speeches and written effusions, we firmly reject.

Furthermore, we reject the *"Yes-Buters,"* those who *"generally agree"* but always have a *"But"* ready regarding certain points.

It is different if, for instance, a programmatic point is misconstrued by outsiders or maliciously exploited by political opponents, as has already happened. In such cases, an official commentary must and will be provided.

Thus, Article 17 of the 25 programmatic points, torn from its context, has found a malicious misinterpretation and slanderous insinuation by our opponents. Adolf Hitler, upon my proposal, has therefore issued the following clarification regarding Point 17 on April 13, 1928:

Clarification

In response to the dishonest interpretations of Point 17 of the program of the N.S.D.A.P. by certain hostile opponents, the following clarification is necessary.

Since the N.S.D.A.P. stands on the foundation of private property, it follows that the clause *"Expropriation without compensation"* refers only to the creation of legal possibilities to expropriate land that was acquired unlawfully or is not managed in accordance with the interests of the public welfare, if necessary. This accordingly is primarily directed against the Jewish land speculation companies.

Munich, April 13, 1928.

Signed, Adolf Hitler.

It goes without saying that there can be no question of the N.S.D.A.P., restricting the German landed property in the city and countryside in its well-acquired property rights, as was falsely asserted in the last election campaign by the Landbund, the Farmers' Party, and the German Nationals. No party pursues a clearer and more targeted land policy than we National Socialists. From the sense and spirit of our overall program, it is absolutely clear that expropriation can only pertain to such German land and soil that, especially during the inflation, was swindled from the German owners for a so-called pittance by foreign or domestic speculators and profiteers, mostly Jews, or also to such large landed estates that are not managed in service of the general public for the nourishment of the people.

It is the task of the National Socialist Library to publish, over time, fundamental treatises on all areas of public life touched by our program, in the spirit of our program.

It is the intellectual forge for our liberation struggle.

Murnau on Lake Staffelsee, September 1928.

CHAPTER 16

PROFIT SHARING

First printed in *"People and Community,"* monthly journals for National Socialism and local politics, edited by

1. The Problem

It is indicative that in Social Democracy the demand for profit sharing is one of the most hotly contested issues. Capitalism has long since solved the problem in its own way. The holder of a share or a stock certificate in any company is profit-sharing in the earnings of the company without any effort or work. The money alone *"works for him."* It is precisely this form of profit sharing that has led to the greatest and most glaring injustices, indeed, to a complete separation of capital and labor.

Without the capitalist even needing to know where the production facilities are located from which he owns shares, bonds, stock certificates, etc., without having to be active in any way for *"his"* company, without the slightest interest in the quality, economic necessity, or goodness of the products, without being in the least concerned about the social conditions, hygienic and sanitary provisions in the interest of the workers employed there—the capitalist, the shareholder, bond or stock certificate holder, is the sole one entitled to profit.

That such a system must provoke the sharpest criticism in a moral and social sense is quite clear. That the main task of every production facility—the increase of yield, the continuous improvement of production— must also suffer from it is equally clear. Here, capitalism reveals its fatal effect.

For the capitalist, however, there is certainly nothing more convenient and comfortable than this form of exploitation of the labor power of all those involved in production.

Therefore, it is only natural that the demand arises for the elimination of income without work and effort derived purely from capital ownership and that one strives to direct the profits of enterprises to those who earn these profits. Social Democracy has simply coined the slogan: *"Down with capitalism!"* However, the direction in which this demand operated was by no means against the harmful interest-capitalist form of shareholding, but rather most unilaterally aimed at the entrepreneur who is in possession of the means of production, which bring him unjustified profits. He should be socialized. Here, again, it becomes quite unmasked that Social Democracy is by no means concerned with the elimination of an obvious and cruel injustice but with the denial of personality and the merits arising from it. Not against the capitalist system, but against the high-value personality, the entrepreneur, the economic leader, the Marxist struggle was directed. The one who makes the foundation, who takes the risk, who organizes the work, who opens up new markets, is considered by Social Democracy as the exploiter against whom it mobilizes the rage and envy of the masses.

The driving force of the Marxist demand for profit sharing is therefore not socially ethically founded, but rather a manifestation of the mobilization of the lowest instincts among the masses.

In this way, the demand for fair profit distribution, which is essentially based on such a high ethical level, is constantly at risk of being either capitalistically or socialistically distorted, all the more since this demand opposes egoistic instincts, indeed, even springs from them. The demand for profit participation, as we National Socialists understand it, must therefore equally keep itself pure from both capitalist and Marxist deviations. It will certainly not be entirely easy in practice to always avoid these two reefs. This seems generally possible only if the universally binding guideline *"Common good before self-interest"* is adhered to.

I have repeatedly pointed out the extraordinary difficulties of a personal and direct profit participation.

The formulation: *"We demand profit participation,"* initially makes it the duty of the legislator to clearly outline the concept of *"We."* Are the *"We"* the workers, employees, and civil servants employed in the individual enterprises, or does the *"We"* cover the entirety of all working people, or is the *"We"* limited to the National Socialists or even the National Socialist state, which, as the representative of the totality, claims a share in the profit yield of production? From the superior standpoint of breaking the bondage of interest, personal, direct profit participation in the sense of introducing workers' councils must be rejected. This is preferably advocated by capitalist quarters, especially when socialist incursions threaten. In such cases, one prefers to throw a piece to the nasty brutes to content them, while still allowing the big capitalist to continue to draw his plunder, albeit somewhat reduced.

2. When is Profit Participation Justified?

We must fundamentally be clear that profit participation is morally and economically justified only when the one who claims the right to profit participation has also contributed to the profit through special personal performance. It would fundamentally contradict the sense of social justice if every day laborer who performs any incidental work, who sits as a porter at the entrance, who is obligated to carry out cleaning and maintenance work in the factory spaces, or even the one who has to perform a specific, unchanging task within the framework of overall production, who operates machinery or distributes or delivers raw materials, were to claim that their activity has any substantial influence on the operational results and thus on the profit of the entire enterprise. Indeed, diligence and conscientiousness must and can be demanded from such tasks, which must then also be compensated through appropriate remuneration. Just as little would it be justified to undervalue such tasks, as they are all indispensable.

However, they are not of equal importance for the economic yield of an enterprise. Whether it is Meier or Huber who shovels the incoming coal wagons into the bunkers is entirely inconsequential for the enterprise's yield. But it is not inconsequential whether the technical director invents an efficient, labor-saving construction, whether a chemist devises a new preparation that significantly boosts sales, or whether a commercial director creates a flawed calculation. Such *"intellectual achievements"* are of decisive importance for the success or failure of an enterprise. On these depend the profit or loss of an enterprise.

It is certainly important that the technical personnel invests their best efforts with genuine interest and here and there suggests improvements, just as it is important that the operational managers continuously devote their attention to a general increase in performance in the sections under their supervision—but even then, these individually valuable and yield-enhancing measures cannot so substantially influence the final result of the entire enterprise that one could derive a legal claim to the profit of the overall enterprise from these particular achievements. It is entirely conceivable that a series of excellent technical improvements in one part of the operation might be conceived, ordered, and implemented by an engineer or foremaster, while a deficient or clumsy handling of the technical department in another section renders the improvement completely illusory, just as the possibility exists, and unfortunately often occurs, that a shrinking economy nullifies even the most brilliant improvements and deprives an enterprise of its profit share. Conversely, it is entirely unclear why a disinterested or indifferent technical officer, who merely sits through his office hours, should participate in the profit that has been achieved solely through the brilliant propaganda activity of the sales manager, technical improvements in another production site, or even through a genius-like reorganization of the entire enterprise.

One can see that here the extraordinarily numerous practical difficulties lead to great injustices, so that the entire problem must be examined with the utmost caution. Such complicated questions are least of all resolved by slogans. It appears entirely correct and fair and appropriate that special compensation be granted for special achievements. How often, to point to some extremes on the other side, have the most brilliant inventors perished as poor devils, how often is the profit from a technical achievement not reaped by the engineer or foreman who devised it, but by a shrewd capitalist who *"financed"* such an improvement! And yet, a deep moral kernel lies within the demand for profit-sharing, as long and insofar as profit-sharing benefits the one who has primarily generated the profit through his own achievement.

The demand for profit-sharing carries within it a profound moral core, as long and insofar as the profit sharing accrues to the one who has primarily generated the profit through his or her performance.

How often have we heard: The National Socialist state must be a state of work and achievement! For us, the value of personality stands at the center. Not the mass as such and not the individual as such has claims to make, but each according to his or her diligence and ability. Profit-sharing, therefore, can only lie within these overarching perspectives in the National Socialist spirit.

3. Who has a claim?

The scope of the claim to profit-sharing logically cannot be greater than the area in which the individual is active and can influence the outcome of his work through his performance and ability. A simple metal turner, for example, undoubtedly has a claim to profit-sharing in his workshop if the workshop significantly increases its output—its yield—through skillful techniques that he himself has devised. Similarly, the facade mason who achieves double the output compared to his colleague next to him undoubtedly has a claim to the profit generated by his measures within the overall context. Of course, the higher one's rank and position within a company, the higher their fixed remuneration, their salary, and this already generally includes profit sharing. That is why one is a director or plant engineer, so that they continuously devise, order, and carry out improvements—in service to the whole.

If such a director or plant engineer demanded special profit-sharing for each individual improvement that, however, falls within the scope of their duties, it would be in stark contrast to the idea of duty. After all, state or municipal employees are expected to forgo profit-sharing from the outset. Where would one end up if all senior government officials and railway presidents, all wagon inspectors and workshop workers at a public service enterprise, such as the state railways, demanded profit-sharing?

Undoubtedly, profit-sharing contains a powerful incentive for all work. Undoubtedly, a fair system of profit-sharing, or better said: value distribution, could significantly increase the yield. From this perspective of increasing yield, profit-sharing must somehow be resolved in a positive sense.

4. Previous attempts at profit-sharing

The attempts to involve workers in the profits of the commercial enterprises where they are employed date back to the beginning of the last century. Particularly in England and France, various attempts in this direction have been made, some of which were abandoned after a short period. Bohmert, J. St. Mill, LeronBeaulieu, and others have praised this *"wage system"* as a radical means of improving relations between employers and employees.

To see a *"solution"* to the social question in this, however, goes far too far. To gain insights, Professor Böhmert already conducted a survey in 1878 on the experiences made. In 1883, the French Ministry of the Interior conducted an inquiry. In 1900, an international congress to promote profit sharing even took place in Paris. Out of the multitude of these attempts however, only relatively few can be cited that can claim to be of real value.

A certain form of profit-sharing has proven truly successful only in fishing, particularly in sea fishing and whaling. The companies, which naturally cannot supervise the crews of the various fishing vessels and sea fisheries, involve the fishermen in the profits. These are motivated by the prospect of profit, in addition to their fixed wages, to greater diligence, care, and discipline. (Here, however, let it be noted that this involves a completely self-evident process and circumstances where it concerns a strictly limited group of individuals with a narrowly defined task, the fulfillment of which lies exclusively with this group of individuals.)

Attempts with profit-sharing have also taken place in agriculture, some of which were accompanied by favorable success, but all of them more or less rooted in the more patriarchal mode of operation in agriculture. Thus, the renowned estate owner S. v. Thünen introduced a genuine profit-sharing system for the village residents employed on his estate Tellow in Mecklenburg. According to this, each of the approximately 20-30 workers on his estate received a share of a hundredth of the surplus yield that exceeded a certain sum he had set (18,000 Marks). The resulting amounts were not paid out in cash but were deposited into a savings account. They were to be available to the beneficiaries from the age of 60, ensuring them a carefree old age. The system is said to have proven successful. Naturally, it ceased with the sale of the estate in 1896. In this case, it can also be expected that the social sense and the care in the patriarchal sense of the employer for his workers were the deciding factors for the economic peace between the estate ownership and the village residents. More recently, the Reich Land Workers Union has recommended sliding wages with profit-sharing.

In industry and commerce, we must from the outset discard the form of profit-sharing that is limited to bonuses, gratuities, and special allocations to higher-ranking officials and employees. For these, sound and entirely appropriate forms have long been found in various companies and have proven successful. However, it must not be overlooked that this in no way constitutes profit-sharing in the sense of a general and direct profit-sharing of all productive employees. This form of profit-sharing is better characterized by the term performance allowances or premiums. Such performance allowances also usually do not stand in a direct proportional relationship to the net profit achieved by the entire enterprise.

Otherwise, it is precisely the large-scale industry with its thousands of commercial employees, its apparent or real profits, that is the target of those who strive for any form of profit-sharing. It must appear striking that the attempts are by no in proportion to the enormous number of enterprises, and that of the well-known attempts, which again mostly owe their origin to the special social responsibility awareness of the respective owner, proprietor, or manager, only the very fewest can claim truly positive results. It can be very clearly traced that real encouragement for the increase in yield can only be spoken of where it involves special quality work. Well known is the enterprise of the French building painter Leclaire, who as early as 1843 involved his painters, upholsterers, and decorators in the business profit. Here we are dealing with a relatively restricted circle of individuals with pronounced quality performances in a craft business. On a larger scale, we find a similar attempt in the factory for sewing machines and buckles Dequenne and Co., which employs up to 1600 workers. The profit-sharing introduced in 1876 was mainly used for the establishment of grandiose welfare facilities (workers' housing, consumer facilities, insurance funds, childcare institutions, libraries, etc.).

In England, a well-known case is that of the Des Steinkohlenbergwerk Briggs Son and Co., Westnorthire, where, after endless labor disputes, a certain profit-sharing in 1865 led to the establishment of a better relationship. Briggs converted his enterprise into a joint-stock company, retaining two-thirds of the shares for himself and distributing the rest among the employees. Initially, this system worked to satisfaction, but it soon became the cause of new disputes and was subsequently abandoned. In England, from 1865 to 1920, a total of 330 such profit-sharing attempts become known. More than half of these (192) were abandoned again. The existing ones are distributed among gas works (36), commercial operations (26), food and drink businesses (16), machinery and shipbuilding (14), weaving (17), printing (13), agriculture (8), bank and insurance (5), and building trades (3); hence, an extremely small proportion of businesses. The profit-sharing quota reached an amount roughly equivalent to about two weeks' wages. In Germany, where there are around 20,000 joint-stock companies and 50,000 G.m.b.H.s alongside several hundred thousand private partnerships and sole proprietorships, profit-sharing was implemented in 29 enterprises in 1922; 66 enterprises had abandoned profit-sharing. In 13, there was capital participation, and only in 16 enterprises was there profit sharing in the true sense. 13 of these had adopted the Thünen principle, according to which the profit share was not paid out but was instead deposited into a savings account to be paid out upon reaching retirement age, upon leaving the company, or upon death. The combined profit and capital participation, as is relatively commonly practiced in America and Great Britain, has been recorded only once in Germany. In a few cases, the entire workforce was collectively involved in the enterprise. However, the share allocated to the workers was not particularly significant, and for this reason, a real increase in yield could not be spoken of. It was more a consequence of the socialist revolution, which prompted some entrepreneurs to promise the workers a portion of their profits in order to placate them. Historically notable in Germany is the case of the Borchardt mine in Berlin, where, after deducting a 6% preferential dividend on the capital, the remaining profit was split equally between the company and the employees. However, this system was abandoned after just five years, as the prospect of a minor share offered too little incentive for diligent individual performance, and favorable buying and selling conditions—in other words, the economy—were of far greater significance for the net profit. Otherwise, profit-sharing experiments have only been conducted in the Salle machine factory and the Carl Freese blind factory in Berlin.

Finally, mention should be made of the Zeiss company, in which Ernst Abbe, the later sole owner, without disregarding the fundamental reservations about profit-sharing, paid out a wage and salary adjustment based on the earnings of individual business years. In good business years, this wage and salary adjustment was indeed implemented. Here, too, it must not be overlooked that the focus of social welfare measures lay in other areas, as Ernst Abbe initially and as the most important prerequisite for the lasting success of his company made significant funds available for preliminary economic work so that Zeiss could always maintain its world renown as an optical institution. Furthermore, he did much for the development of the city of Jena and especially the workers' districts, and otherwise ensured the founding and maintenance of workers' settlements in the most generous fashion. Nevertheless, conflict arose immediately here as well, when under the influence of the war and the revolution, the profits of the enterprise dwindled and no *"wage adjustment"* could be made. Jena was one of the reddest Communist strongholds in Germany.

In America, profit-sharing is purely capital-based. The American steel trust offers its employees shares.

5. Is Profit-Sharing for Increasing Production?

Regarding the problem of profit-sharing, two practical considerations come into play. Namely, whether one aims to increase production through the introduction of profit-sharing, or whether profit-sharing should serve social ethics in the sense of facilitating the organization and management of the enterprise by fostering mutual trust.

An increase in overall production as the aim of profit-sharing can only be expected if the individual workers have sufficient insight into the overall operation. This includes understanding the difficulties of a technical, commercial, and even political nature, which can naturally only be expected in the rarest of cases. Furthermore, the operational peculiarities of the individual enterprise are of decisive significance. In largescale operations that are subject to global economic fluctuations, that set prices through the formation of cartels and trusts, where everything depends on maintaining the operational facilities at the most modern level, which are under constant operational control on a scientific basis, not even the greatest efforts of individual diligent workers can have any noteworthy influence on the final production outcome. The individual worker at the forge or in the pit cannot possibly oversee the operational, commercial, technical, communal, and fiscal factors, and even if he could, the overwhelming multiplicity of all these factors would likely have more of an inhibiting than a motivating effect on his work ethic.

Furthermore, it must be added that in large enterprises with significant labor forces, the proportional profit shares, even in good years, are extraordinarily low, reaching only in exceptional cases 7% of the total wage bill, but usually remaining below 5%. The hopes placed on the effect of profit-sharing for increasing production mostly stem from ignorance of the fundamental circumstances. Far more effective for improving the economic situation of an individual enterprise could be arrangements targeted at the very sphere of activity of the worker themselves. For example, if a worker before the war could earn 50 Marks hourly, by working overtime, say, up to 80 Marks to 1 Mark more, which was typical for brickwork labor, allowing them to earn 2400 Marks over 300 ten-hour workdays instead of 1500 Marks, such a system undoubtedly has far greater significance for increasing the willingness to work and thus for boosting productivity than even a profit-sharing scheme that constitutes 10% of the wage; all the more so since, even with the most accommodating arrangements, the workers would still feel shortchanged.

6. Social Ethical Effects of Profit-Sharing?

If the social ethical aspect is to be regarded as the main purpose of profit-sharing, one cannot stop at mere profit-sharing but must inevitably proceed toward co-ownership and co-determination rights; in other words: one must add the democratic principle to the capitalist principle of profit-sharing and be willing to introduce parliamentarism into the business as well. What might be gained through this approach in terms of mitigating tensions between employers and workers—by giving the workforce insight into the countless factors and difficulties of organizing and managing an enterprise—would be lost again due to the endless obstacles that arise through workers' councils, works councils, and, in short, the entire parliamentary administration of such a business. For small and specialized enterprises, such possibilities are entirely feasible and should by no means be opposed. But one must be entirely clear that all such efforts depend on mutual understanding, and a willingness to understand can certainly not be enforced by legal prescriptions. We will need to delve much deeper here to bring about a change in attitudes, especially among entrepreneurs. However, a new ethic of economic thinking can only be initiated if the fundamental flaws of purely capitalist thinking and business practices are mitigated or eradicated by the National Socialist worldview.

The conflict between unrestrained individualism on one hand and Marxist Communism on the other can only be resolved here by National Socialism in a universalist spirit.

The objection raised by the workers against profit-sharing cannot be lightly dismissed: *"The employer wants to give us workers a portion of his profits only because he believes he can secure his large gains this way."* Certainly, this idea of profit insurance was also the motivation behind most employers' attempts—especially after the war—to share profits with the workforce.

A growing understanding on both sides, that of the entrepreneur and of the employer, regarding the mutual dependencies and interconnections within the entire production process, is likely to pave the way for a satisfactory solution to the problem of profit-sharing in the future. Fundamentally, the demand for profit-sharing is far too real and technically-economic in nature to theoretically consider its practical success as impossible. Personally, I find the current approach of combining profit- and capital-sharing, which organizationally requires the participation of eligible parties in the management of individual enterprises, to be not promising. In political life, we have already made the worst experiences by introducing the co-determination rights of financially obliged citizens into the parliamentary system. Agriculture has so far successfully (apart from works councils) resisted parliamentary methods and has fared well by doing so.

An evolving insight, both on the side of the entrepreneur and the employer, into their mutual dependencies and interconnectedness within the context of the entire production process will undoubtedly pave the way for a satisfactory solution to the problem of profit-sharing in the future. Fundamentally, the demand for profit-sharing is far too real and technically-economic in nature to theoretically consider its practical success as impossible. Personally, I find the current approach of combining profit- and capital-sharing, which organizationally requires the participation of eligible parties in the management of individual enterprises, to be not promising. In political life, we have already made the worst experiences by introducing the co-determination rights of financially obliged citizens into the parliamentary system. Agriculture has so far successfully (apart from works councils) resisted parliamentary methods and has fared well by doing so. Profit-sharing is also only appealing and interesting for the participants as long as the company thrives. Loss-making years, economic downturns, and competitive struggles quickly diminish interest in it, and instead of finding support and assistance in times of crisis, the company will only suffer under the increased complexity of its management structure.

7. Legislative Measures

Attention should also be drawn to some legislative measures that were taken in various countries to pave the way for capital formation in this manner, especially where existing legal regulations concerning joint-stock companies excluded so-called *"small shares."*

In Germany, the nominal value of individual shares was significantly reduced after the adjustment following inflation. Moreover, in Prussia since 1912, a law has been in place providing for profit-sharing by higher-ranking officials in state-owned mining operations. The German Jurists' Congress in 1921, however, rejected a legislative mandate for profit-sharing and wanted to limit legal regulation to facilitating the voluntary standardization of certain typical forms of participation.

In England, the great enthusiasm that had prevailed for profit-sharing around the mid-nineteenth century has subsided. The major miners' strike in 1921 was settled through government intervention, and the workers were granted a share in the company's profits.

In France, the so-called *"labor share"* was introduced, where the basis of the share is labor performance, not capital contribution.

In 1922, Norway, through a special committee, recommended the statutory mandatory introduction of profit-sharing for certain enterprises.

The various forms of profit-sharing are as follows:

a) According to the object.

1. Participation of the employee in the company where they are employed.
2. Participation of the entire workforce of an industry in the total profits of that sector.
3. Participation of all in the overall economy of the country. Practical significance has so far been gained mainly by the possibilities under No. 1 of individual profit-sharing, as opposed to the more collective-economic forms under 2 and 3.

b) According to the circle of persons.

Here, one can distinguish:

1. Individual participation of each worker in the form of a certain percentage of their annual wages-designated and assigned to them.
2. Collective participation, where the assigned profit shares are not paid out to individuals but used for the benefit of the workforce for welfare facilities, etc.
3. Mixed systems, which arise from the combination of the two aforementioned forms.

c) According to the basis of profit attribution.

Here, the distinction is as follows:

Profit-sharing 1. based on membership in the firm, i.e., labor performance in the relevant enterprise; 2. based on a (usually earned) capital participation (small share); 3. a combination of both types.

It is in the nature of things that there are a number of intermediary forms. Exemplary for collective participation was the approach of the Krupp company, Essen, which year after year spent significant sums, up to 20 million Marks, to create various welfare facilities. The value of these facilities cannot be overestimated in terms of maintaining the health of the workforce, improving living conditions, particularly in the home environment, and enabling physical training through baths, sports halls, laundries, etc. It is noteworthy that these expenditures were entirely voluntary, without any obligations.

However, the best possible use in the service of the workforce was ensured. Certainly, few would consider this as profit-sharing in the strict sense of the word. If, however, one compares the actual benefits with the amounts that would have come to individual workers through individual profit-sharing, namely at most 5% of their wages, the extraordinary superiority of this form of collective participation of the workforce in the earnings of a company over the individual method becomes evident. 5% more in the household budget of a working-class family would never suffice to significantly improve their general standard of living.

If in each case these amounts had been saved, such tremendous achievements for the common good as mentioned above would have been made possible.

8. The Economic and Scientific Aspect of Profit-Sharing

Profit-sharing is the result of certain economic circumstances. It primarily concerns the question of the necessity of an allocation beyond the fixed wage from the company's earnings. Secondly, it concerns whether it is possible to grant the worker something extra beyond the fixed wage from the margin between production costs and market prices. As far as the latter is concerned, the possibility can undoubtedly be affirmed for a whole range of industries, as it is well known that even with uniform market prices, individual enterprises are run with varying degrees of efficiency, thereby increasing the profit opportunities of the better-managed enterprises compared to those less well managed.

For the less efficiently managed enterprises—and these are the majority—the possibility of profit-sharing becomes even smaller and narrower the more additional unfavorable factors come into play, such as tax burdens, unfavorable locations, expensive rail connections, etc. A legal regulation of compulsory profit-sharing thus presents extraordinary difficulties, and if introduced, it would ruin the many smaller enterprises, while the few highly modernized businesses could still show significant profit margins, as they could expand their operations even further due to the elimination of competition—if not monopolize them through price dictatorship.

Of particular importance in all this remains the overall economic situation. It will never be possible to determine with any certainty which production factors are responsible for specific shares of the total earnings. Therefore, there can be no general, economic-scientific proof in favor of the workers' right to profit-sharing.

For the large mass of unskilled workers, for the mass of workers in heavy industry, textiles, and the chemical industry, for transportation companies, considering the state of rationalization in the organization of operations, the influence of labor performance in terms of quality and intensity is diminished. From this, a moral right to profit-sharing can hardly be derived, especially for the masses of industrial workers. Certainly, profit-sharing does not grow theoretically on the basis of an ethical postulate. It has always arisen from the will of the entrepreneur, who thereby demonstrated his social sentiment, especially when he did not operate profit-sharing in the narrow capitalist sense of individualistic profit distribution but, out of a social spirit, took collective care for the entirety of his workforce. In doing so, the concerned parties have also, for the most part, best ensured the productivity of their enterprises, have awakened the workers' interest in the overall company, and have best worked to bridge the class-struggle tensions between employer and employee.

CHAPTER 17

THE BETRAYAL OF THE PEOPLE BY THE REICHSTAG

Speech on the Young Plan on March 7, 1930

Stenographic Reports, Pages 4229-4232; see also "Völkischer Beobachter" from March 15, 1930

I am of the opinion that there is no better illustration of the *"relief"* that the Young Plan brings us than the new tax laws. Precisely what one has always heard in the radio broadcasts, the *"relief"* for the German economy, has turned into its opposite. No less than 700 million in new taxes are to be imposed; the beer tax will be increased by 75 percent, amounting to 240 million. The gasoline and benzol tax will yield 65 million, tobacco is supposed to bring in

30 million more, the mineral oil tax 40 million, and the industrial burden will be retained, although it was to be reduced according to the Young Plan—it is to be set at 280 million, etc.

One must truly wonder, in light of these facts, how there are still people in Germany who advocate in favor of adopting the Young measures. I do not want to go into the details of the payment table, it is enough if one keeps reminding the German people that according to the Young Plan, they are supposed to pay an average of 2 billion annually for 58 years, while essentially under the Dawes Plan, the payments should have ended by 1961.

The living and practical fact is that we must pay 2 billion gold marks annually in foreign currency, and at this point, the first fundamental question regarding the feasibility of these payments arises. It is not without interest to cite the most prominent figures of this republic with their statements on this matter. Herr Gustav Stresemann, certainly one of the most prominent figures in modern German politics, declared on June 24, 1929, in this house literally: *"Do you believe that any member of the government would declare: I guarantee that the Young Plan is feasible?"*

So this is how the German government's certainty stands, that it can implement the Young Plan.

Around the same time, the Prussian Minister-President Braun expressed his doubts about this view with the following statement: *"I have strong doubts whether, according to the proposal of our experts and in light of the heavy burdens of the past, it will be possible to raise 1,640 million Reichsmarks for 37 years."*

The *"comrade"* Wels spoke in a similar vein in May 1929 in Magdeburg: *"We must reckon with the fact, which can no longer be erased by any party resolution, that a significant portion of the proceeds from the labor and production of the German people cannot serve the common good of our own country but will flow to the reparations creditors for decades to come."*

There is no doubt about Herr Dr. Schacht's position. His memorandum from December seems to have been completely forgotten by the subservient government. I also recall the German delegate in Paris, Herr Bögler, who at least by resigning his mandate has shown the German public that he cannot, under any circumstances, lend his name to such an impracticable matter. I do not understand how you, Herr Dr. Curtius, can be so eager to push for its adoption. Your argument that maintaining the Dawes Plan would mean a crisis is the most peculiar from your party's side. It was you and your party who elevated the Dawes Plan to the highest level.

Dawes Plan above all, for you did not consider it a silver lining on the horizon, but a mark of the highest economic reason that you accepted the Dawes Plan. Herr Stresemann called the Dawes Plan the *"Bible of the economy."* And now all that you praised to us at that time is bad and miserable. Your current stance is a single judgement of condemnation on the whole previous policy. It is not merely that—it is also an admission of political dishonesty. It signifies nothing other than that you now wish to distance yourself from your previous policy.

We National Socialists have no intention of defending the Dawes Plan; for it was precisely we, in contrast to our present allies, who were the most resolute and direct opponents of the entire policy of fulfillment in the battle against the Young Plan. This of course does not prevent us from always pointing to the one advantage that the Dawes Plan might offer for Germany in the present crisis, if we had a government that truly represented German interests and was not eternally subservient to the will of the enemy coalition. I refer to the transfer protection.

First, a few words about the prehistory and development of the Young Plan. At the Paris Conference, Germany was represented by experts—not government or state officials, but bankers and economic leaders— which is itself indicative. This German delegation in Paris was given only one directive: *"No agreements should be made that, after conscientious examination, would endanger the standard of living of the German working population."* This was the mandate they tried to follow. It is known that Dr. Schacht initially intended to bring a proposal of only 800 to 1,000 million to Paris.

I repeat: they ended up accepting 1.64 billion, to which the Prussian Minister-President Braun has already raised strong concerns.

Then came the second stab in the back, the statement in *"Vorwärts"* that one should not allow oneself to be overly dependent on the proposals of these economic experts but had to exceed them for political reasons. It was Comrade Severing, in his notorious speech at the time, who declared two billion to be completely negotiable and bearable. In the further course of events, it was specifically ordered that the average annuity of two billion can be accepted, and this, as you know, was also signed in Paris.

I can only place the behavior of the German government on the same level as the November betrayal of the year 1918. Such behavior is treason, a charge which the SPD, far from taking as an insult, regards as a badge of honor, as expressed by Herr Gendewig. Herr Gendewig, in the socialist student community at the FürstBismarck School in Berlin, declared: *"It is therefore an unreasonable demand when we ask the Entente to relieve us of our reparations. The accusation of treason is for us a badge of honor."* Similarly, the Social Democratic senior school director Dr. Ramerau, head of a gymnasium in Berlin, in a lecture in the spring of 1929 on *"The Struggle for the German History Book,"* stated: *"We demand that Germany's guilt in the World War finally finds its way into German history books."* In the same vein, the Social Democratic deputy Rosenfeld in Stettin expressed: *"It is the task of the SPD to ensure that Germany does not violate the Versailles Treaty: for Versailles is German Reich law, and in a rule-of-law state, no illegalities should be tolerated."*

Rely on this, gentlemen; these things will be entered into the great ledger of the German people, and in the not-too-distant future, you will have to answer for these things before a German state tribunal, and in the coming state, treason will be punishable by death.

Equally untenable is the position of the Center Party. The chairman of the Center Party, Prelate Kaas, has clearly stated in Saarbrücken: *"The acceptance of the Dawes laws can only be considered hand in hand with the regulation of the reparations question."*

Yesterday, from the convoluted explanations of Herr Hilger, we could discern that the complete flip-flop of the Center Party is being prepared.

As for the Democrats—though I see not a single member of this dying party here—one expects nothing but anxious fence-sitting between the two large neighbors. They are, after all, living solely on the mercy of these two parties and the large Jewish press. But precisely here, I must point out the political spinelessness with which today's Democracy supports the Dawes laws and joins in the ludicrous panic cries of the government, as if we were not in the midst of a crisis. Aren't we indeed in the midst of a crisis, Dr. Curtius?—In March, when the Paris Conference threatened to collapse, the *"Berliner*

Tageblatt" declared: *"Pure fear of adverse political and economic consequences of a rejection of the Dawes Plan; the result would only be a retention of the Dawes Plan, whose transfer protection provisions would have to come into force in the shortest possible time, so that our opponents would get less than they would now receive under the new figures of the Dawes Plan."*

A few words from the speech of the Bavarian Minister-President Held for the Bavarian People's Party as well. The Bavarian Minister-President Dr. Held expressed himself in the Bavarian Landtag as follows: *"It is a matter of financial control over Germany. The decision over the fate of the involved peoples is placed in the hands of a few financiers."* Finally, the Bavarian Minister-President Dr. Held pointed to *"the most disgraceful sort of dishonesty,"* when parties bind the German people to promises of so much to deliver, themselves doing nothing to achieve a financial policy capable of allowing us to fulfill these obligations. He added: *"One has promised a fiscal reform in January which was to bring tax relief. This was a giant swindle, and the German people have never been treated so shoddily as now. I cannot say yes if I am convinced the demands are unsustainable."*

That then, ladies and gentlemen is the mind of the Bavarian People's Party; a party that, perhaps against expectation, presently shows itself as ready and ripe to commit to ratifying these treaties.

Summing up we note: Within this rabble of lofty airs yet base means, not one among the governance has said they see the fulfillment of the said Young Plan as tenable. Moreover – and given the matter in contention's supposed inescapable finality (which by the intentions at stake must be dealt with); it constitutes a serious dishonesty, before the treaty's contractual partners, should any such figure sign off on affairs held presently impossible of realization! Only a scumbag promises more of it than he can deliver.

Summing up further, I put before the present governance several questions.

1. Given the aforesaid; do you view possible the new Plan's fulfillment? Yes or No? Dr. Curtius – platitudeslike *"I decline to prophecy"* do not become an answer deemed of the responsible statesmen. If yes, then you bear the responsibility; if no, why do you sign it then?
2. Do you truly consider the New Plan a step forward, if you seriously believe that the Dawes Plan offers the possibility of a reduction, or even a suspension, of reparations payments?

3. Will you explain the peculiar clause in the Young Plan: "*If Germany is unable to meet its obligations, the Bankers' Conference will consider contributing to the expansion of world trade by financing German enterprises—especially in underdeveloped countries—which would likely not be undertaken with the usual available financing methods? Does this not contain the terrible danger of an obligation to human exploitation in the event that we cannot raise the necessary billions in foreign currency? What does "underdeveloped countries" mean? It is known that this World Bank plans a motorway from Cairo to the Cape. This plan is feasible. But who will carry it out? This is one of the cases where German workers will indeed be exported and turned into slaves. How do you intend to protect the German population from this horrific prospect of the future? From the prospect of being exported as white slaves?*"
4. Are you prepared to answer for your actions with your head before a future state tribunal?
5. Are you prepared to submit the draft bills to the Reichstag in the shortest possible time, which logically result from your claimed full restoration of Germany's sovereignty, as we have laid out in our motions Nos. 1704 to 1708? These motions read:

- **Motion No. 1704:** The Reichstag shall resolve: The War Equipment Law of July 27, 1927 (Reich Law Gazette I, p. 239) is repealed with immediate effect.
- **Motion No. 1705:** The Reichstag shall resolve: The provisions of the Versailles Peace Treaty and the related agreements, whereby Germany's naval strength may not exceed 100,000 men, shall no longer be recognized by the German Reich following the possible adoption of the Young Plan.
- **Motion No. 1706:** The Reichstag shall resolve: Simultaneously with the possible adoption of the Young Plan, the German Reich shall resume full sovereignty over German rivers and streams. The provisions of the Versailles Treaty that oppose this shall no longer be recognized.
- **Motion No. 1707:** The Reichstag shall resolve: The resolution of the National Assembly of December 18, 1919, whereby Article 61 Clause 2 of the Constitution of the German Reich was rendered null and void, is repealed.

This concerns the annexation of German Austria.

Motion No. 1708: The Reichstag shall resolve: Article 178 Clause 2 of the Constitution of the German Reich shall be rendered null and void simultaneously with the possible adoption of the Young Plan.

This actually concerns the German Basic Law, whereby the provisions of the Versailles Treaty take precedence over the provisions of the Reich Constitution. If you truly describe the Young Plan as the liquidation of the war and as the final settlement with the enemy states, then the adoption of our motions is the logical consequence.

I conclude: The position of the National Socialist German Workers' Party on the Young Laws can leave no room for doubt. In unshakeable

In unshakeable consistency with our entire political stance against the entire fulfillment policy, we reject the Young Laws outright. I declare on behalf of my faction: We see in the adoption of the Young Laws a deliberate and conscious betrayal of the people.

The ministers and party leaders who have carried out and signed this betrayal of the people will not only bear the responsibility before history, but we hope to bring them before the state tribunal of the future Reich in the near future.

We National Socialists deny this Reichstag and this government, which, according to yesterday's remark by the Reich Foreign Minister, feels like the *"pawn of the Reparations Agent,"* the right to speak for the German people today.

We National Socialists speak today not only in the name of the six million who have already voted against the Young crime in the national referendum, we speak today for countless masses of voters from the camp of the government parties, especially from the camp of the Social Democrats, whom you have misled. We speak today for the entire German people, who demand their right to life, who are slowly awakening from the paralysis of the November crime of 1918, and who do not want to see the future for their children and grandchildren miserably betrayed and gambled away by you. Dissolve this Reichstag! Call for new elections! Then the response of the German people will be different than under the bondage of a cowardly, spineless policy of fulfillment!

CHAPTER 18

REFLECTIONS ON THE YOUNG PLAN

First published in the "National Socialist Monthly," Issue 6, September 1930

Since the end of the war, no political event has stirred the German population more intensely than the struggle over the adoption or rejection of the Young Plan.

What needs to be said historically on this matter has been expressed by our deputies and speakers in the most emphatic manner. Less highlighted has been the fact that this event, too, must not be viewed in isolation, but rather as a provisional endpoint in a long series of political developments, and above all as the culmination of a tragic struggle in the character of the German people, as a heavy defeat of the Germanic race against the organized forces of subhumanity.

In all such broad historical analyses, we must, while carefully observing the immediate phenomena, delve deep into the sources of the German people, their strengths and their weaknesses, in order to comprehend the present fate inwardly and to draw from it the insights needed for the constructive reshaping of German life.

It has always been Germany's fate that in its mighty marches, it founded great empires and achieved cultural pinnacles; yet time and again, it fell back into internal discord, into shame and impotence. In a heroic surge, the young and vigorous Germanic people shattered the world dominion of Rome, spilling their best blood in broad streams; but all the Germanic realms on ancient Roman soil sank and vanished again because greed and envy, discord, and above all, the mixing with the subjugated peoples, hollowed out the inner strength of the ruling class. We observe the same tragedy in the later history of the German Empire. A repeated rise to dazzling splendor, to world dominion: Charlemagne, Otto the Great, Frederick Barbarossa and Frederick II, the Hohenstaufens, Frederick the Great and Wilhelm I—and two generations later, always a pitiful collapse. With Louis the Child, the proud Carolingian dynasty went to the grave ingloriously; Otto III, the son of Theophanu, was ashamed to be a German and died as a youth; Conradin ended on the scaffold in Naples (1268); at Jena and Auerstedt, Napoleon annihilated the Prussian army; Wilhelm II fled across the Dutch border.

Yet even this external fate of Germany, which one could read from history books as a last resort, is overshadowed by the most terrible German tragedy, the Thirty Years' War. Even these religious struggles are noted by historians, but rarely does anyone dare to point to the deeper essence of these conflicts, as Alfred Rosenberg does in such a spiritually clear and comprehensive manner in his latest work, "*The Myth of the 20th Century.*" In a grand synthesis, Rosenberg exposes the deepest roots of these struggles that took place within the German Volk: honor and freedom and "*love*" and blind obedience as thesis and inner contradiction, through which the soul of the Germans became sick and broke down.

Siegfried and sagas, Arminius and Segest, Gedan and Tannenberg—then Versailles and the Young Plan. Jubilant victory, shattering defeat, betrayal, and treachery. Light and darkness—God and the devil.

What does this have to do with the Young Plan?

Much! Almost everything. Because Versailles and the Young Plan, seen from a racial perspective, signify the deliberate binding and slaughter of the German spirit, German labor, and the German soul by the organized subhumanity.

With deepest dismay, we are witnessing the German tragedy of fate in our own time. Glorious victories. On all the battlefields of Europe, the best of German youth spilled their red blood, while behind the front lines, shadowy men and schemers, marrists and Jews, forged the chains and sharpened the dagger. Unaware and trusting, without deceit, the German essence does not comprehend that others are different.

Kaiser Wilhelm II's words: "*I no longer know any parties, I know only Germans*" are infinitely revealing of the complete blindness to all the forces and powers that sought Germany's downfall. These words betray a total ignorance of racial laws, express the most dangerous German naivety and false Christian brotherly love. Instead of simply locking up the social democratic rabble, they were allowed to continue their destructive work unhindered until the proud German Empire, the mightiest military power on earth, was stabbed in the back by Jews and Marxists and lay on the ground.

With full intention, I have placed these brief reflections at the forefront, for only when the young, awakening Germany becomes clearly aware that the great and terrible events of recent years are not merely ordinary struggles and political inevitabilities, but rather a grand, ultimate decision, a world struggle, a final confrontation between idealism and materialism, blood and money, labor and capital, light and darkness— only then can we hope that from this deeply racial understanding, redemption and liberation will be granted to us, and that the Third Reich will endure longer than the proud rise of the Wilhelmine-Bismarckian era.

These fundamental insights—and insights they are, far more than mere knowledge—do not, however, relieve us of the duty to examine with the utmost precision the particular forms of the current political and economic conditions.

Knowledge is power—but only knowledge and will give birth to action.

Only by embedding political events within the recognition of the grand connections and polar opposites of world history does one comprehend the path that led to the Dawes Plan, the historical precursors, recognize the intentions of the enemies, see the consequences, and thereby also discern the measures for defense and the prerequisites for them.

The Dawes Plan is the final link in the chain of political events aimed at the subjugation of Germany. n

With the Dawes Pact, it was said: Only the Entente can help us! We must be grateful that we have finally regained the trust of the Entente. Only with foreign capital can we rebuild the German economy. This was told to the German people in every conceivable tone, from Mosse to Scherl, from the Social Democrats to the German Nationalists, no differently than by the government itself—until the Pact was accepted.

How we National Socialists were hated because we opposed this political monetary murder of Germany with all our might! How our resistance against the acceptance of foreign credits was met with mockery and scorn by the traitors and swindlers! We saw more clearly and deeply, we predicted what was to come, what the purpose and intention of the Dawes Pact was, and we expressed our position in the state political declaration that I read in the Reichstag on August 29, 1924, on behalf of the faction.

In contrast to this National Socialist stance, the Reich government and the fulfillment parties praised the Dawes Laws as a salvation and celebrated them as a great success of Stresemann's fulfillment policy. I quote the most telling statements.

According to the official stenographic reports of the Reichstag on August 23, 1924. Reich Chancellor Dr. Max said:

"The experts' report has been accepted by the government as a suitable basis for the resolution of the reparations issue."

"A rejection of the London Agreement means, first of all, the destruction of all the hopes cherished by the German people and our brothers in the occupied territory. Industry and agriculture will continue to suffer increasingly from the credit crisis.

The rise in unemployment and the general distress are certain consequences of rejection (!) ... An enormous responsibility rests on the German Reichstag. Its decision will, in my deepest conviction, mean blessing or curse."

Thus, *"blessing"* meant the acceptance of the Dawes Pact according to the opinion of Dr. Marx, Reich Chancellor by the grace of the Center Party. And Dr. Hans Luther prophesied on the same day:

"Only through the acceptance of the London Agreements can the necessary relief for our economy (!) be provided, namely, the adjustment of our tax system to the economic and social necessities and a tangible reduction in railway tariffs.

As soon as the London Agreement is accepted, the foundations for the loan are laid!"

Thus, for the hopeless, interest-bound indebtedness of Germany. He was followed as the third of these parliamentary Graces by Gustav Stresemann, who, in equally lengthy and meaningless words, described the *"benefits"* of accepting the Dawes Pact.

Within five days, the laws were then pushed through and, without amendment, passed with an inaudible two thirds majority by the German Nationalist yes-men, the Social Democrats, the Center Party, the German People's Party, the Economic Party, and the Bavarian People's Party.

*

Now it was believed that what had been desired had been achieved. Germany lay shackled on the ground, politically defenseless through brazen manipulation, stripped of its sovereign rights, ripe for international exploitation.

Six years have passed since those terrible August days of 1924, and today we can determine the results of these *"advantages"* and reliefs. 2,740,000 unemployed in the Reich, 16,000 deaths by suicide per year. 50,000,000,000—fifty billion in debt of the Reich, the states, the cities and municipalities, of agriculture, industry, and trade.

11,000,000,000—eleven billion in Reich taxes for 1930, in addition to 4,000,000,000—four billion in property and business taxes and 660,000,000—six hundred sixty million Marks annually in direct payments from the Reichsbahn to the Reparation Agent, now to the International Bank of Payments in Basel, moreover 300,000,000 Marks—three hundred million annually in interest payments from the industrial burden to the Reparation Agent.

Financial misery and tax torment, judicial scandals and the complete state bankruptcy looming on the horizon, moral decay spreading widely, one corruption scandal after another.

"The Experts' Plan has functioned satisfactorily," reported Parker Gilbert in a deceitful manner to his employers—the Allied and associated governments—but they could not shake a certain concern: the Dawes Pact contained some clauses that a nationally-minded government could have exploited in Germany's favor, the so-called transfer safeguards. Furthermore, the most significant uncertainty factor remained: the Dawes Pact was a political act, and the Dawes payments were political debts; the high finance had not yet entirely liberated itself from its political instigators, political constellations, the collapse of the Entente, even a merely latent moral resurgence of Germany, the desire of one of the Allies to see Germany regain its capacity for alliances, or an actual alliance could still disrupt the ruthless plan of high finance. Money had not yet definitively triumphed over blood.

The clever General Agent therefore sought a renegotiation of the Dawes Pact for years. It may also have made him uneasy to think of the inevitable collapse in Germany and the then blatant failure of the Dawes Pact.

His goal was to impose the responsibility for the payments on Germany itself, particularly for the transfer of payments, and above all, he wanted to transform Germany's political debt into a purely private-capitalistic, contractual obligation towards an unpolitical body in neutral foreign lands. This swindle was called the *"Liquidation of the War"* and the elimination of the transfer safeguards—the restoration of Germany's full sovereignty and the abolition of the burdensome control bodies.

It is unnecessary to say that the German fulfillment politicians eagerly fell for this brazen fraud, and that they welcomed the Young Plan with the same enthusiasm, recommended it with the same words, and spoke the same phrases about the *"relief"* that this product of the most tenacious diplomatic appeasement work of the *"greatest statesman of the German Republic,"* Gustav Stresemann, would bring to the German people.

Let us now examine the Young Plan soberly according to the official text. The experts of the Paris Conference declare with beautiful candor that they approached their task as—businessmen.

"We have," the report continues, *"set the amount and duration of the annuities and made provision for the conversion of the reparation debt from a political to a commercial obligation."*

In other words: Germany Must Pay:

Period	Amount (in million RM)
Sept 1, 1929 – Mar 31, 1930 (7 months)	742.8
Apr 1, 1930 – Mar 31, 1931	1707.9
Apr 1, 1931 – Mar 31, 1932	1685.0
Apr 1, 1932 – Mar 31, 1933	1738.2
Apr 1, 1933 – Mar 31, 1934	1804.3
Apr 1, 1934 – Mar 31, 1935	1866.9
Apr 1, 1935 – Mar 31, 1936	1892.9
Apr 1, 1936 – Mar 31, 1937	1939.7
Apr 1, 1937 – Mar 31, 1938	1977.0
Apr 1, 1938 – Mar 31, 1939	1995.3
Apr 1, 1939 – Mar 31, 1940	2042.8
Apr 1, 1940 – Mar 31, 1941	2155.5
Apr 1, 1941 – Mar 31, 1942	2180.7
Apr 1, 1942 – Mar 31, 1943	2194.0
Apr 1, 1943 – Mar 31, 1944	2194.3
Apr 1, 1944 – Mar 31, 1945	2207.5
Apr 1, 1945 – Mar 31, 1946	2208.3
Apr 1, 1946 – Mar 31, 1947	2199.5
Apr 1, 1947 – Mar 31, 1948	2215.2
Apr 1, 1948 – Mar 31, 1949	2210.0
Apr 1, 1949 – Mar 31, 1950	2216.5
Apr 1, 1950 – Mar 31, 1951	2359.2
Apr 1, 1951 – Mar 31, 1952	2348.2
Apr 1, 1952 – Mar 31, 1953	2346.2
Apr 1, 1953 – Mar 31, 1954	2353.3
Apr 1, 1954 – Mar 31, 1955	2364.6
Apr 1, 1955 – Mar 31, 1956	2359.8

Apr 1, 1956 – Mar 31, 1957	2354.2
Apr 1, 1957 – Mar 31, 1958	2361.8
Apr 1, 1958 – Mar 31, 1959	2393.8
Apr 1, 1959 – Mar 31, 1960	2370.6
Apr 1, 1960 – Mar 31, 1961	2380.5
Apr 1, 1961 – Mar 31, 1962	2398.3
Apr 1, 1962 – Mar 31, 1963	2390.2
Apr 1, 1963 – Mar 31, 1964	2402.6
Apr 1, 1964 – Mar 31, 1965	2402.1
Apr 1, 1965 – Mar 31, 1966	2428.8

Continued(1966–1988):

Fiscal Year	Amount (in million RM)
1966/67	1607.7
1967/68	1606.9
1968/69	1616.7
1969/70	1630.0
1970/71	1643.7
1971/72	1653.9
1972/73	1662.3
1973/74	1665.7
1974/75	1668.3
1975/76	1675.0
1976/77	1678.7
1977/78	1685.4
1978/79	1695.5
1979/80	1700.4
1980/81	1711.3
1981/82	1687.6
1982/83	1691.8
1983/84	1703.3
1984/85	1683.5
1985/86	931.4
1986/87	931.4
1987/88	897.8

In addition to the above annuities, the amount of 660 million Reichsmarks is to be paid annually without deduction, i.e., without any right to a deduction of any kind, in equal monthly installments in foreign currency.

In total, the annuities amount to 114 billion gold marks, which are to be paid in dollars!!

The interest-based economy of Germany is thus imposed on three generations of the German working population.

The despotism of high finance over the most industrious people on earth is thereby sealed.

4 billion in war reparations was demanded by Germany from France in 1871.

6 billion in war reparations was demanded by Germany from Russia in 1917.

114 billion is being demanded by the *"experts"* of the Paris Conference from Germany, and its representatives, Dr. Schacht and Curtius, place their names under this most terrible document in world history despite the protest of 6 million Germans, who have expressed their opposing will in the national referendum.

114 billion—without even accounting for the approximately 50 billion that Germany has already paid over the 11 years since the end of the war, in cash, in reparations deliveries, or through the loss of the stolen colonies or the sequestered German assets abroad, etc.

Germany must pay—must pay to the utmost limit of its ability—no, far beyond that.—That Germany would have to pay, and indeed much more than it could afford, was already clear to the foreign experts long before they came to Paris.

The hearing of the German delegates was mere shadowboxing. Schacht originally intended to approve at most 800-1000 million for the year, was then negotiated up to initially 1635 million over 37 years, but ultimately signed an average of 2050 million annually over 59 (!!) years.

Here we can confidently assert that organized subhumanity in the form of

Marxist agitators has lent support to the capitalist oppressors.

Carl Severing declared on August 31, 1929, before the Reichsbanner in Duisburg: *"The Young Plan brings political and financial benefits of immeasurable magnitude."*

And the gentlemen Curtius and Grzesinski, Guérard and Schmidt, in their infamous radio speeches, expounded the *"advantages"* and reliefs of the Young Plan, misusing the radio. They can be certain that the State Court of the coming Reich will once again pose the burning question that I directed to Minister Curtius in my speech on the Young Plan on March 8:

"Are you prepared to answer for your actions with your head before a future State Court?"

*

The war is being liquidated—by transforming the political debt into private legal obligations. This was actually the far more difficult task for high finance. In fact, discussions in Paris lasted a full 3½ months over the form, the how—and to whom the payments were to be made, while the amount of the payments was effectively dictated to the German negotiators in the final 3½ weeks of the conference.

One must always consider—high finance, which is not inherently identical with the Allied governments, wants to remove the plunder of Germany from the hands of the Allies, and gain control over the billions of German tribute payments itself. This must be made palatable to the nationalistically inclined governments with intricate sophistry. This is naturally much more difficult than dictating to the spineless German delegates. Personally, it remains incomprehensible to me how, for example, such an eminently nationalconscious country as Italy could not see through this villainy of high finance. I therefore, with full intent and in full awareness of the significance of this point, discussed it in my speech at the Nuremberg Party Congress on August 2, 1929:

"I cannot imagine that a proud and self-conscious nation, such as Italy, could tolerate the idea that claims fought for through blood and iron could be settled through a stock exchange deal—albeit of worldwide scope—with the potential risk of falling into disfavor with an international banking consortium domiciled in a

neutral country outside its sovereign territory, and then only receive, after endless delays and pretenses, its due payments in part or not at all.—Italy, for example, would possess no means of power or pressure."

It is precisely at this sensitive point that a determined German foreign policy should have intervened, in Paris, in The Hague, and in London, to sow justified distrust among the former Entente powers, distrust especially against the supranational regulation by an international financial consortium. For Germany, the siren song was calculated: It is now high time that we extricate ourselves from the sphere of eternal war and post-war peonage. Germany should finally be freed from the feeling of still having to pay war debts to the evil France, England, and Italy. It should feel itself as an equal member in the great community of nations, the payments, which should be reduced to a level that Germany itself will acknowledge through its signature, should in the future no longer be made to the formerly hostile governments, which would always leave a sting behind, no, the payments should be made to a neutral trustee committee, in which Germany also has a seat and a voice. Thereby, the possibility for the largest international credit transactions should simultaneously be opened. The German payments should no longer have the character of war tributes, but should rather have the character of private-capitalist contractual obligations.—With this, the bothersome political controls by the Reparations Committee etc. can also be abolished. Germany can regain the feeling of complete sovereignty when it makes the payments to the International Payments Bank on its own responsibility.

It is no wonder that our government officials were delighted by such hypocritical talk and forgot that it was completely irrelevant to the working German population, to the German taxpayer, both in terms of the amount of the payments and in terms of the threat to German state finances, whether the German tribute had to be paid directly to Paris, London, Belgrade, etc., or via Basel.

What was not irrelevant, however, was that through the provisions of the Young Plan, the so-called transfer protection clause was abolished.

*

The transfer protection provisions of the Dawes Plan were the only effective leverage for a revision in favor of Germany. The transfer protection clause was dictated by a remnant of economic reason that did not want to let the goose that lays the golden eggs die, born from the realization that genuine reparations payments can only be paid from export surpluses.

The bridge of understanding for the inextricable connection between transfer and trade balance is not so easy to cross, but we must strive to gain complete clarity on this matter.

Transfer refers to the transfer of tax payments made in Reichsmarks etc. to the allied governments in their respective national currencies. The transfer was within the task scope of the Reparations Agent. This agent therefore had to convert the German market payments received into foreign currencies (dollars, francs, pounds, lire, etc.) and then remit them to the various governments.—To the layman, this may at first seem very simple, assuming that the Reparations Agent simply buys $1 for RM 4.25, £1 for RM 20.20, etc., on the stock exchange and then remits it—the layman here only thinks in small terms, while in reality we are dealing with the need to exchange at least 2 billion into foreign currencies annually—which cannot be raised in the whole of Germany—because the German trade balance is passive!

But before I elaborate on this, I would like to point out what was understood under transfer in the Dawes Plan. In Annex 6, Section X of the Dawes Plan*), it was made the duty of the Reparations Agent to carry out the conversion of German market payments and the remittance to the Allies only to the extent that the Reparations Agent managed to obtain foreign currencies without endangering the German currency.

If this could not be done in the normal way, no payments were to be made.

At first glance, this would still not have meant any relief for the domestic market, because even if no transfer payments could be made, Germany's obligation continued to deposit the agreed market amounts into the account of the Reparations Agent—albeit up to a maximum sum of 5 billion gold marks.

However, this sum was also subject to the restrictive provision that even before reaching this sum, reparations payments had to be reduced or completely suspended if *"such an adjustment poses a threat to Germany's financial and economic situation."*

It can be no doubt that this provision would have effectively protected against the complete bleeding of Germany, and that this very provision of the Dawes Plan would have been an extraordinarily effective means for achieving a revision of the Dawes Plan had Germany had the necessary government.

*) The Dawes Plan according to the original text of the Expert Committee of April 9, 1924, and comments by Dipl.-Ing. Gottfried Feder, Member of the Reichstag. Part 7 of the National Socialist Library. Published by Franz Eher Nachf., Munich, Thierschstr. 11. 144 pages. Price: M. 2.-, hardcover M. 3.-.

Now back to the trade balance.—Even the most fulfillment-ready government cannot ignore principles and basic facts of world economics. One such principle is: If Germany has no export surplus, then there are no foreign currencies at the German currency centers, then the Reparations Agent cannot buy dollars, francs, and pounds etc., then transfer is immediately out of the question, then the Dawes Plan stops functioning on its own. Even the layman will understand that in Germany we can only get dollars if we sell our German labor products in America and get paid in dollars; with these dollars we must first buy the foreign raw materials that we unquestionably need to maintain our German processing industries.

We must, under any circumstances, buy cotton if our entire large textile industry is not to collapse and hundreds of thousands more workers are to be thrown onto the streets; for the same reason, we must buy wool. For our rubber industry, we need latex; for our enormous electrical industry, we must have copper; iron ore for our iron and steel industry, etc., etc.

It requires the most intensive work of the German economy to earn enough foreign currency annually by supplying dyes, medicines, light bulbs and motors, iron goods and machinery, precision instruments and optical products—to name just a few—to be able to pay for the absolutely necessary import goods.

The fact that hundreds of millions are spent on importing coffee, butter, fruit, vegetables, or even bananas and other tropical fruits—items that are not essential for life—is a scandal that once again demonstrates the pitiful and lamentable weakness of the so-called German postwar governments.

From this weakness arises the catastrophic deficit in our foreign trade balance. For years, Germany has been importing more than it can pay for with its exports. —Germany, therefore, has no active trade balance in reality, from which alone the foreign currency could flow to pay the genuine tributes to the enemies.

One can see how, behind the transfer problem as a colossal factor of global economic significance, the German foreign trade problem looms large.

Now, to be sure, even this does not exhaust all the possibilities for at least temporarily executing the reparations payments. One such possibility is the internal sell-off of Germany to foreign countries through the continuous creation of new interest-bearing debts and the mortgaging of German assets to international high finance.

In principle, Germany could be coerced into this by its own government. Who forces the cities and municipalities to build sports fields and stadiums, to pay their mayors salaries higher than those of federal ministers, who forces industry and agriculture, state and local governments, to plunge into hopeless debt accumulation? Foolishness, short-sightedness, and the utter inability of the Reich government to conduct a rational and sound financial policy.

Instead, an utterly insane debt economy has developed.

According to capitalist principles, high finance naturally only parts with its money if German goods are mortgaged as security and the sums lent are heavily interest-bearing.

Thus, in addition to the tribute payments, there are also the interest payments for the foreign loans. The interest-based economy is complete, and high finance smugly reaps, via the detour of reparations payments, the billions it receives in interest from the loans!!!

The Reparations Agent can rub his hands, buying and reporting foreign currency: *"The Dawes Plan has worked to satisfaction!!!"*

To make this swindle of world finance clear even to the simplest mind, here is a brief example:

Berlin needs, let's say, 100 million for the Stadtrats, the grandees and majesties of the bureaucracy, as well as for the expansion of municipal operations, for the unemployed, etc. The tax capacity of the population is already exhausted, so they do what all bigwigs in Germany do: they take out a loan in America. That is, they incur debt; the treasurer Böß travels to America to bring home the golden fleece and returns, let's say, with a loan of over 20 million dollars.

Berlin cannot even use the dollars, since all payments by the city must be made in Reichsmarks—but the Reparations Agent is already waiting for these German geniuses, who are then just happy when the Reparations Agent graciously exchanges the 20 million dollars into marks, of which he has more than enough from the pockets of the German taxpayers. The dollars then make their way back to America at the fastest speed, the unemployed in Berlin are paid—naturally—from German tax money, and all that remains as a lovely souvenir is a high-interest-bearing bond for 20 million dollars, the interest on which will burden Berlin's budget with annual payments from now on—plus, part of Berlin's assets will be mortgaged to some American bank Jew.

Sell-off of Germany—interest-based economy over Germany.

The Young Plan, in contrast to the Dawes Plan, has no so-called transfer protection. According to the Young Plan, Germany must, under all circumstances and without

Regard to its economic situation, pay annually through some means two billion marks in dollars (the exact yearly figures are listed above). There is only one clause that allows a part of these payments, namely 1.3 billion, to be deferred for a maximum of two years—but in the third year, the deferred and current amounts become due—and then the complete collapse is inevitable—then Germany must declare state bankruptcy— or it must perpetrate the swindle of a new inflation—or Germany must pay with people if it cannot pay with money. Export of people to compensate for the reparation payments. Germany, the slave reservoir for the phantasmagoric plans of high finance!

Let us now, at the end, cast another glance at the consequences of Germany's policy of fulfillment under the yoke of the Dawes Plan and its supplement, the Young Plan.

It is superfluous to say that all the promises of the German government have proven to be rotten swindles— instead of recovery and stabilization in economic terms, we are in the midst of the most dreadful reparation crisis.

Hilferding, Moldenhauer, Dietrich appeared before Parliament almost every month with new tax demands. Wailing, Hermann Müller stood before the Reichstag before Christmas with the dire confession: Our cash deficit amounts to 1.7 billion!! and demands *"coverage."*—In New Germany, *"coverage"* means short-term promissory notes!—Bank debts—debts to the Reparations Agent—debts to the Post and Railways—debts to Ivar Kreuger, the matchstick magnate—debts and coverage! A month later, Moldenhauer stands before the Reichstag and declares that a new genuine deficit has been discovered, and demands new taxes—shortly before Easter, by the German nationalists as auxiliary troops for the Brüning cabinet, out of fear of dissolution, 526 million, new millions are approved. No two months pass. Before Pentecost, Moldenhauer delights the Reichstag with the renewed revelation: Now I need another 836 million in new taxes.—Moldenhauer vanishes into oblivion. Hindenburg appoints Dietrich as the tax enforcer over Germany—he too knows nothing else to do but, supported by the parliamentary reparations criminals, to submit the new tax bills to the Reichstag. Tax robbery from the civil servants and salaried employees (this is called Reichshilfe), surcharges to the income tax, bachelor tax, *"citizen"* tax and community beer tax, exploitation of the unemployment insurance, reduction of the benefits of the social insurance. The Reichstag balks—Hindenburg enforces the Young-Hindenburg taxes using Article 48. The Reichstag does not comply. Hindenburg blows and scatters the Reichstag.

The organized financial piracy and its supporters have prevailed, chaos over Germany, in Germany itself a tax Bolshevism, financial misery, unemployment, hunger and destitution, collapse of agriculture, collapse of commerce, collapse of industry, loss balances in the cities and municipalities, deficit upon deficit in the budgets of the Reich and the states, murder and manslaughter every day, crisis of parliamentarism, crisis of the government, crisis of the judiciary, crisis in the arts. Jewish literary trash comes to the surface, theaters and cinemas are spoiled, Negro culture impudently spreads, Jews, bastards, profiteers of all kinds with fixed grins, Marxist inferior officials in high government positions, corruption upon corruption.

There the last ones gather together. Instinct stirs! Knowledge is power, but only knowledge and will give birth to action.

The ancient sun symbol becomes the sign of a new rising life. Germany awakens in the National Socialist movement.

CHAPTER 19

RECKONING WITH THE POLICY OF FULFILLMENT

Gottfried Feder's great Reichstag speech

Stenographic reports of the Reichstag session of December 4, 1930, see "*The Flame*" of December 11, 1930.

Before us lie, to come to the theme of today's session, the 1931 budget, a voluminous book of about 1,000 pages that was only distributed yesterday, and two emergency decrees, containing hundreds of paragraphs. We already have before us the third emergency decree of this year, the one that was rejected by the old Reichstag, the second that was issued on the 26th of July after the Reichstag was driven out, and now the third of December 1, 1930. But oddly enough, there is a gap here. The 1930 budget has not yet been presented to the new Reichstag, which has to decide on it. We know that the deliberations in the old Reichstag only progressed to the second reading before its dissolution. There is absolutely no doubt that the decree of the Reich President is not a budget law in the sense of the constitution according to Article 85. I would particularly like to emphasize that even the emergency decree itself contains the declaration that the budget must still be specifically adopted by the Reichstag if the Reichstag so demands. There is absolutely no doubt about this. If the Reichstag relinquishes this right, then it ultimately relinquishes its *raison d'être*. After all, a parliament is fundamentally the body that is supposed to decide on a state's expenditures. That was the evolutionary history, which ultimately led to the Parliament and the legislative bodies seizing all legislative powers altogether. Now, if you abandon the most noble, the first fundamental right of this parliamentary system, my gentlemen, then you can simply remove yourselves from the process altogether.

It is very noteworthy what the Reich Finance Minister noted at the end of his speech yesterday:

"The Reich government has in its measures avoided anything that might conflict with the constitution, and even if the adoption of the budget is accompanied by an emergency decree, this does not take the decision making power away from the Parliament."

Thus, the emergency decrees are to be accepted or rejected; there is no debate.

But the government itself, strictly speaking, is not constitutional. Of course, it claims to be *"legitimate."* I do not wish to contradict this, provided I may separate the words: it is rightfully legitimate. But this, in my opinion, does not achieve what the constitution intends. According to the Reich constitution, it is well known that in order for the ministers to exercise their office they require the confidence of the Reichstag. By virtue of Printed Matter No. 324, to give the Parliament the possibility to confidently express its trust (positively), we brought forth the proposal:

"In order to create the constitutional conditions for the capability of the Reich Cabinet (Dr. Brüning) and secure the legal basis of its existence finally. By avoiding the otherwise relevant requests, notices and formulas of the agenda concerning the present Reich's Government, the Reichstag declares its confidence in the Reich Cabinet of Dr. Brüning."

So, you have the opportunity, ladies and gentlemen, to respond to it. One fact is certain: The composition of this government does not accurately reflect the public result of the September Election. The government however acted as if this Reich election does not even exist for them. In the current cabinet, there are ministers today who, in the strictest sense, cannot rely on the small and tiniest of factions, just like Herr Treviranus is. Just, as Herr Reich Finance Minister Dietrich, until yesterday, he could not claim parliamentary legitimacy either. I would like to mention, that the person of Herr Treviranus or of Herr Dietrich is without doubt more favorable than some other personalities in cabinet, such as the man, who considers the oath of allegiance as merely an ideal and also Herr Wirth, a man who expressed himself on multiple occasions, speaking to which I will comment on in conclusion hereafter.

Strangely enough the largest Government Party, the SPD, holds no power despite the current cabinet, not being represented. In respect to any single poll, we can verify the SPD is the most loyal support of Brüning. Unfortunately, the SPD stands outside being incapable of governing. We, the National Socialists, support clear fronts. Herr Treviranus, Herr Dietrich and probably Herr Wirth, perhaps with the intention to get around delivering a portfolio in charge of Social Democracy, and there again hoping to obtain the support of the Social Democratic now have this in mind: a veiled dictatorship, presently emerging.

Ladies and gentlemen! There are two things that bind people together: Idealism or mutual criminal activity (lively exclamations from the Socialists; amusement from the National Socialist side). What holds this system together today results in one thing alone: The fear of accounting. This fear, its only propelling impetus, what you witness in all its occurrences here. This fear drives the frantic budding of this present parliamentarian system. The system has even been toying with ideals of a coup. My attention is drawn upon to the rumor spread upon General Sommerstein. I cannot verify it as there is not a foundation for such statements, much less in his position, to even be considered, allowing for just reason to cause misunderstanding that some may wish to disseminate. I remind you, that one brings individuals like Brüning, Luther, Geßler, Schleicher among others whose names we speak forth. It is obvious that if it is not necessary to carry out an open coup, so much the better if it can be avoided. And we rejoice over Herr Brüning, how skillfully he drives the Social Democrats into a corner, how he gradually wears them down, how he strips them of their last credibility among the people. With emergency decrees—to use a phrase from your old fighter Bebel—with exceptional laws, any fool can govern. I do not claim that I am referring to the current government with this. I merely wish to cite this interesting quote. The fact is that in this way, of course, all parliamentary difficulties can be overcome. (Dr. Goebbels interjects: *"There are still donkeys who can't even manage that!"*)

A further word on Herr Dietrich's statements. Mr. Minister, you suggested: there is a danger that a parliament, in which large parties, purely negative in their stance and rejecting all responsibility, are seated, will see its influence diminish. We National Socialists are pleased that this realization is slowly dawning even in government circles. The parliament is losing its influence. But please, Herr Dietrich, do not blame us for this, but rather take the blame entirely upon yourself, upon the parliamentary system, which was simply incapable of pulling Germany out of the quagmire but instead allowed it to sink ever deeper. Do not believe that we are opponents of the republican form of government. Oh no, when the leader of this republic is once called Adolf Hitler and the cabinet consists of National Socialist ministers who are decisively anti-Marxist, we have nothing against the republic.

A few brief remarks on the 1931/32 budget, which, as Herr Dietrich said, is already before the house. Why this suspicious haste? Nothing else is usually rushed. They forgot (!)—as I mentioned earlier—to present the 1930 budget.

Now the 1931 budget is already on the table. Is this meant to help gloss over the unpleasant issue of the 1930 budget? You said, Mr. Minister—and this is very good to hear—the 1931 budget is lower by 1,153 million in the ordinary budget and 272 million in the extraordinary budget. Yes, but when one hears your own justification, it is a very awkward matter. Salary cuts! The civil servants will not thank you for this suppression of the budget figures if you cut their salaries. Reduction of transfers to the states! You will receive little gratitude from the states if you further restrict their rights even more. Making the unemployment insurance self-sufficient! This is, of course, a trick that the treasury will have used to eliminate this *"uncertainty factor"* from the budget. And if you make the unemployment insurance self supporting, if you demand a 6% contribution, then I ask: who has to pay that? Once again, the broad masses of the population. So this is ultimately just a budgetary relief and reduction of the household.

You have explained that the main reason for the confusion is that in the 1930 budget you had only accounted for 1.2 million unemployed. With this you admit that you were mistaken, that your forecast was wrong. We were not mistaken. Even your later estimate of 1.6 million unemployed has been surpassed by the grim reality by 100 percent. Today we are already well over 3.2 million unemployed. The counterpoint to this, of course, is the decline in revenues by 900 million, and you are even pleased that this decline has not been exceeded.

Now come your further statements about the increase in revenue figures, particularly in the area of taxes on unnecessary luxuries. The only gift you believe you can bring to Germany is that for the coming budget years, fixed budget figures for 1932 and 1933 of a total sum of 10,867 million are binding. However, on the question of where savings could actually be made, you regrettably skimmed past rather quickly. You very neatly explained that the actual Reich budget itself is very small. Namely, in the total budget there are 3 billion in transfers to the states, 4 billion in external and internal war burdens, 1 billion in interest and repayments, and only 2.5 billion actually constitutes the Reich budget. On this, save as much as one might, there is not much to be saved, and you once again mentioned salary cuts, pension reductions, savings, etc.

Quite unsatisfactory were your statements about capital flight. You only mentioned that only in part is there actual capital flight, that for the most part the *"capital flight"* is due to the withdrawal of foreign credit. I would be very grateful if these figures were made accessible to the Reichstag so that we can understand the ratio between actual capital flight and the naturally expected withdrawal of capital. For if one takes on short term credits, one must know that these short-term credits must be repaid.

That you have described the financial situation as favorable is a pious belief. Since you have repaid last year's bridging loan of 350 million and also foreign credits amounting to 210 million, you really should not forget to point out at this juncture that just a few weeks ago we took up a new bridging loan of 500 million. You have furthermore admitted that indirect and direct taxes have reached the highest level that a people can bear. But you then concluded with the reassuring statement that *"the dangers for your state have been eliminated."* The government's will, you said, is to create prosperity, so that we *"remain creditworthy abroad."* With this, you have articulated what we most vehemently oppose: Jehovah, grant that we remain creditworthy abroad! This is precisely what we resist with all determination and strength, for this means interest slavery for Germany.

I would just like to return briefly to the second and larger part of the total Reich budget, to the 4 billion in internal and external war burdens.

This is precisely the point to which you and the entire government should have responded. For this is what drags the state, the people, and the economy into the abyss. But not a word, not the slightest hint of resistance to this tribute policy, which costs us 4 billion in this fiscal year of 1931.

And now I will briefly lay out for you the reckoning of the November crime of 1918, which has led to the financial end result we see today. The November Revolution stands at the threshold of this historical epoch of Germany, with the slogan: *"We do not want Germany to bring its war flag home victorious."*

The result for Germany, which then, in accordance with your will, did not bring its flag home victorious, was the immeasurable loss of material goods; but what pains us National Socialists even more bitterly is that through this peace treaty, German soil and German honor were lost, for disarmament means dishonor for every German man.

After the peace treaty came the civil war, murder and manslaughter, hostage killings. Then came the conferences. From conference to conference, one hoped: Spa, Brussels, The Hague, Genoa; one hoped for the first London conference, one hoped for Paris, and finally, it came to the point where the second London conference could take place. The result was that the Dawes Plan was simply imposed on us, without discussion, according to the recipe: Take it or die! We experienced this in 1924: no changes were possible, these Dawes laws had to be accepted en bloc. You called this: the success of the policy of fulfillment.

Alongside this went a second crime, the crime of inflation, a crime that was knowingly committed.

This crime had to end and did end with the complete bleeding dry of the entire economy, from which operating and savings capital had been entirely withdrawn. With this, the prerequisite for the establishment of the worldwide dominance of Jewish high finance over Germany was created. We lost our financial and transport sovereignty and, in exchange, took on an annual tribute burden of 2.5 billion.

When the Dawes Plan proved untenable, the era of the Young Plan began, and it was always claimed that under the Young Plan we would have far less to pay. On this point, I would like to state once again quite clearly that under the Dawes Plan in 1924/25 we only paid 1 billion, not, as now, 2 billion. In 1925/26 we paid 1.2 billion, in 1926/27 1.5 billion, in 1927/28 1.7 billion. When we then attempted for the first time in 1928/29 to pay the 2.5 billion, the entire German Reich budget collapsed entirely.

The result we see is the ongoing credit and financial crisis of recent years. A year ago, here stood the Reich Chancellor Müller with the embarrassing declaration: *"I am bankrupt."* We had a financial deficit of 1.7 billion at that time. (Call from the NSDAP: Herr Silverding was present.)—Of course, Herr Silverding was always Müller's faithful subordinate. We have then experienced that there was naturally no escape from this disastrous circle. If you, Mr. Minister, consider these 4 billion as unalterable, you will never emerge from Germany's misery.

The Young Plan was supposed to represent, in your opinion, an improvement over the Dawes Plan. And the result is the complete collapse. Moreover, the Young Plan means the introduction of the transfer protection clause, the elimination of the gold clause, a very dangerous matter, and finally, as the most dangerous element, the commercialization of German obligations, which I would like to particularly emphasize once again in this context. In order to bind the German population to the tribute obligations, it was deemed necessary to stipulate the lie of war guilt, thus establishing a moral guilt of Germany for the war. The gentlemen who adopted and propagated this lie knew very well that it was a lie. But this lie was needed initially. High finance knew exactly that material demands could be built upon moral guilt. Thus, it was the task of the conferences to turn this moral guilt into political guilt. Out of German war guilt, German interest bearing war debts were to be made. This succeeded through the conferences, especially through the first London conference, when 132 billion war debts were established as political debt. But the collection of these debts seemed impossible. The subsequent conferences then brought us the Dawes Plan, the loss of financial sovereignty and transport sovereignty, through which these tributes could be secured and collected. After this further financial securing of the German political war debt had been achieved, the uncertain element of *"political"* debt still remained, and the efforts of global politics were directed towards commercializing this political war debt, i.e., turning the political war debt into a private law, contractual obligation. This was done through the Young Plan. This is actually the main significance of the Young Plan compared to the Dawes Plan. The elimination of the transfer protection clause has been repeatedly criticized by us as particularly dangerous; for in this way, the current government has deprived itself of any possibility to demand a reduction or suspension of the tributes.

When I now draw a brief cross-section through the misery of contemporary Germany after this historical development, there are three things that form the basis of this misery, not unemployment as such, it is merely a consequence, but the following three fundamental facts. (Shouts from the Socialists: First, the lost war!) I have just reminded you of that. You indeed did not want Germany to win this war. The highly celebrated Rathenau also spoke the words, *"World history would have lost its meaning on the day Emperor Wilhelm rode through the Brandenburg Gate as a victor on a white horse!"* Three things determine political and economic events: first, the tax burden, second, the indebtedness, and third, the state of the German trade balance. A Reich budget amounting to 12,000 million—the recent reduction to 10,876 million is very dangerous, for it only comes at the expense of the taxpayers -, such a budget, which only includes Reich taxes, is unimaginable in any country of the world. To this must be added—I ask you not to forget—the equally popular trade and property taxes. That is another 4,000 million. Furthermore, the Reichsbahn's contribution to the Young tributes amounting to 660 million. That totals roughly and neatly 16-17 billion in tax liabilities to the public purse. Under such tax pressure, the economy must collapse.

I do not wish to go into details here and come to the second point, which is all too often overlooked. That is the indebtedness of the public purse and the indebtedness of the private economy. A few days ago we were presented with this thick book, which bears the lovely title: *"The Public Debt in the German Reich"*. Colored charts are included, and in this book we are informed that the total sum of public debt has now reached the figure of 24,000 million. That is only the public debt of the Reich, states, and municipalities. But that is still far from all. I ask you to add the debt of German agriculture, which today also amounts to roughly 15,000 million. To this must be added the debt of trade, commerce, and industry, for which no exact statistical figures are available, but which amounts to at least 20,000-25,000 million. This amounts to a total debt of state and economy in the range of approximately 50 to 60 billion. You must never forget this when assessing Germany's internal condition; this is what we call *"interest-based economy."*

This debt burden is particularly heavy because it includes 26 billion in foreign debt alone. According to your view, the interest on this must be paid under any circumstances. With an average interest rate of 10 percent— as we must calculate for foreign tributes—this means an annual amount of 2.5 billion gold marks, which must be transferred abroad in addition to the war tributes. The total burden on Germany thus reaches around 5-6 billion gold marks, which flow out of the German economic body into foreign lands year after year like an open wound. This is the result of the fulfillment policy you have pursued for the past twelve years.

A third essential factor is the state of the German trade balance. When a country tolerates the annual import of 600-700 million marks worth of foreign wheat, the import of half a billion marks in butter, when it tolerates the import of vegetables that could be produced domestically, and fruits to the tune of a quarter billion, when the total import (Interjection by Dr. Silverding: What about exports?)—I will address that, Mr. Silverding—of foodstuffs, which could mostly be produced in Germany, amounts to 4.2 billion, then you should not be surprised if the German trade balance becomes catastrophically passive, as has been the case in recent years. (Interjection by Dr. Silverding: It is active by 1.2 billion!) You will soon be satisfied, Mr. Silverding. (Interjection by Dr. Silverding: The opposite of your assertion is correct!) We are not so foolish as to believe that in today's highly intertwined global economy, we could live in a closed trade state.

We National Socialists are well aware that we need an extraordinary amount of raw materials. We must have wool and cotton for our vast textile industry. We do not want another hundred thousand unemployed on the streets. We naturally need jute and sisal, hides and pelts. We undoubtedly need copper for the electrical industry. We have enough work just to cover and pay for these necessary imports. We must supply endless machinery, rails, and pharmaceutical products to pay for these essential imports. So do not believe that we are such complete economic utopians! On the contrary, because we think socially and nationally and see the necessities, we also appreciate the enormous significance of the great statesman Mussolini for his country. I consider one of Mussolini's greatest achievements to be his law *"bonifica integrale,"* through which he managed in a few years to increase Italy's agricultural output from 35 million double quintals of bread grain to 75 million double quintals. The Duce accomplished this in just five years in a country that is by no means among the most fertile; apart from a few fruitful areas, Italy is a rocky country, traversed by mountains from north to south.

This was a feat of the highest order. Do not come with the objection that we do not have enough land to produce the necessary agricultural products ourselves in Germany! (Shouts of approval.)—Very well, ensure that what today benefits foreign countries through our imports benefits German agriculture for just one year, for even half a year, and then German agriculture, which is already of such a high standard, could easily be elevated to a position where it could supply Germany with the products we currently import.

First and foremost, gentlemen, it is of course the right of the opposition to criticize. We, as the opposition, do not inherently have the task of laying out the paths we will take.

We will demonstrate those to you in practice when the time comes. Only after we have been in government for 12 years will you have the right to criticize, as we now exercise our right to criticize you. Nevertheless, we have never hesitated to point out ways where something can be done or achieved. I remind you that we did not just recently, but already in 1926 in this house, submitted a motion to tax banking and mining profits. In 1926/27, the numerical surplus value of shares at the end of the year was around 12 billion. The value of shares in Germany rose from about 10 to 12 billion to 22 to 23 billion. Had you intervened back then, you could have collected several billions and placed the taxes on those who were capable of bearing them. But at that time, we were met only with ridicule and scorn. I remind you of our motions to skim off the war profits, of our proposals to take action against profiteers and black marketeers; I remind you of our motions to restore the assets destroyed by inflation. Above all, I remind you of our political stance, which with unwavering consistency demanded the rejection of the entire fulfillment policy practiced thus far.

The rejection of the Dawes Plan, the rejection of the Young Plan, and generally the rejection of the entire debt-based economy.

Let me ask whether these were not enough practical proposals. You respond anxiously: What would have happened if we had rejected this treaty?—My God, then another conference would have been convened. What would have happened if you had said *"no"* in Paris? Dr. Schacht himself declared it intolerable. Even within your own cabinet, there were members who repeatedly stated that the burdens were unbearable. Minister-President Braun in Prussia stated that he considered it impossible for Germany to bear a burden of even 1.64 billion for 37 years. These are people from your own circles. On the other hand, Wels, *"the small tailor from Bielefeld,"* as his friend Stampfer called him in the *"Vorwärts,"* believed that 2 billion could be paid quite easily.

No, gentlemen, you cannot conduct politics in this manner if you are always stabbing your own representatives abroad in the back. Then you must simply come to terms with the fact that foreign countries take what they can get, while dealing you further blows.

I must also point out one fundamental misconception: your belief that the tributes would be eased if the budget were in order. If the debtor *"gets back on his feet,"* the creditor would be an idiot if he were to forego extracting the last ounce from him.

You have no right to accuse us solely of negative politics.

Our politics affirm the vital interests of the German people.

Your politics, gentlemen, for a decade, have consistently only gratified the outrageous demands of our external and internal enemies. We were always right with our prophecies, thank God, and you were always wrong. What did Herr Stresemann from this rostrum say about the implementation of the Dawes Plan? What did Herr Luther talk about regarding the Dawes plan as a matter of salvation? Then it was said: There definitely would be reductions in railroad tariffs and an easing of the tax burden. It always was the same refrain, and soon thereafter it was always the same bitter awakening that the broad masses had to pay the price.

We have never needed to revise our program. Never once have we changed an iota of what we laid out programmatically as our principles.

You, on the other hand, spin a politics of constant makeshift arrangements, a politics living from hand to mouth.

Finally for conclusion, I should like to lay down a few programmatic declarations concerning the economic and financial policy of the coming National Socialist Reich. I must admit straight away that I shan't allay the doubts of worried minds concerning certain planned measures we would enforce for the economic revival within the new and future 3rd Reich. This gives you an opportunity though, to familiarize yourself a little with our literature. For instance our National-Socialist literature and party programs, whose present editions exceed 200,000. It is becoming, I believe, one of the most read today world wide. Kindly thus familiarize yourselves too; pick up the book once! Simply please don't come telling me about certain half-wits who declare—when questioned: Oh me doesn't know nuffin' about your theory etc, oh sure doesn't approve but certainly condemned!. One of the most powerful contributing factor for Germany's recovery, particularly for her economy is the restoration of the National Will to Self-Determination, has long and often been sabotaged by you.

I merely wish today to address various widespread fallacies or conscious falsehoods circulated about our program and to clarify the record. One of the favorite propaganda weapons against us, is the allegation the national Socialists are opposed to private property. National Socialism is fundamentally based on private property which it places under Government protection.

The first possibility is: I deny private property, I do not recognize it: *"Property is theft,"* as your friend Proudhon (according to Lints) put it, *"Property is theft."* The other possibility of the fundamental attitude toward private property is the unlimited, boundless recognition of private property, insofar as it is based on any legal means. This, of course, ultimately leads to the expropriation of an entire nation: for the legal titles under which Germany is being expropriated today are called Dawes Plan, Young Plan, i.e., interest-based economy over Germany, complete surrender of the entire German economy to foreign countries, impoverishment and depersonalization of the German economy under the dominance of international anonymous companies and international financial corporations. That the recognition of property rights also entails the recognition of inheritance rights is self-evident to any thinking person. We National Socialists fundamentally recognize property as long as it arises from one's own efforts and abilities, but we fundamentally reject so-called acquired property resulting from fraud, speculation, and deceit, like that seen in the Barmat scandal.

In connection with this fundamental declaration, allow me to briefly state our stance on the issues of socialization or the free economy. Here, too, we are faced with two absolute extremes. Some say: *"Everything must be socialized."* Yet nothing has been socialized. But what has been nationalized is what should have been socialized.

What was denationalized was what absolutely belongs in the realm of the state: the monetary system and the judicial system.

The government relinquished these two most important things, and after it handed over sovereign finance, the Reichsbank and the Reichsbahn, it could ignore the socialization of the production process. We National Socialists sharply distinguish between the spheres of tasks that must absolutely remain free from all state interference and the other spheres of tasks. The first sphere is the realm of the productive economy, in which all the imponderables essential and important for yield—diligence, skill, the honor of the honest merchant, entrepreneurial initiative—play a role, on which the yield of any economy depends. What lies between production and consumption is another realm: the realm of trade and the monetary system. The monetary system, alongside the trade system, is the great mover, and here different factors come into play.

The monetary system is the most social affair of all: for everyone is equally interested in a clean, incorruptibly managed monetary system. Therefore, these matters must be under the sovereignty of the state (21dg. DauchHamburg: Yet there is a danger in state monetary economy: we have indeed experienced inflation!)—Herr College Dauch-Hamburg, I must confess to you openly today—I am the most determined opponent of the idea of handing the Reichsbank back to Herr Silverding. The prerequisite for an organic economy is, of course, that we live in an organically structured state. Socialization in the areas that are absolutely of decisive importance for the community, and a free economy in all parts of the economy where the free and self responsible individual must assert themselves!

Now, some fundamental remarks about the forms of organization in the economy. It is quite clear that a complex economic system requires various forms.

The very possibility of dynamic growth from small to medium, from medium to large enterprises has characterized the pre-war economy. The concentration into mammoth corporations, on the other hand, always signifies the death of a vibrant, free economy.

Another remark on the organization of the banking system in the future state! Do not believe for a moment that we intend to exclude the solid private banker or dispense with his cooperation (Shouts from the Communists: 3. 8. Herr von Strauß! Herr von Strauß is reassured!). On the contrary, the cultivation of the solid private banker will essentially contribute to the revival of personal credit, which can hardly be nurtured today; for in the large banking corporations, everything operates according to fixed rules: credit is granted only to those who can provide the necessary documents, and not to the individual who has earned trust.

A final word about yield and interest!

In our opposition to interest, some believe we must also oppose economic yield. Nothing could be further from the truth—we National Socialists indeed aim precisely to restore the German economy to its greatest possible yield potential by eliminating the Interest System and thus the complete subjugation of our entire economic life to the demands of international finance. I am convinced that in this struggle against interest, we will not find the Church as our ally. For the canonical prohibition of interest was always one of the most beautiful pearls in the crown of the Church. The Imperial Police Ordinances of 1530, 1537, and 1570, as is well known, also made binding for the laity what the canon law had prescribed since Pope Leo I, the Great. Only modern scholasticism has seen fit to assume an *"accidental fertility of money,"* and has thus aligned itself with the desires and wishes of high finance, which naturally finds in this a convenient justification for what the ancient Church Fathers always labeled as sin and usury.

A few more brief comments on the questions posed to us by the four professors, whose work has been widely and comfortably circulated throughout the German press. The learned gentlemen have expressed concern that the banks, upon a reduction of interest to 5 percent according to our proposal, might only be able to pay their depositors 2.5 percent. Well, how much does one currently receive from the banks? Until recently, it was only 0.5 percent, and since recently, 2.5 percent! What was it like in the past? Did one perhaps receive more than 2.5 to 3 percent in a regular account at savings banks and banks in the pre-war period?

I have already made brief remarks elsewhere about the flight of capital abroad. It is self-evident that only a strong, ruthless state can halt this capital flight. Those who handle the profiteers with kid gloves will never achieve the goal of stopping the big profiteers from moving their capital abroad. But if you hang the first and the second, the others will think twice before shifting their money abroad.

Breaking the Interest-Based Economy is the core of our entire policy. The breaking of the interest-based economy—I would like to explicitly state this—is not, internationally speaking, a question of money and credit systems, but rather a question of power. The current powerless government will never be able to remove even a single gram of the interest-based economy from our nation. We have been able to observe the extent to which our demands have already made the foreign country take notice, and a National Socialist government is ready to make concessions. The foreign country knows that in a few years it will have to choose between a National Socialist Germany or a Communist Germany. There is no other option. Whatever lies in between will be irrevocably crushed.

Internally, the breaking of the interest-based economy means a radical restructuring of the most important organs in the German body politic, in one word: a return to the best traditions of German history. And to you, Mr. College Dingelden—I don't see him at the moment—I recommend that when you speak about National Socialism in your parliamentary sessions, you should at least acquaint yourself with our literature, for you have no reason whatsoever to accuse us of any *"socialistic"* tendencies as you understand them. (Stormy shouts from the Socialists and Communists: Hear! Hear! – Rep. Torgler: Excellent! Bravo! The millions of workers should hear that! Outside you say the opposite!) – For these *"socialistic"* tendencies (to the Social Democrats and Communists), the German people thank you! – You know very well what we mean by the term *"Socialism,"* in contrast to your Marxism, which destroys the people and the state.

To you, gentlemen of this crumbling center, I can only say one thing: You must make a decision. *"Because thou art lukewarm, and neither cold nor hot, I will spew thee out of my mouth."* And that is what the German people will do with you if you continue to pursue the politics of the cowardly bourgeois center. Finally, do not overlook, gentlemen—I also address this to the Center Party the religious foundation of our movement.

It is characterized by the highest moral qualities of humanity: sacrifice, dedication, and holy strength. We are those who see ourselves as the best followers of the Savior when we drive the moneychangers and swindlers out of the temple, and I warn you, gentlemen of the Center Party, against the culture war you have partly instigated against National Socialism!

You are driving millions out of the Church if you continue as you have begun in Mainz. You have allied yourselves with political atheism on the left. It is highly necessary that you dissociate yourselves from it, as it is also the command of the Briton. The Center Tower has many cracks and holes. I advise you, finally sever this unholy alliance with the Marxists and deniers of God! One cannot continuously play with tuberculosis bacilli without getting infected. Fill your followers with the sacred fire against everything base and vile! Only then can you join us in praying the much-maligned school prayer of your Mr. Wirth: Father, in Your almighty hand stands our people and Fatherland. You were their source of strength and protection, and You are our best shield and guard, so free us from deceit and betrayal (laughter and noisy interruptions from the left), make us strong for liberating deeds! Grant us the heroic courage of the savior! Honor and freedom be our highest good! (Laughter and cheers from the left.)

Our vow and our pledge shall be: Germany, awaken! Lord, make us free!

CHAPTER 20

SOCIAL DEMOCRACY & NATIONAL SOCIALISM

Conversation on *"Deutsche Welle"* on January 3, 1931, between Prof. Dr. Nolting from the Academy of Labor in Frankfurt a. M., member of the Prussian Landtag, and the National Socialist Reichstag Deputy, Dipl.-Ing. Gottfried Feder. Based on a stenographic record, published in *"Der Flamme"* on January 8, 1932.

Feder: Professor Nolting! A mountain of newspaper clippings, which the management of *"Deutsche Welle"* has presented to us today, proves the extraordinary resonance our conversation of December 16 has found. An equally large or even larger pile of personal writings proves the same to me. From this, three things seem to me of importance. The first is the remark of the "8-*Uhr-Abendblatt*," which explicitly confirms the tremendous propaganda value for National Socialism, the second is (to my regret) a personal defamation by "*Vorwärts*," which, as the only newspaper, has not maintained the restraint observed by all other parties. And the third is that I am being reproached: I did not answer the last question you directed at me, the question of how we stand in relation to economic democracy. Now I would like to briefly clarify my position on this matter. We reject both works democracy and economic democracy in the narrower sense, as they achieve nothing but the introduction of parliamentary forms into the economy itself. This inevitably leads to the detriment of labor and thus of the working class. For productivity declines when the mess begins. We have had more than enough of political democracy and its parliamentary expression; economic democracy would completely destroy what remains of the economy. This does not, by any means, imply that I would not particularly welcome it if workers were given the opportunity to inform themselves as extensively as possible about the overall situation of the enterprises in which they are employed. This information will, of course, also lead to a rapprochement between employer and employee. But what is unbearable is that what happens here is voted on in parliamentary forms. This only leads us into works councils and soldiers' councils governance.

Prof. Nolting: Mr. Feder! It is very interesting that you feel compelled to provide a supplementary definition to what you recently stated, but I do not know whether the working class will be much happier with what they hear from you today. It is interesting that you say: Any participation of workers in the enterprise can only amount to mere chatter. That the working class should be reduced to harmless economic lectures where they are innocuously enlightened—I believe this does not sufficiently correspond to their interests. I have, in fact, used the Christmas period to review your book' once more, and I must say, my astonishment at your rejection has only increased. For you do not merely reject economic democracy; you reject works councils. Here on page 76 it states that works councils represent "*an overburdening of the enterprise with a large number of persons*" who are "*dispensable.*" You reject insurance officials. You are, it says, against excessive unemployment insurance, against a state minimum subsistence level. And what particularly shocked me, Mr. Feder, is that you seem to praise the economy of Wilhelmine Germany wholesale. For you explicitly declare: "*The German State on National and Social Foundations,*" Verlag Franz Eher Nachf., Munich on p. 69: "*On the whole, the overall economy of the German Empire,*" meaning: of Wilhelmine Germany, "*met* *the fundamental requirements that we also place on a healthy national economy."*So you only discovered the issue in the capitalist soup starting from November 9, 1918; until then, you were in complete agreement with everything. You are not a real opponent of capitalism, Mr. Feder. At most, you are a Savonarola, preaching sermons of repentance against it.

Feder: Well, Professor Nolting! You know very well that the worker was better off in old Germany than in today's Germany.

The complete collapse of our entire economy, including the working class, is reflected in the unemployment figures. But if you allow me, I will immediately address the topic of the 'interest-based economy and breaking the *'interest-based economy.'* This is necessary because it involves a new concept coined by me, and I will briefly define what is meant by the interest-based economy. The interest-based economy is the state in which the German worker, the German economy, the German farmer, the German cities, the German states, and the German Reich currently find themselves—namely, a state of excessive indebtedness to pure financial and loan capital: where income from pure monetary assets, without work or effort, triumphs over the earnings from labor. This is precisely expressed in the following forms: First, in tax Bolshevism, under which the entire nation, and most severely the working class, is suffering. You know very well that in the old, as you like to call it, 'rotten' system of the past, the worker did not have to pay income tax. You know that the burden of indirect taxes was minimal compared to today's burden of indirect taxes, to the creation of which you have always contributed in the Reichstag. You know—secondly—that the indebtedness of the Reich, the states, cities, agriculture, industry, and trade has reached a maximum, with the total debt figure today amounting to a nice round figure of 60 billion marks. A figure that is particularly painful for Germany because no less than 26 billion of this debt is owed to foreign countries, meaning approximately 2.6 billion in annual interest payments must be extracted from the German national body solely due to this foreign debt. Due to the brevity of the speech, I cannot delve into the damages that the German economy has suffered from the state of the German trade balance in recent years—that would be the third point—but I will also remind you of the most important point—and this is the culmination of the interest-based economy—the fact of the existence of the Young Plan, to which you contributed to its adoption. You hailed the Dawes Plan on August 29, 1924, as the greatest achievement of social democratic politics. The 'improvement' of the Dawes Plan, as you like to call it in your public pronouncements, the improvement through the Young Plan, imposes an annual burden of 2 billion marks on Germany. This is what we understand by the interest-based economy.

Nolting: Mr. Feder! I do not get the impression that your concept of the interest-based economy is such an absolutely original invention. For you have here a mental gallery of ancestors, even including Jewish names.

I remind you of Proudhon, I remind you of Marx?! Of course, one must read up to the third volume of 'Capital,' where very harsh words are found about stock speculators. I remind you of Hilferding, of his famous book on finance capital, which was published as early as 1910. To me, a socialist, you should not accuse me of not recognizing usury interest. Naturally, there is financial usury. But, Mr. Feder, there is also wage usury, price usury, land usury, rent usury, and tariff usury. Capitalism is the breeding ground for every kind of extortion. I must only object to your one-sided view of the world.

Marx and Hilferding are Jews; Proudhon, 1809-1865, the founder of anarchism, was French.

As I told you recently, not every factory is good, and not every miser is always bad, so today I must tell you: Not every lender is a Shylock and every borrower a poor wretch. That is a medieval notion. Today, it is precisely the industrialist, Mr. Feder, who takes on credit. And in reality, there is not even the hostility between earning and creating capital that you always return to; there is instead an intimate entanglement. This is precisely the essence of finance capital, that there is a common exercise of control, that there is an exchange of share rights and board positions from both sides. The banks are by no means always the dominant power; often, they are the instrument of the producers. In fact, I do not believe this at all. That one should speak so abstrusely of an interest-based economy in general. Interesting shifts of power have occurred in the last decade and a half. During the inflation period, the banks served as tools for the flight into tangible assets, but after stabilization, the tables turn: the entrepreneurs stripped of their business capital then fall into a dependence on the banks. And often this dependence increases due to the speculative losses suffered by the entrepreneurs because they pay too little attention to their businesses and spend too much time in the stock market. Then comes the third stage, the consolidation phase, and through this the banks, which must finance the consolidations, often lose their dominant positions. The consolidations achieve extra profits, they achieve self-financing: the third has become independent, has its own land banks.

Feder: Do you believe, Professor, that these deductions, that these explanations will be understood by the workers who today are hanging by the hundreds of thousands at their radio sets? No one will understand this. We must now discuss what measures need to be taken to carry out the breaking of the interest-based economy. Precisely this concept of interest-based economy is so all-encompassing, is much more all encompassing than your focus on pure enterprise capital. We National Socialists see these measures for breaking the interest-based economy in domestic policy in the following individual measures: We must demand and will implement, when we are in political power, the nationalization of the Reichsbank. This is a completely selfevident demand of a sovereign state that cannot tolerate that pure finance capital leads an independent life within the framework of the national community, within the framework of the state. Politically, you are responsible for the fact that this so-called Reichsbank is today not an institution of the Reich, of the nation, but an international institution that essentially serves only powerful money interests. Secondly, we must finally move away from the way of financing major public tasks as was done before, namely through making debt. If it is not possible according to the old Prussian method to finance major public tasks through tax funds, that is, through community contributions to the state, then there is an opportunity to still carry out these major tasks if we remember the sovereign fiscal authority of the state. By this we mean—according to my proposal—to finance public tasks through the issuance of state treasury notes. We thus create money from our own right. This monetary creation from our own right is definitely permissible and will not lead to inflationary phenomena because we are creating new values. The third measure we will implement is to set up socialized construction and economic banks in order to get out of the muck with our own power, especially on one of the very key areas—that of housing shortages, and so will we tremendously be capable of addressing unemployment. The central thought is the same. Time, however, is lacking to make single considerations of such important things. A fourth issue will be tackling the restructuring of repayments in an respectable, socially just way: in the same pattern as where billions of marks have been obliterated by the destruction of savings, it is just as possible to obtain a major proportion of the losses back to the country by a well organized remodeling scheme of repayment. Another needed measure will see the enactment of state controlled, real credits. A further needed change will likely arise when the repayment of the mortgages are due the coming year—it becomes fundamentally necessary for the Reich to absorb the mortgages in place of causing a new chaotic onslaught of anarchy from which the nation will issue sovereign bonds directed in payment thereof.

Nolting: Feder—I am not worried that our workers, our followers on whom such ideas have impelled them like the tide, have missed the gist; I will indeed answer what you have posed—in answer to what may perhaps have been a partial insight is that I am quite happy with the socialization of the banks. We very much can agree on this in truth—but, do make it not only a single, lone instance; follow it with more wide ranged socialization measures into the realm of production, as I have said before and must reiterate it now, born of socio-economic cognizance, and not born out of petty crusade aimed towards that Jewish dominated banking capital. As to points in the interim, I should add: In taking the banking structure thus from these considerations you must make certain that thus prepared you ensure the credit worthiness of the German Nation remains before that of the world, that stands in the forefront and not the opposite. Now concerning for the credit worthiness, this has, however, fallen from the ceaseless threats ever given from those National Socialist voices throughout the country already thus prepared and must be restored otherwise in the interim.

It was very interesting what you said about your Feder money. Yes, I fear, Mr. Feder, that the Third Reich of Adolf Hitler will become a great inflation shop again. I was reminded of the old children's tale about the *little-lend-me-away*. You say that the state has the right, by virtue of its minting sovereignty, to create as much money as it wants. I can give you an example here. If you build a house that costs 100,000 marks and this house brings in a rental income of 8,000 marks per year, then in the first years only these 8,000 marks will flow back to you as a counter value, all else aside. The 92,000 marks in construction bills that you have issued, however, remain uncovered and will act inflationary. Then we also need a currency standard of international significance, Mr. Feder. In the current state of the world economy, we still need a metallic basis. Even Knapp, your witness, says so, the one you like to refer to so often. Perhaps you know that law which says that the worse money always displaces the better. The people would have to content themselves with the inflation money, while in large-scale trade foreign exchange and gold money would circulate. That is a very dangerous situation. I have the feeling that through the Third Reich, it wouldn't just be the rustling of Wodan's sacred trees, oaks, or beeches that we would hear, but also the noise of the printing presses, which would have to increase their rotation speed to print inflation money, Mr. Feder. And we would like to avoid that. Gladstone once said that most people are made fools by love and money. We both want to protect ourselves from this fate, Mr. Feder.

Feder: Mr. Professor Nolting! The German population shudders at the memory of the time of the social democratic finance minister Dr. Wirth, who was certainly a master at setting the printing presses into action. Isn't that right? So you have no reason to hold the fear of inflation against me. Because in contrast to the Marxist monetary policy of Mr. Wirth, we stand on the principle—and this is understood by everyone, even the simple man understands this: Inflation only occurs when new money tokens are printed without the creation of new values. Inflation will not occur if new values are created, and if I may call on a witness in this context, it is the professor of economics at the University of Vienna, Professor Othmar Spann, who has expressed very clearly in relation to my theories: *"However bold these thought processes of Feder may appear, anyone who does not stand on the ground of metallism must recognize the core of them as theoretically correct and practically sustainable."* Undoubtedly, the banknote based on economic expansion has no inflationary effect, unlike the case when one simply prints to cover non-productive state needs, as the Marxist state has done.

Nolting: Yes, Mr. Feder, I believe we should not dig into the dunghill of the past. We are all burnt children who fear the fire. We have had enough of inflation and do not want to prepare a new inflation. And that's why I warned you. Moreover, I would like to pose a question to you: Do workers fare much better in countries with low interest rates? And the second question: Why do workers in countries with dictatorships—Poland, Hungary, Italy—fare so badly? In Italy, the worker lives on 13 marks a week, as we recently read in the press.

Feder: Mr. Professor! Our task here in Germany is to look after the German workers. We cannot always look outward at how things are going there. It is not our task to investigate the specific reasons for the poor condition of workers there. We have to take care of that, and to pick up on a second question you posed earlier—we must free ourselves from the gold madness. It is madness to base a currency on gold. We ourselves in Germany have set an example for the world that one can free oneself from the gold madness by creating the Rentenmark. Yes, the Rentenmark was also not backed by liquid assets, as you previously demanded for the *"Feder-money,"* as you expressed it. The property parcels are also not immediately redeemable.

Nolting: Yes, but, Mr. Feder, we only had a circulation of the Rentenmark of 400 million in total. The Rentenmark was spared any practical test of fire because it could always be exchanged for other banknotes.

That's why its rate held up. But, Mr. Feder, I believe, we must get back to what you said earlier about the Dawes Plan. First of all, I would like to state: There is no one in Germany who enjoys paying. And we Marxists are, God knows, no reparation-crazed fulfillment fanatics, as you so often portray us. The problem is simply this, Mr. Feder, that we have to pay. The enemy's collection agency is at the door. Beautifying one's life by not paying debts is an old student trick. Perhaps we both tried this as students and didn't get very far with it. Foreign policy cannot be conducted to the tune of *"The Old Fraternity's Glory."* Certainly, the path of fulfillment is a via crucis, but it has not been a dead end. Allow me to remind you of the numbers, Mr. Feder. Yes, despite your objection. We have gone from the 340 billion that was discussed in Versailles to the 123 billion of the London Ultimatum and then to the 47 billion of the Young Plan. And we also have the impression that the Young Plan cannot be the definitive solution, that it is only a stage. That this Europe must still drag its weary body to many conference tables. Without the Young Plan, we would be following the corpse wagon of Europe; with it, we follow the sickbed of Europe. There is, God knows, no reason to burst into joy over this. And if you believe that it was national unreliability that led us to support the Young Plan, then I would like to draw your attention to the fact that Hindenburg, against whom you surely would not dare to raise this accusation, signed it. Do you really want the unilateral repudiation of the Treaty of Versailles? That means war, Mr. Feder! And the field of skulls would be higher than the mountain of tribute. The problem would remain, but with reversed signs.

Feder: Mr. Professor Nolting! Just briefly for clarification. Firstly, it is not correct that only 400 million Rentenmarks were in circulation. You know full well that 2.3 billion Rentenmarks were put into circulation, and then another 2.5 billion Goldmarks. Of the Goldmarks we have today, only one-third was backed by gold. So at least 4.5 billion were in circulation without the so-called backing you desire. Furthermore, it is incorrect, as you previously stated, that initially a claim of 340 billion was made. That was never the case. Read the Treaty of Versailles again, and you will find that first 40 billion were demanded, and if those were paid, an additional 80 billion would be sought. In the first London Treaty, 132 billion were demanded—a number you also did not correctly represent earlier—and now, through the Dawes Plan, which set no final sum, the Young Plan has added another 114 billion to the approximately 50 billion already paid up to last year.

You then asked me: Do you believe we could have freed ourselves from this externally? Yes, obviously, externally, the breaking of interest bondage is not a question of free personal German decision. For there we encounter a will opposed to us. This is a highly political question and thus naturally a pure question of power. Here we can no longer rely on any financial theoretical or economic-political considerations; here it is purely a question of whether we have the power to cast off these chains. If we do not cast off these chains, then at the end of this via crucis, Mr. Professor, as you so poetically put it, lies crucifixion and death. Therefore, we must cast off these chains. We must also clearly and distinctly distinguish between private debt obligations to foreign countries and political debts. As far as the German foreign debt, which I previously quantified at 26 billion, is concerned, these are actual private loans, most of which have been converted in Germany into values and investments that bring us economic returns. Thus, a future National Socialist government—after a precise examination of the situation—will ensure the swiftest possible repayment of the borrowed funds, which naturally does not exclude that we, through negotiations with foreign creditors, seek a reduction of the interest rates and possibly even the entire claim. This would only serve our nation and thus the German worker. The future government will be guided by the principle that performance and counter performance must stand in a just relationship to each other. May I just point out that, measured against the gold index, our burdens have already become significantly heavier today than they were back then? Since some of the incurred financial obligations involve purely political claims, which are not matched by any actual performance on the part of the Allied and Associated Governments, we do not recognize their legal bindingness. If you have followed the declarations of the daily press as of January 16th, you could not have missed that the idea of revision is making progress, and not only in Germany but throughout the world. Naturally, our highest political goal is not just revision, but the annulment of these treaties, these dreadful treaties, which in my conviction and in the conviction of many worldwide are ultimately the deepest cause of the economic misery in Europe and in the whole world. This shedding of burdens, this liberation, is our highest political goal. Naturally—and on this we are entirely clear—this goal can only be achieved step by step. We will encounter immense resistance, which must be overcome, but we will also find allies everywhere. With gratitude and satisfaction, we recall Mussolini, who in his message to the American people coined the phrase that even treaties have their time. I remind you of the statements of the Swede Cassel and the Englishman Keynes and various American senators, who have clearly expressed the futility of the Dawes and Young payments. In this context, we must, of course, also exclude the mutual guarantee obligations of the League of Nations. We must disengage from this League of Nations and rediscover ourselves nationally. We National Socialists can proudly say: We have now awakened the nation. With joy, we note that the year 1930 was a year of awakening, and that the year 1931 will follow as a year of action.

Nolting: Mr. Feder! I do not know if it was very appropriate to address this vote of thanks to the Italian Duce. It seems to me that we will not escape the dreadful situation in which we find ourselves by splitting Europe again into two new military camps. For we need the pacification of all Europe. This fawning, this frantic search for alliance politics, this chasing after Mussolini with raised forefinger: *"I'd like to join!"*—this will not advance us and, moreover, does not correspond to the national dignity. For I believe it is not worthy of a nation to serve as mercenaries again and to snatch at the crumbs that fall from the table of the great. I also wish to point out to you that Italy has once before been our ally. What remains for you besides Italy? Perhaps Soviet Russia, Mr. Feder? A curious combination: Mr. Stalin on one side, Mr. Hitler on the other. That would create a wild confusion of *"Heil Hitler"* and *"Hail Moscow"* cries. And Germany—and this is the worst of it —Germany would become the battlefield in such a war. It is, at any rate, commendable that you at least recognize the private debt obligations. However, your speech was very obscure on this point. For you say that you will consider how you will later fulfill these debt obligations. I believe that a unilateral determination on your part would lead to very sharp countermeasures. A threefold blockade would be imposed on

Germany: a blockade on raw materials, a blockade on exports, and a blockade on credit. And I must remind you that we have approximately 6-7 billion in short-term loans in Germany. Why are our interest rates so usurious? They are so usurious because an enormous risk premium has been added. And it has been added because Germany smells of danger, because you have introduced the stench of impending civil war into the country. A conversion will only occur if trust in us is restored externally. First, the quagmire beneath our feet must be turned into solid ground before we can think of such a settlement. But by rattling our sabers or by unilaterally committing ourselves to a specific mobilization policy, we certainly will not advance but rather lose the ground we had. When you said earlier that crucifixion awaits us at the end of this path to Golgotha, I can only reply that one should not commit suicide out of fear of death. Your policy would only lead us to crucifixion all the sooner.

Feder: Mr. Professor! It is strange when a Marxist poses as the standard-bearer of German dignity. Do not take this amiss! For your comrade Crispien was the man who coined the phrase: I know no fatherland. That Germany stands for. But let us move on. You ascribe to me once again warlike intentions. I must state with all decisiveness that this, our will for national self-determination and preservation, in no way implies any animosity against any nation. We are not driven by thoughts of revenge, which would lead to warlike entanglements, but we demand the right to expand our national defense measures in accordance with the threat to our people, or, what we would much prefer, a reduction in the armaments of the opponents, as the Versailles Treaty also envisions. But all these are, as mentioned, matters of power that cannot be resolved through theoretical discussions and clever remarks but only through a clear and unambiguous alliance policy. You evidently favor *"splendid isolation,"* this glorious isolation of Germany, and seek neither affiliation with Italy nor with any other side. Honest and clear words would have a much better effect on our creditworthiness abroad than the repeated declarations of submissiveness and the constant striving to fulfill unfulfillable demands. The ultimate and deepest reason for our opponents' violent hostility—to say just a few words briefly on domestic politics—against the fulfillment policy of the Reich government is that the thesis of the Brüning administration and the Finance Minister Dr. Dietrich, which he expressed in his budget speech, is always reiterated: first stabilization, then revision. To this, we National Socialists oppose the demand for immediate revision, because a stabilization of German finances is impossible as long as the insane tribute burdens remain without any reciprocation. Even in private life, no one will grant a debtor relief if he stabilizes himself and this stabilization proceeds only through incurring debt according to the proven recipe of today. Then we will sink deeper and deeper into subjugation abroad while simultaneously acquiring the reputation of unreliable partners.

Nolting: May I first say this: alliance policy always leads to a point where one becomes entrenched in armament, and then the guns go off by themselves. And second: you once again accuse me of lacking national sentiment and begrudge the Marxist for even speaking about his fatherland. It is the same old accusation: we are tearing the nation apart. The nation is torn by class antagonisms, which we deplore. And as long as we cannot remedy this by altering the property regime, the nation remains divided into two peoples. National community first arises on level ground, and if you quoted Crispien's words: *"The worker has no fatherland,"* we have always added: *"Well then, we will create one for him."* Classes are not formed because we have given them a sociological conceptual identification, nor will classes be abolished because you deny them. As long as class antagonisms exist, there will always be class struggle. For only through class struggle can the shifts of power assert themselves. And please, do not always recoil at the mention of this term! For this class struggle has a long history. It extends from our ballot papers to the scaffolds where, according to Mr. Hitler's prophecy in Leipzig, our heads shall one day roll, Mr. Feder. If you travel through the East of Berlin and then proceed to the West, you will see why the class struggle exists. In the days of old Prussia, if among 13 senior presidents, there happened to be one bourgeois, he would have been even more reactionary and foolish in his servility than the rest; when people called us *"enemies of the empire"* and did not consider us *"fit to be night watchmen,"* then indeed, this too is a class struggle. You must learn to see the world as it is viewed from below. May Day is just as political, Mr. Feder, as the Emperor's birthday, and even you are stoking the class struggle. By stirring up the capitalist intermediaries, you are only adding the middle-class struggle to the proletarian battle. Whether this class struggle has become any nobler through your gestures, Mr. Feder—I can only observe that for now it has become louder.

Feder: Professor Nolting, it is precisely the concept of class struggle that we in the National Socialist movement strive against and hate so vehemently. Class struggle, indeed, is the most vicious attack on the unity, solidity, and thrust of our nation. Our opposition to Marxism is for three reasons:

First, the Marxist theoretical assertion of *"equality"* represents the destruction of the individual values upon which National Socialism is founded. This is not an attitude that enhances national efficiency.

In the second place, we condemn Marxism because of its historical materialistic interpretation of things which contradicts our entire value-oriented view of life, culture, soul and peoples' traditions.

And third: The Marxist promises of social justice, peace, fraternity, etc. were false and misleading. National Socialism desires to realize social justice within the German nation, but never at the expense of our national culture, our strength and defense capability!

Nolting: And it is all these things, Mr. Feder, that fill the worker with rage if you wish to reduce the achievements of the republican era today to meaningless catchwords. Millions lie on the streets, and not freedom, peace, and bread, as you promised.

Feder: We National Socialists cultivate the will for self-preservation and the idea of national community internally. We are the guardians of the German defense idea externally. You, on the other hand, are the spokesmen for pacifism, that is, for submissiveness. We want to restore the German worker to his rightful yield. Because we hold the national community dear, we hate Marxism. Because honor matters more to us than profit, because we prioritize the national community over class struggle, and because we place the will to defend above pacifism. And if you still smile today at our ideas, Professor, the utopias—as you call them—of today will be the realities of tomorrow. History will one day decide who was right.

Nolting: It is very nice that you begin your declaration of national community by expressing indelible hatred against the Marxists. I already told you earlier: national community is not so cheaply won through mere declamations, and the class struggle, which we recognize, distinguishes itself from other class struggles in that it is not an endless, ever-repeating event; rather, above the Marxist class theory lies the shimmer of social prophecy. It tends toward self-abolition. For with the socialization of the means of production, the conditions of class antagonism are also eliminated. And thus, peace grows out of struggle, and love springs from hatred. For the class is not just a vessel in which negative emotions accumulate, hatred against kings, hatred against exploiters, but rather, the class struggle is the form in which we transform these stored-up emotions into a dynamic force. From our hatred against institutions grows that historical movement which is to bring about better conditions.

Feder: That is the romanticism of a dying system, Professor.

CHAPTER 21

FUNDAMENTAL PRINCIPLES OF NATIONAL SOCIALIST ECONOMIC POLICY

First print in the Yearbook for 1932

1. The Task and Purpose of the Economy

The national economy in its entirety has the task, first and foremost, of adequately covering the three basic needs of all compatriots—food, shelter, and clothing—and beyond that, to satisfy all cultural and civilizational needs in accordance with the current state of technology and income levels. The economy in its entirety is a serving limb within the overall organism of the nation; it is, in the best sense, service to the people for the greatness and welfare of the nation.

The economy of a nation is not an end in itself; it is not there to enrich individual economic leaders at the expense of their officials, employees, and workers, nor is it there to serve as an object of exploitation for international high finance.

2. Forms of the Economy

There are three possibilities for conducting an economy:

1. Free economy without any constraints (capitalist-liberal),
2. rigid, bound planned economy (Marxist-collectivist),
3. a corporately structured, genuine national economy (universalist-National Socialist).

The completely unconstrained capitalist economic form leads to ever sharper contrasts between rich and poor; it generates exploitation methods that result in the depersonalization and degradation of the entire economy, and unleashes continuous economic struggles that the state itself must watch, powerless and inactive. The rigid, systematically planned Marxist economic form of the socialization of the means of production leads to the exclusion of the most powerful economic factor, the creative personality. Such an economy stagnates and ultimately declines in its productive wealth.

Only the organically structured national socialist economy, which clears the path for the creative personality free from capitalist exploitation and Marxist leveling, can, under careful state supervision, become a source of true welfare for the entire nation.

The class-dividing split between employers and employees must be bridged by the national socialist slogan:

Workers of the brow and fist, unite!

Only in this way can each person, in their place, give their best for their people and, in doing so, for themselves as well.

3. State and Economy

In the liberal era, the organic management of the economy was dissolved, and a wild struggle for power developed between the state and the economy.

This power struggle can produce two outcomes: Either purely materialistic-capitalistic interests triumph over the state and thus over the population (interest-based economy), or the political leaders seize control of the entire economic apparatus (socializing it), then the entire state itself becomes an economic machine and descends to the level of a forced labor institute, as in Russia.

National Socialism unconditionally assigns the state priority over the economy, for the state as the representative and guardian of the power, honor, and existence of the nation, as the expander of the empire, may not engage directly in productive economic activity, as it would soon be drawn into the interests of individual economic sectors and could no longer freely serve the common good.

This results in the following principles regarding the relationship between the state and the economy:

1. the state's right to supervision over the economy, and
2. the state's right to intervene through police, administrative, and fiscal (tax) measures, whenever the collective interest of the state demands it.

4. Foundations of the Economy

Creative, fulfilling labor, the labor of the brow and fist, is the foundation of all economy. To labor, therefore, belongs the first, the honored place in the entire economy. Wealth, property, gain, profit from material goods of all kinds, money, capital, buildings, factories, means of production, machines, and even arable and cultural land are all first the fruits of productive labor. The foremost task of the state to come will be the protection of the creative personality and the safeguarding of labor power from exploitation. Every laborer is worthy of his wages, and every labor must yield its appropriate return. It follows that the yields of diligent and efficient labor, whether it be cultivated land or tools and goods, must pass into the free possession and ownership of the laborer and be protected by law and justice. The same applies to intellectual property rights.

National Socialism fundamentally recognizes private property and places it under state protection.

However, it binds the right of property to moral duties toward the national community.

National Socialism also recognizes the right of inheritance, since for it the family is the most important state cell.

The right to the fruits of labor must not be understood to mean that it would ever be possible to base wages on the market value of a product. In the prices (market prices) of products, the very numerous costs must be included for raw materials, machine wear and renewal, buildings, support staff, commercial and technical management, social and sanitary facilities, as well as for education and the next generation, old age and health care, for state institutions enabling and securing production, administration of justice, trade contracts, and even for national production through police and sea power, etc.

Alongside this most widespread form of private property, it is naturally also possible to have collective ownership in the form of state and municipal property, cooperative ownership, or ownership by legal entities under civil law, etc. In contrast to the capitalist and Marxist systems, the National Socialist state will once more enable every productive individual to attain property.

The property-less proletarians in the National Socialist state shall attain property through diligence and efficiency. They shall feel that they are full citizens and participants in the entire national production.

5. Work and Capital

Capitalism has managed to completely subjugate labor, to exploit it and render it interest-bearing. It has thereby turned the natural and healthy relationship between labor and capital (money) upside down. The current state of affairs in the state, in the municipalities, and in the economy shows the most terrible consequences of this unhealthy, indeed deadly development. National Socialism calls this condition: the interest-based economy.

The despotism of loan capital is no longer satisfied with the simple forms of money lending; long ago, through transformation (conversion of economic enterprises into joint-stock companies), it deprived the creative personalities of the best part of their functional possibilities and reduced the economy from its original task of meeting needs to the pure profit standpoint. Beyond this, financial capital has succeeded in turning the financial management of the public hand to the disastrous lending system (read: debt-making), and on a worldwide scale, the appalling state treaties between Germany and the Allies (the Versailles Treaty, the Dawes Pact, and the Young Plan) signify the completion of the interest-based economy of high finance over German labor.

The breaking of the interest-based economy is the greatest and most significant economic-political task that the National Socialist state has to solve. It is the prerequisite for the restoration of the economy. Details about the measures intended by the N.S.D.A.P. are sufficiently outlined in the party's official writings.

During the transitional period, the National Socialist state will make moderate use of its right to create money for the financing of large public tasks and housing construction in the sense of my well-known proposals (Building and Economic Bank, etc.).

6. The Organic National Economy

The National Socialist economic structure: The economy is an organic structure. The existing cross-connections today (workers, employees, civil servants, entrepreneurs, special interests) lead to the fragmentation of the economy into various interest groups, which stand in open or hidden conflict with one another.

The genuine, true economy strives for the dissolution of these inorganic cross-connections and for the unification of employers and employees in the various economic sectors in the sense of a professional, corporate organization.

The National Socialist state regards it as one of its most essential tasks to lift the relationship between employer and employee out of the poisoned atmosphere of class struggle and racial chaos and to align all those involved in the production process with loyalty and responsibility toward the common goal of national labor.

By granting extensive self-administration, the professional corporations will have to regulate wage and vacation conditions; they will above all work for the restoration of professional honor and regulate all personal relationships between those employed in the businesses and their leaders. These professional corporations will be organized into district, regional, and state associations and will culminate in a central body at the Reich level.

Alongside these chambers that regulate personal relationships, a new phenomenon in economic life will emerge: the so-called economic chambers, composed of independent men personally invested in the economy itself in no way or dependent on it. The economic chambers have the task of assessing the significance of individual professional branches, overseeing them in the spirit and service of the interests of the general public.

A particularly important task of these economic chambers will be the cultivation of the domestic market and the careful oversight of foreign trade.

The economic chambers will be united in the Reich Economic Council, which will safeguard the general interests of the entire nation against special desires and interests of individual economic sectors.

Example:

In the years 1925-1930, the Saxon textile industry experienced an extraordinary boom due to the fashion of light women's stockings, which were exported worldwide. At the same time, German knitting machine manufacturers offered their machines across the globe. Every knitting machine sold abroad meant competition for German textile workers, unemployment, hunger, and misery. The economic chambers of the Third Reich will have the task of making such mutual competition impossible; knitting machines that take bread away from German textile workers must not be exported. A modern example on a large scale is the orders from Soviet Russia, which were given to German industry to open up a terrible competition against the German economy.

7. Trade Policy

The principle of National Socialist foreign trade policy is:

All products that can be grown or manufactured in Germany must not be sourced from abroad. This means protecting the German economy in both city and countryside from foreign competition.

Since today Germany imports around 4000 million worth of foreign foodstuffs (wheat, barley, fruit, vegetables, butter, eggs, fish, meat, etc.), this means misery and hardship in German agriculture, unemployment, and a constant drain on German national wealth. (Example: The import of frozen meat.) Equally appalling is the fact that over 2000 million worth of finished goods (clothing, footwear, machines, automobiles, iron goods, etc.) were imported into Germany from abroad. A German who buys an expensive foreign automobile pays about 3000 RM in wages to foreign workers. German workers, who could perform the same work, remain unemployed, and German taxpayers must still pay 2000 RM.

Prohibition orders will be strictly imposed on every such initiative. The ban on importing superfluous foreign goods does not at all signify a foolish and impracticable isolation from abroad and from the world market. Rather, just as foreign countries still need high-quality German products for a number of years, we urgently require the raw materials that our processing industry absolutely needs: cotton, wool, copper, hides, furs, mineral oils, iron ores, etc.

8. Transitional Measures Elimination of Unemployment.

Upon assuming political power, National Socialism will encounter an almost terrifying situation in the German economy. An army of 5 million unemployed demands reintegration into the production process; the state finances are devastated; the state and the economy are completely indebted; the tax and purchasing capacity of the population is exhausted; the state coffers are empty; agriculture, industry, trade, and commerce are on the brink of collapse. Added to this is a system of irresponsibility, corruption, and party-political cronyism, and the spirit is poisoned by class struggle ideology.

Here, a tremendous cleansing and educational effort must first be undertaken.

Work and bread must be created.

The introduction of compulsory labor (a concept outlined elsewhere in this work) will initially liberate half a million German compatriots from the curse of unemployment. The necessary revision of rent legislation will first take the form of relieving at least half of their tax burden for those subject to the housing tax, provided they can present receipts for repair work on their properties. Hundreds of thousands will be provided with sustenance, and hundreds of thousands will be reintegrated into the economic process.

Following this, the construction industry will find employment through the promotion of building and settlement activities, by providing cheap (interest-free) loans according to my proposals, and through the establishment of social building and economic banks.

Under state pressure, extensive import restrictions will be implemented, and demand will be redirected towards the domestic market. Agriculture will be vigorously supported through interest reduction, debt restructuring, tax relief, and the provision of cheap loans to enable the production of milk, fruit, vegetables, meat, butter, etc., on German soil and to bring them to market. It must succeed in rendering at least 2 billion worth of food imports superfluous through domestic production. This would allow the reintegration of at least 1 million unemployed into production. The same goal will be achieved by eliminating the import of foreign industrial products in the German domestic market. And again, hundreds of thousands will find employment in the revitalizing economy. On the financial policy front, the strongest measures and simplifications will be achieved through the abolition of high interest rates, initially by nationalizing the Reichsbank and other note-issuing banks.

The nationalization of real estate credit and the conversion of high-interest mortgage bonds will bring a massive revival to the real estate and construction markets.

The nationalization or the placing of major banks under state supervision will initiate the loosening and resolution of wider economic areas from their interest-bearing indebtedness.

The nationalization of the electricity supply will lead to a significant reduction in electricity prices and have an invigorating effect on overall production.

Alongside these measures, which signify a tremendous revitalization of the domestic market, come the major foreign policy tasks, which can only be hinted at here:

The abolition of reparation tributes, the expansion of our economic space through trade agreements, etc. A vigorous alliance policy will ensure the reestablishment of a German state of work and achievement, which, far from imperialistic goals, will see its sole aim as securing work and bread, freedom, and honor for the German population.

CHAPTER 22

NATIONAL SOCIALISM & PROPERTY

First published in *"Die Deutsche Volkswirtschaft"* in March 1932 (Issue No. 2)

National Socialism understands in complete alignment with the historical development of the term, ownership as *"the regulated power of disposal over things."* With the term *"regulated,"* the concept of ownership enters the sphere of legal institutions, and thus the most general concept of ownership can be described as the legal regulation of the dispositional power over things. There is undoubtedly the possibility of an impairment of the free power of disposal over things, both for individuals and for communities, through external intervention, so that property, in its ultimate essence, can never involve an unrestricted power of disposal. The most formally correct and accurate explanation of *"property"* will therefore likely be the one that sees in property only the final right of decision over a thing, after other persons or the public authority have previously asserted rights that, in practice, under certain circumstances, are capable of annulling the free *"power of disposal over things"* in the broadest sense.

Of greatest importance in this context, it seems to me, is the hierarchy of the claims of others. In the first place, there is always the precedence of the public authority, followed by the limitations of property through the claims of private persons in the form of mortgages or pledges of claims. Particularly significant for our consideration is undoubtedly the precedence of the public authority, that is, of the state. Undoubtedly, the state can completely abolish the property of an individual, as it can, through expropriation, intervene in private property by means of an authoritative act of coercion, even to the point of entirely abolishing the property.

However, not even the most beautiful fundamental state law, such as Article 153 of the Reich Constitution, which declares private property inviolable, can provide protection against this.

After these very general brief guidelines and formal considerations about the concept of property, which, despite the strong possibilities of restriction, must be characterized as the ultimate decisive legal relation in itself,

it will be necessary to take a very brief look at the history of property, especially since National Socialism fundamentally rejects making any utopian demands or forming concepts that are not historically derived from an organic shaping and consideration of the nation.

In ancient German law, there was no property in land. The land was folk land, which was granted to individuals as **fiefs**. It was only with the penetration of Justinian law that land also became declared as individual property, in order to secure it against princely power and the arbitrariness of the courts. This transformation of private property even into land in the legal codes of the Middle Ages was not even interrupted by the French Revolution, and I would like to emphasize at this point, with all emphasis against Marxist phraseology and Bolshevist practice, that Article 17 of the *"Declaration of the Rights of Man and of the Citizen"* explicitly stipulates: *"Property being an* *inviolable and sacred right, no one can be deprived of it except when public necessity, legally established, expressly demands it, and only under the condition of a just and prior compensation."*

It can therefore not be the slightest doubt that the general conception of the inviolability and protection of private property as the foundation of human society has up until the most recent time been common to all civilized nations.

Section 903 of the *"Civil Code"* stipulates: *"The owner of a thing can, insofar as the law or the rights of others do not conflict, deal with it as he pleases and exclude any interference by third parties."*

In this legal conception of the law currently valid in Germany, it seems to me particularly noteworthy the explicit stipulation that the owner *"as he pleases"* and under the exclusion of the interference of *"third parties"* can dispose of his thing, while the possibility of legal restriction or the limitation by prior rights of others is only mentioned in a subordinate clause. Certainly, the practice of the last decades has taught the German owner of things or land in a rather unpleasant manner that this subordinate clause has now become the main clause and that the German working populace has entered an era of unrestrained expropriation.

The sharpest and strongest justification for private property in contrast to the theoretical dissolution of all private property in anarchism has been given by Aristotle, who declares: *"All community is dangerous and conditions easier and stronger strife than the legally separate position of the individual. The separate property will be an incentive to work, since everyone then does it for himself. But also with regard to the joy and obligation of possession, the conception that it is something our own stands much higher, especially since it alone makes possible the virtue of generosity, which falls entirely flat in communal life."*

In ancient Rome, the jurists ranked private property among the institutions of the *"jus gentium"*: a right that is protected among all peoples. In a clever manner,

Hobbes thoroughly grounded property rights—though he first starts from the communist idea of *"omnia omnibus," "all belongs to all," "everyone can freely take what is within their power and defend what they have taken possession of"*—but then immediately follows this with the insight that this would mean a war of all against all. The right of all to everything cannot therefore be maintained, and only the establishment of private property, i.e., a legal regulation of the power of disposal over things, assigns to each individual his rightful domain.

Herein lies the connection between the object and the person. Property, in the sense and according to the understanding of modern legal doctrine, becomes, as it were, a part of the personality.

Attacks have been raised against this grounding and development of the concept of property from the idea of an ordered human society, of which the following should be briefly mentioned: It is claimed that early Christianity rejected private property. This, however, is by no means correct; only the charitable element was strongly accentuated, the members of the community supported each other fraternally and helped one another. Among various sects of the Middle Ages, such as the Cathars, Waldensians, Bohemian Adamites, Anabaptists, and others, the call for communal living replaces the free exercise of charity. On the other hand, the Catholic Church has never demanded the community of goods or condemned private property as an obstacle to salvation. However, this recognition of private property was always accompanied by the reminder that the owner is merely a steward of his possessions before God, from which he should share with his needy fellow humans, and that exploiting them by virtue of ownership is particularly reprehensible. Herein is also embedded the Augustinian doctrine of interest, which is extraordinarily closely related to the National Socialist perspective.

The utopias of Thomas More, Campanella's *"City of the Sun,"* in which even the community of women is demanded, up to Bellamy's *"Looking Backward from the Year 2000,"* can be conveniently passed over as fictional constructs. In contrast, Babeuf's utopian socialism appears worthy of note as the intellectual soil for Marxist theories. Babeuf asserts that all goods belong to the people and coined the phrase: *"Everyone has a right to everything; complete equality of goods will be established."* The same demand is made by Fourier, who calls for the abolition of all private property, and Proudhon is the source of the famous statement: *"La propriété c'est le vol"* (*"Property is theft"*).

Marxist socialism, according to its materialist interpretation of history, sees private property in the means of production as an unjust institution through which the owners can dispose of the fruits of others' labor and extract surplus value at the expense of the workers.

In a consistent development of these ideas, Bolshevism has abolished private property. However, it has not eliminated exploitation but instead replaced the potential and actual exploitation of workers by individuals with the exploitation of workers by the masses.

This brief historical overview of the concept and content of private property, its justification and rejection, was indispensable in order to explain, present, and justify the position of National Socialism toward private property. The previous views can undoubtedly be classified under the two extremes: recognition of private property and rejection of private property. The denial of private property leads to collectivist-communist economics, to coercion and misery. An unrestricted recognition of private property, as demanded by Western capitalism and as it has sought to guarantee through privileged claims by state treaties (Dawes-Young Plan), likewise leads to the dissolution of private property for individuals and thus to hardship and poverty.

National Socialism, as our program clearly and unequivocally states, is based on the recognition of private property with the explicit general limitation that, as far as it owes its origin to individual capacity and achievement, whereby my commentary explicitly includes the pre-achievement of fathers and ancestors. Inheritance is thus also recognized. However, this, too, is fundamentally incorporated with the moral obligation: *"What thou hast inherited from thy fathers, acquire it, to possess it."*

National Socialism thus seeks a refinement of the concept of property, both in the direction that it establishes the demand for one's own value creation in accordance with the principle of general performance and, on the other hand, incorporates the social obligation that allows unrestricted disposal over private property only if it serves the community: *"Common good before self-interest!"*

A third factor is of particular significance: The precedence of the state as well as its right to intervene and, if necessary, the right of expropriation over private property that is mismanaged or detrimental to the common good. Precisely this latter thought should, will, and must replace the mindset of individualism with its liberal capitalistic recklessness in the unrestrained exploitation of private property. Especially the tendencies toward ruthless and unrestrained exploitation, which have been introduced into the economy through the modern forms of pure financial and loan capital, must disappear.

The centralization, the form of the shareholder society in the economy, led to an alarming decay of the economy, to a depersonalization and degradation, which became the most dangerous breeding ground for Marxist-communist ideas. Thus, National Socialism, which recognizes the personality as the most significant factor in state and economic life, is compelled to take a sharp stance against mass hysteria and money power, opposing certain forms of private property recognized today.

National Socialism sees in a legal order that enables the diligent and capable to acquire private property and guarantees the possession of what has been earned, the best foundation for the revival of the economy, the personality, and thus also the prerequisite and basis of all culture. The interventions of the state should generally occur only when higher state necessities demand it, and even this should generally happen with corresponding compensation, unless general sacrifices in the interest of the whole (war taxes) must be demanded. That the state itself as well as other public legal entities can possess collective property is self evident. Indeed, the National Socialist state, in the spirit of the party program, which in Article 13 demands the nationalization of all already socialized enterprises, will nationalize various areas of work that previously lay in private hands during their economic development, such as electricity supply and fuel supply. It must be explicitly emphasized here that nationalization in the realm of production is not intended, as it is sustained in its productivity by the free, creative personality.

Entirely different principles apply, however, in the realm of circulation, that is, in the field of administration and supply of the population with the most essential goods in the realm of transportation and, above all, in the field of money and credit. The nationalization of the entire money and credit system has become a central point of the National Socialist program, and all opposing or half-hearted solutions that would leave the monetary system to financial capitalism or individual professional groups are fundamentally rejected. It should be particularly noted that in the hands of loan capital, interest usury was one of the most dangerous instruments for expropriating private property and home and land ownership, as no fewer than 100,000 bankruptcies in Germany during the last decade prove. The massive wave of expropriation during the post-war period through inflation is further evidence of how dangerously Marxist ideology combined with capitalist banditry affects the preservation of private property.

The fundamental recognition of private property in the National Socialist state is in no way shaken by the frequently cited Article 17 of our program, which calls for the creation of a law for the gratuitous expropriation of land and soil. A government that does not have the courage to expropriate unlawfully acquired possessions, even if they have taken the form of legally recognized property, and without compensation, is in no position to protect honestly acquired property from loot, robbery, and theft, especially in the modern forms of banking and stock exchange fraud.

All in all, National Socialism thus stands on the foundation of private property, which it places under state protection. However, the welfare of the people sets a limit to the excessive accumulation of wealth in the hands of individuals. Usury and profiteering as well as ruthless enrichment at the expense and to the detriment of the people will be punished with death.

Through the breaking of the bondage of interest, i.e., through the liberation of the state and the economy from its terrible foreign policy interest and tribute obligations (a political act), through the nationalization of the money and credit system with the ultimate goal of making cheap, indeed interest-free credit available for economically important tasks, debt restructuring, interest and tax relief for the distressed agriculture, trade, commerce, and industry, the rebuilding of private property will first be made possible again, which in recent years has been shaken to its foundations, burdened, and completely expropriated in all segments of the population.

A radical reorganization of the money and credit system, in conjunction with the detachment from the gold standard, initially in the domestic market, and thus the enabling of money and credit creation, corresponding to the requirements of the expansion of production, will first create the prerequisites for the reintegration of millions of fellow countrymen, currently exposed to the curse of unemployment, into the production process. The exploitation of significant technical innovations will unexpectedly enliven the labor market and lead to a significant resurgence in the undoubtedly leading global economic crisis in the field of technical production, allowing nations to care for the welfare of all fellow countrymen at a higher level of culture.

This fundamental stance of National Socialism towards property will be of particular significance for the currently destitute masses of urban workers.

The National Socialist state will pay special attention to ensuring that the working class can once again grow close to the German homeland through resettlement from their hopeless rootlessness in the big cities. They should once again become rooted in the soil, should come into the possession of small, hygienically and technically impeccable own settlement houses; they should receive enough land to enable them to sustain themselves through gardening and small animal husbandry during times of crisis and need. In good times, their own garden will represent a highly welcome augmentation of their income.

Naturally, this presupposes a systematic redistribution of the population in the sense of de-congesting the big cities and resettling to the countryside and smaller country towns in the spirit of the great population policy inaugurated by Adolf Hitler.

In the greatest possible number of free, independent existences, National Socialism sees the best and most secure foundation for a robust, flourishing, physically and racially healthy state of work and achievement.

A later age will also recognize a great achievement in the field of reshaping the concept of property within the National Socialist idea, removing endless strife and conflict from the life of nations by creating clear hierarchies and delineations between state power and private property, by expropriating plunder and usury and thereby creating a new legal certainty within the nation and among nations.

CHAPTER 23

FUNDAMENTALS ON THE FINANCING QUESTION OF THE EMPLOYMENT CREATION PROGRAM

First published in *"Die Deutsche Volkswirtschaft,"* May 1932 (No. 5)

A Reply to Dr. Brüning:

Gregor Strasser presented the outlines of a National Socialist job creation program during the Reichstag session on May 10, 1932. Reich Chancellor Brüning responded the following day during the session, among other things, as follows: *"I listened with great interest to the remarks of Representative Strasser, as they largely coincide with the measures the Reich government is preparing. Mr. Strasser stated that he agreed with the gentlemen on this side (indicating the left) regarding job creation; therefore, I probably do not need to express that I agree with them. The spirits diverge, however, on the question of financing. I, for my part, will under all circumstances refuse, and for both domestic and foreign policy reasons, to do anything that might bring temporary slight relief, that might be temporarily popular, but would place the currency in grave danger... we must go down paths that are very clear."*

The Reich Chancellor is entirely correct in his demand that in the financing question, very clear paths must be taken. I and with me the N.S.D.A.P. have always demanded clarity in matters of state finances and have strived—with success—to bring about a clear separation of views. I would therefore like to respond in the following, as the eldest and most qualified authority of the N.S.D.A.P. in the field of monetary and credit policy, to Herr Reich Chancellor Brüning, in order to avoid misunderstandings and to clarify in which camp there is actually clarity on the financing question, with some fundamental principles. The Herr Reich Chancellor has deemed it appropriate, in the last electoral campaigns, to accuse the N.S.D.A.P. and specifically me personally of wanting to bring about inflation. The proof for this assertion, as the Herr Reich Chancellor and many others who have made and continue to make this claim, is supposedly in the so-called *"Feder money,"* which the N.S.D.A.P. allegedly intends to introduce after the seizure of power.

Formally, it must first be stated that the N.S.D.A.P., from any responsible authority, has never intended or announced the introduction of a new currency after the seizure of power. The word and concept of *"Feder money"* was coined by my opponents to discredit my monetary and credit policy theses. Thus, the lie about Feder money entered the arsenal of political slogans in the battles of recent years. *"Feder money"* became an untenable concept in monetary and currency policy discussions, so that today every proposal in the field of monetary and currency policy that in any way opposes the strange principles of the gold-standard-friendly Reichsbank leadership and central bankers is subsumed under the term *"Feder money." "Feder money"* has been stamped as the archetype of all *"unsound"* money.

It is beyond doubt that the current economic crisis is not an ordinary business cycle crisis. The economy is not capable of accumulating from within itself the forces necessary to overcome the present state of affairs. Even the previously used stimulation methods, such as discount rate cuts, tax reliefs, etc., are no longer capable of having an *"invigorating"* effect. Not even state subsidy policy has been able despite unprecedented activity—to halt the contraction process of the economy. The pressure of dreadful unemployment—almost one in three Germans live in some way on public support—has become so strong today that the government is forced, against its will and spirit, to actively intervene in production. Work is to be created through the state. So far, there is agreement among the major parties according to the statements of the Herr Reich Chancellor. There is no agreement, however, over the most important organizational question of the entire action: the question of financing work creation.

For the N.S.D.A.P., the path that must be taken is the one that signifies a completely clear, radical overall solution. Before any effective activation of production can be initiated, the Reichsbank and the major banks must first be completely nationalized, and then Germany must immediately abandon the gold standard and adapt the face value of the Reichsmark to the requirements that have become necessary with regard to the German workforce and the changed valutaric world conditions (almost half the world has abandoned the gold standard). The courage must finally be found to break free from the fiction of stable exchange rates and to end that calamitous policy based on the thesis once voiced by Reichsbank President Dr. Luther: to squeeze *"the last drop of blood"* from the body if the *"stability of the currency"* requires it.

If these prerequisites are created, then a strictly controlled credit emission (book money creation) must form the basis for the implementation of the large tasks of the National Socialist job creation program. The instruments of book money creation will be the *"Construction and Economic Banks"* I have planned, which are to be either newly established or formed from the apparatus of the nationalized major banks.

When I said above that the nationalization of the banks is the prerequisite for the implementation of any large-scale job creation, it is for the following reason:

The National Socialist state will claim the full *"monetary sovereignty,"* that means to possess the exclusive right of money creation. The current state does not have this right. It would not have had it even if the so called Reichsbank had been in the exclusive possession of the Reich. Let us consider this: The Reichsbank limited its activity essentially to the issuance of paper money, while it completely left the creation of giral[1] money to the major banks! This meant that the state essentially confined itself to providing the payment mediums of the consumer economy (consumer money according to Dr. Wagner). Thus, out of approximately 6.4 billion state payment means, the small-denomination notes (up to and including 100=RM notes) alone, including token coins, amounted to 5.16 billion RM (end of 1930). The rest consists of large denomination notes (1000-RM and 500=RM notes). The Reichsbank giral money is of entirely subordinate significance. In contrast, the major banks' giral money in normal times is generally estimated at about five times the total state money. With 6.5 billion in state money, we thus have approximately 33 billion in major bank giral money. The liberal state had therefore left the creation of money for the production economy (producer money) to the private major banks. True, the state had taken away the right of note issuance from the major banks, but with the introduction and enforcement of cashless transactions, payments that previously could only be made with the help of the transfer of notes could now be accomplished in the same way by transferring giro balances from account to account. Further, if one takes into account the fact that the banks in normal times on average operated with a reserve of state (cash) money of perhaps 8-10 percent, it is evident what a tremendous credit pyramid the credit-creating banks could build. The granting of a balance on current account—whether against security or on a pure trust basis—was, due to the changed payment habits, the same as the issuance of new banknotes in the past.

The essential function of the major banks in the course of highly capitalistic development now consisted in the fact that, through additional giral money creation beyond their own resources and deposits—even under circumstances beyond the capabilities of the economy!—they enabled the financing of all major technical innovations and inventions, as well as purely speculative and occasionally fraudulent manipulations. This was not the only, but the most important method of financing capitalism. All major investments were initially made possible in this way. The means that normal saving activity provided would hardly have sufficed to carry out the technical revolutions. The future higher profits and increased saving activity were, as it

---

1 **Giral money** (***also called scriptural money, from the German Giralgeld***) refers to non-cash money held in bank accounts that can be transferred electronically or by check. It is essentially money created through bookkeeping entries by banks—not printed currency or coins, but digital or ledger-based balances.

were, anticipated and only made possible by giral money creation. This proves that capitalism—even the creation of *"big money"* for the production economy —was carried out entirely according to the principles I have proposed. The rules of the so-called *"classic"* money creation (note creation based on the circulation of cash) applied only to the (state) small money of the consumer economy.

If therefore *"Feder money"* is said to be *"illegitimate money,"* then all giral money of the capitalist economy is *"illegitimate"* money and thus *"Feder money"* by measure. If additional money creation for investment purposes is said to mean inflation, then inflation was the *"initial ignition"* of the capitalist economy par excellence; if it is said that *"Feder money"* creates capital *"out of thin air,"* then the major banks have done nothing else. Why should it now, after the nationalization of the major banks, be forbidden what was previously legal practice?

If in the capitalist system credit expansion was primary relative to increased saving activity, why should in the future the opposite alone be correct?

If today one comes to me with the fairy tales of national economic textbooks from the last century and counters: Investments can only be made with savings, then I can only admire the ignorance or audacity of my critics. It is an elementary fact that, for example, if one takes the current situation as a basis, one must first get the economy running in order to make saving activity possible at all. Thus, giral money creation is primary relative to savings accumulation. Not the other way around.

The fear that, after the nationalization of the major banks, the limitation on giral money creation that had hitherto been necessitated by the need to maintain sufficient liquidity for the banks would disappear for the state, is entirely unfounded. On the contrary, the national socialist state, by ensuring that additional giral money creation will occur solely according to national economic viewpoints, will apply stricter principles to money creation than previous practice. I have—as I explicitly state here in response to the objections of numerous opponents of my ideas—never held the view that I want to replace the gold standard with a commodity standard. On the contrary, I have defined money as a *"claim on performed labor,"* i.e., economic goods. According to this view, the *"backing"* of a currency with the value of money or the insurance of money has nothing directly to do with it. Rather, any currency that is based on land or arbitrarily expandable material goods invites the danger of inflation. Thus, the so-called *"miracle of the Rentenmark"* cannot be explained by the fact that land as backing ensured the stable value of the Rentenmark; only the fact that the Rentenmark was issued in relatively small and strictly limited quantities can explain the stability of this currency.

Although I have repeatedly pointed out in my book *The German State on National and Social Foundations* the *"commodity backing"* of the money to be issued by the planned *"Construction and Economy Bank,"* this should not mean that the *"backing"* is what precedes the creation of money, forming, as it were, the basis for the subsequent emission—money can never be *"covered"* by already existing material goods -, but it should mean that the *"backing"* is what the creation of money is supposed to create in the first place. The decisive factor is whether the use of the additional money creation serves productive or consumptive purposes.

Therefore, when Selfferich is cited as a witness against my ideas by quoting the following passage from one of his Reichstag speeches: *"If you believe that the Reich can create a real, value-stable means of payment by implementing the confiscation of material goods, then you are mistaken, for you may confiscate as many material goods as you like, but you will still not have money in your possession, and you will never be able to make money out of these goods,"* those who do so are on the wrong path. In this matter, I am entirely on the opposite side of Selfferich. I have consistently and emphatically rejected the disastrous notion that one could create money out of material values or on the basis of material values. Thus, *"Feder money"* has nothing to do with projects that aim at a land mart, a rye mart, an iron mart, a labor rent mart, or anything similar.

Regarding the financing of the employment program, given the billions of marks involved (if the task is to be comprehensively and effectively addressed), the primary consideration is the path of additional capital creation—under the conditions I have already mentioned above.

The Free Trade Unions and the Brüning government have rejected this path and believed that they had to choose the method of raising funds through a loan (premium loan). All proposals that were limited to currency reform or even just the demand for deflationary banking policy were indignantly dismissed with great pathos, while I was given the honor of being seen as the influencer behind all these proposals.

Thus, the deputy federal chairman Eggert said the following at the conference of the Free Trade Unions: "*Finally, financing must be made possible through a popular employment bond. The employment bond must be designed in such a way that it draws out the saved-up money from the stocking. To the extent that the loan certificates are not fully placed on the capital market, they should serve as a basis for the banks to provide interim financing for employment. This interim financing occurs in the form of bills of exchange being drawn on the credit societies to be founded by the entrepreneurs tasked with the employment projects. The banks commissioned with the issuance of the loan discount these bills, with the loan certificates serving as additional security. The banks, in turn, can discount the acquired bills at the Reichsbank.*"

It is self-evident that Mr. Eggert was also aware that the popularity of the planned loan, as well as the loan itself, would be a very problematic matter. Extracting liquid funds amounting to 1.5 to 2 billion from the private sector is, at present, pure fantasy. The most important aspect of the project is undoubtedly the interim financing. This can mean nothing other than additional issuance of means of payment (d. h. Giral money plus state money). This is certainly a necessity. However, it is inexplicable why the state should additionally be burdened with debt and interest in the same amount. If, therefore, any inflation risk arises from the employment program and its financing, then it is not due to the additional creation of money, but rather to the utterly senseless and superfluous prior establishment of state debt in the amount of the money to be created.

Vladimir Wontinftn, the theorist of the Free Trade Unions, remarked very aptly in the January issue of "*Arbeit*": "*Whoever speaks of employment creation has spoken of credit creation.*" Wontinftn develops a complicated financing plan, into which I will not delve here, but in which an employment creation loan also plays the decisive role. Wontinftn, out of fear of "*Feder money,*" has fallen into the thicket of liberal theory and has hopelessly entangled himself in it. I fully agree with him when he asserts that the whole question is not about "*the reckless use of the printing press, but merely about the attempt to organize the economic forces.*" However, it is incomprehensible to me that the state should have to borrow the funds that simply have to be created in order to eliminate unemployment. Wontinftn seems to have sensed something similar, for he says: "*The loan path does not mean that the employment creation action would depend on to what extent it succeeds in interesting the capital market at home or abroad in the matter.*" (March issue of "*Arbeit.*")

No, Mr. Wontinftn, here there is only an Either-Or! Either a genuine loan or a genuine credit expansion.

Every compromise is a highly dangerous expedient! Wontinftn says: *"Instead of loans, I could say 'credits' or 'credit expansion', and: 'Loans represent the best economic basis and at the same time the simplest banking form of credit expansion.'"* This is theoretical wordplay with the aim of making a virtue out of necessity. I pointed out ten years ago that the issuance of state loans must cease, as they are unworthy of the state and furthermore only favored the swindle maneuver of finance capital, which, by exploiting the source of Giral money creation of the banks, ultimately provided the liquid funds for the loans from additional purchasing power. It has been left to the Marxist Mr. Wontinftn to glorify the whole loan swindle and to call it the "best economic basis" of credit expansion. The opposite is the case. State bonds—as well as securities in general— are by no means the best basis for newly created Giral money. Although the large banks, for technical reasons, have preferred "covered" credit in their business practice, in fact, with competent business management, *"uncovered"* credits of a bank have always been the best. Quite apart from the fact that in the interim financing of employment creation on the basis of loan securities, it would simply be a veiled bank credit.

I have been reproached that my financing proposals would result in *"capital being created out of thin air."* In response, I can only counter that never has more capital *"evaporated into thin air"* than during the deflation period, that, if one must speak of *"air capital,"* this designation fits precisely a *"loan"* for which there are no loan subscribers (social insurance institutions and savings banks, which might be forced to take over loan securities, would, of course, be excluded as genuine loan subscribers, since in that case only a capital shift would occur). If, as is no longer in doubt, the employment creation loan is merely a *"banking form of credit expansion"* that the government apparently deems correct, then I can only say that it is the economically most unfavorable and for the community the most expensive, indeed downright dangerous form of credit expansion. For imagine the image of a national economic balance sheet: on the asset side, the national economic-technical real assets, land and buildings, other buildings and inventory, goods stocks, the goods and services; on the liability side, the entire purchasing power (money assets in the broadest sense), both potential (not active on the goods market) and actual purchasing power (mainly money). With the financing method as proposed by

Wontinftn and apparently favored by the government, the purchasing power volume is suddenly increased by a single emergency decree by an amount in the billions (corresponding to the new debt of the Reich in the same amount) even before any activation of production and value creation, and precisely in this fact I see the great danger of inflationary effects. Meanwhile, daily Giral money creation will occur in roughly the same amount, as well as probably an additional note issuance and silver coin minting to cover the additional, not insignificant interest and amortization payments for the loans. In contrast, with my proposal, the creation of additional potential purchasing power is entirely eliminated, as is, of course, the new indebtedness of the Reich and the burdens of interest and amortization; the Giral money creation will proceed in strict accordance with the pace of procurement accordingly. With inflation – which always arises from the budget, i.e., its root causes lie in the increasing and overwhelming indebtedness of public bodies – this has nothing to do. It is downright laughable to always speak of inflation when discussing Giral money creation for productive purposes. Such fear could at best be justified if state investment activities led to mis-allocations or over investments. But that is no argument against the theoretical correctness of my thesis. Moreover, such danger cannot be spoken of if one keeps in mind that in the last year and in the months of the current year, even the ongoing replacement investments have not been carried out to any significant extent. This means that the asset side of the national economic balance has diminished. This indicates that the Marxist economy has already covered its deficits from the substance of the German economy.

We have idle labor forces and raw materials in the country, we have investment needs that cannot be met because *"there is no money."* The exhausted people no longer have any fear of inflation but certainly of the continuation of this insane, value-destroying deflation policy, which has brought about the dreaded economic anemia that threatens to destroy us.

Clear paths must be taken – You are right, Mr. Brüning! – Only our path is clear . . . Yours is dark and unknown.

CHAPTER 24

THE ULTIMATE CAUSES OF THE WORLD ECONOMIC CRISIS

For years, scholars, politicians, and statesmen have been racking their brains over the reasons for the so called world economic crisis, which has gripped both victor and vanquished nations alike. Undoubtedly, the explanations provided so far, both political and general economic, are insufficient to explain the extraordinarily sharp decline of the world economy.

If I point out in the following the most deeply rooted and therefore largely overlooked ultimate cause of the world economic crisis, I would like to expressly state that this does not render the well-known crisis causes obsolete, which have had particularly devastating effects in Germany. On the contrary, precisely because certain and in part unavoidable crisis causes exist, farsighted statesmen and politicians should have all the more ensured the elimination of the political causes for the general misery. Even the most short-sighted politicians on the side of our wartime opponents have come to understand that the insane reparations burden imposed on Germany had to lead to the bleeding dry of the German economy. It has also become common knowledge among large parts of the German people that the red insanity of the post-war period is to be sought as the main cause for the political and thus also the economic decline of Germany. The collapses of the major banks and the enduring crisis in the capital market prove that particularly in this area, extraordinarily grave mistakes have been made.

That the pitiful party politics bears its fair share of the blame for the destabilization of the German economy is also one of the many reasons for the German misery. All these reasons would not, however, suffice to explain the extraordinarily high levels of unemployment in Germany and, increasingly, in the rest of the world as well. We must look deeper. Without a doubt, the reason for this phenomenon is the fact that we stand at the zenith of the technical age.

All the great, significant inventions of the technical age have seemingly been made, the world is essentially equipped with the achievements of the technical age, and upon the unprecedented rise of the technical, industrial age, a collapse in the realm of overall technical installation has followed. The capacity of industrial facilities has grown immensely, while the market's absorption capacity has steadily declined.

I have illustrated this years ago with a curve diagram. (Cf. the diagram on p. 19.) The line of industrial development over the last 70 years shows first a powerful ascent, then an S-shaped curve downward. This curve represents the overall trajectory for the entire technical-industrial development and similarly for almost all significant individual phenomena of the technical age. As an example, consider the development of the railway system, which can be regarded as prototypical for the age of transport and technology.

At the starting point of the railway curve stands, of course, the invention. As with all inventions, the greatest difficulty lies in gaining initial recognition. And painstakingly slowly, the idea of the railway, which has since become common knowledge, fought its way against the resistance of contemporaries. Famous is the notorious report of the Erlangen Medical Collegium against the railway, according to which railway travel was deemed impossible, posing extraordinary dangers to the health of passengers and spectators alike, such that the railway tracks would at least need to be fenced off with boards. As is well known, only the boards in front of the minds of the scholars of that time have been preserved for posterity. The railway system and railway travel slowly and laboriously gained acceptance. Soon, however, everyone was convinced of the extraordinary advantages of the railway, new railway lines were constructed everywhere, the railway became a public means of transport, and the entire industry focused on this vast field of activity. Without interruption, new locomotive factories, wagon factories, rail mills, and auxiliary factories for technical railway supplies were established, countless railway construction companies were founded. The railway construction enterprises received billion-dollar contracts for bridge constructions, the massive station halls in all major German cities were built, the construction industry flourished, tunneling companies had an abundance of work, and numerous auxiliary factories for the required fittings, lighting, and interior furnishings of the wagons emerged. Indeed, it was thanks to this original entrepreneurial and creative spirit that, within a few decades, the entire country was covered with a railway network. The smallest German town received its station, and rail lines of main or branch railways led to almost every village. New factories for railway supplies were continuously established, revenues showed an ever-swelling increase, and German entrepreneurs were lured into ever new investments, as if this would continue forever. Yet, after a few decades—around the turn of the century—Germany was saturated; it no longer needed new railway lines. The existing deliveries were in no way sufficient to fully occupy the factories and enterprises. The excellent quality of the produced locomotives, wagons, and tracks guaranteed a lifespan of 30, 40, or more years; the large stationary facilities, the railway bodies, stations, and station halls, the administrative buildings, etc., were built for centuries. Then, comparatively quickly and abruptly, demand in Germany declined—but the world was vast, and with bold entrepreneurial spirit, German railway builders pushed into the global market to further industrialization abroad and, above all, to build railways there. However, they now clashed massively for the first time with the English-American and French railway industries, which had undergone the same developmental path and now sought sales markets for their products across the globe. Through tenacious struggle, the German railway industry also managed to secure vast sales territories and contracts, until, around the year

1914—in the historic moment of the outbreak of World War I—their efforts, driven to the utmost rationalization in the battle of competition, succeeded in encircling the entire globe with all important and significant railway lines. All major railways in Europe, America, as well as in Asia and Africa had been built, insofar as they held world-political interest in the latter continents.

Thus, the culmination point was reached: the world was saturated with railways. The capacity, the performance capability of all facilities had been elevated to gigantic proportions, and had the World War not brought with it a massive depletion of rolling stock, and the post-war period not necessitated a final massive order for the repair of railway materials destroyed during the war, a tremendous collapse, as indeed occurred around the year 1925, would have ensued even then. There is no power on earth capable of halting this development.

What holds true for the railway is also valid for almost all major technical investments and installations of the past heyday of the technical age. In the same rooms—we will remain in Germany for now—almost all major German cities were constructed, medium-sized and small towns, and the majority of village communities were equipped with water pipelines. These large installations in Germany also brought billions of orders for the German iron and construction industries. Hundreds of thousands of kilometers of water pipes, from the largest to the smallest diameter, millions of seals and fittings, taps and branches, water meters and outlet valves had to be produced and installed. Massive orders for the concrete and reinforced concrete industries were connected to the construction of thousands of storage facilities, water towers, and water collection plants. This, too, has come to an end today. A water pipeline that does not last at least a hundred years without defects has no right to exist. Based on the capacity of pipe and rolling mills, construction companies, and installation firms, one could now provide the whole of Germany with water pipelines a second time within a decade.

The same can be said of the installation of gas in all German cities. This installation also falls within the same short time span, essentially within the years from 1860 to 1910. The massive expansion of the telegraph, telephone, and postal networks provided another tremendous impulse. Sand by sand, the entire German economy was motorized. Hundreds of thousands and millions of horsepower were generated by steam, water, and eventually electricity. The youngest and proudest branch of technology, electrical engineering, took an even faster triumphant march through Germany. It was fortunate that the construction of the very large overhead power lines and large power plants fell into the period after the war, because for the most critical transition period, just as for the railways, there were still many billions worth of work to be done. The technification of agriculture, the clothing and food industries, freed up much labor in favor of machines. Finally, the capacity of the entire German industry in all areas was so increased that there was no longer any demand large enough that could not have been met by the production capacity of German industry. Meanwhile, however, the installation of all of Germany was completed, and in the wider world, the national industries of industrial countries had also so perfected themselves that the fiercest competitive battles were fought over every bit of international contracts. The foreign countries, too, had largely completed their technical installations. Machines had broadly replaced humans, and the human, made unemployed, had lost his purchasing power to buy the remaining goods and thus, in turn, idled the machines. To the tremendous upsurge of the technical age, a descent, indeed a collapse, had to follow with inexorable inevitability. From a purely technical perspective, the global economic crisis is caused by the discrepancy between the capacity of the world industry and the rapidly diminished absorptive capacity of the world market. One should not believe that this is merely a temporary phenomenon that will make way for a new tremendous technical upsurge. The very great technical tasks lie behind us. The conquest of the air is certainly still a final great technical task, but its principle has already been solved. A final, truly great task still remains in the technically perfected provision of heat to the population.

Anyone who followed the great technical installations of the last decades with open eyes must have noticed that, despite an infinite number of technical perfections and details, the latest technical wonders somehow show a tired, decadent touch. Nothing really great and new is shown anymore, something that would make the whole world sit up and take notice and give the global industry new impulses. Anyone who recalls the enormous impression made by the first bicycle, the first automobile, the first electric motor, who remembers the revolutionary significance of the first steam turbine, the Diesel engine, the first electric spotlight, the first large high-speed locomotive, will have to admit that, compared to these, even the great sensations of recent years, radio and film, have been of far lesser significance. We must face this development head-on. We must recognize that the great technical-industrial age is in decline, that it, like other great epochs of world history, represents an impressive uniqueness that will not return, no more than the beauty-intoxicated art of ancient Hellas, the imperialist power frenzy of Rome, or the mighty resurgence of the Renaissance, to name just a few of the great phenomena. The far-sighted statesman must prepare himself for the fact that industry will never again be able to employ the millions of industrial workers as the past century made possible. Certainly, there will still be an extraordinary amount of technical work to be done to ensure renewal and the supply of spare parts for ongoing wear and tear, and certainly, some significant technical innovations, especially in the field of motor and aviation, will provide employment. However, one should not deceive oneself that the emergence of new transportation technologies will, to a large extent, take away the previous tasks. Every tonne-kilometer and every passenger-kilometer transported today by motor vehicles or airplanes takes away the corresponding volume of transportation from the railways. The collapse of the entire German locomotive and wagon manufacturing industry, and ultimately the freight car sector, is far more a consequence of these technical reasons than a result of political mismanagement. No power of the Earth, no financing with borrowed funds or so-called *"federated money,"* nor the takeover of values by the workforce can revive industries and restore them to their former glory. for which there is simply no demand left. Note well, no demand that could exhaust the enormous capacity of these industries and provide lasting work to thousands of people again. The few remaining construction projects can scarcely employ 10% of the capacity of such industries.

It is certain that this relatively sudden and almost abrupt decline in demand could have been mitigated by comprehensive state supervision, and that the devastating consequences of unemployment could have been partially alleviated if large-scale plans, such as those initiated by National Socialist population policy, had been implemented.

This population policy, which envisions the resettlement of uprooted city dwellers and does not indulge in romantic notions of small and rural settlements, demands a very comprehensive re-agrarianization of the German youth. It is important to emphasize, rather than downplay, the devastating influence that finance capital has had on the development of the technical age. This is vividly illustrated by the second curve in the mentioned chart, the interest and compound interest curve, which is exemplary of the development of the explicitly loan-capitalist era. The curve shown is mathematically a second-degree curve, i.e., $x = y^2$, which initially rises very slowly but soon ascends more sharply, ultimately approaching infinity.

I repeat the example of the penny, which, since the birth of Christ, should have been invested at interest and compound interest, so that every 15 years the original capital would have doubled. Today, this penny, invested at interest and compound interest, would have grown to a value whose representation our entire Earth would not suffice, even if it were made of pure gold. Even all the planets and the Sun, twenty times over, made of pure gold, would roughly correspond to the value of this penny invested at interest and compound interest since the birth of Christ.

From this, one can see the fantastical utopia of the interest-driven economy in itself. Theoretically, this curve is easy to draw and calculate, but in practice, the interest is always tied to labor. Therefore, the yield from interest can never exceed the value of labor. The interest curve illustrates, in a way, how insidiously and pervasively a false, anti-economical principle has taken hold, initially slowly and inconspicuously lagging far behind the industrial wealth, while loan capital in the early years of technical development contented itself with modest interest rates, as industry expressed its wealth in enormous dividend percentages, which increasingly whetted the appetite of finance capital.

Now loan capital virtually forced its capital upon the economy, always financing new investments. The standardization of the economy progressed further, personal initiative and entrepreneurial skill were increasingly eliminated, and in place of the great economic leaders of the rising era came general directors, managing directors, etc. The enterprises became dividend factories instead of providers of goods to meet needs. With greedy eyes, international high finance fueled this madness, expecting to reap the fruits of all labor in this way.

its favor. Ultimately, the interest curve, so to speak, intersected the curve of the wealth generated by the entire technical-industrial economy. Through the corruption of public life, attempts were made to completely harness the productive power of technology for the service of finance. In a frenzied whirl, the greed of high finance rose like a fountain over the production of the world;

but just as a fountain lacks internal cohesion or structure, and as so-called "*backflow phenomena*" soon appear, so too have these crisis-like phenomena in the realm of high finance already been evident for years. We stand before the fact that world finance is gripped by a massive crisis, the crisis of the capitalist era, a crisis that, with relentless logic, will drag down the very industries that are meant to sustain it.

Here lies the historical mission of National Socialism: to break the bondage of interest and reconstruct the capitalist system, thereby showing the world new paths for financing major public tasks and carrying out an ambitious employment program for the transitional period. Then, through a long-term national economic and technical program, it must prepare the re-agrarianization of our people, so that within one or two decades our entire nation, at a higher level of civilization and culture, can grow again into a more peaceful era, rooted in the soil and filled with love for the fatherland.

CHAPTER 25

GOLD CURRENCY?

First publication in *"Völkischer Beobachter"* on July 2, 1932

Among the most firmly entrenched preconceptions is the belief that gold serves as a universal measure of value, akin to a meter for measuring length, and that it is suitable for measuring values. For this reason, it was also believed that the currencies of individual countries must be tied to a specific quantity of gold in order to establish a relatively reliable basis for determining the value of goods in their exchange relationships.

We are dealing here with one of the most dangerous errors, which, because of its extraordinarily widespread acceptance, is also extraordinarily harmful. Above all, one must be clear about this: values cannot be measured, they can only be estimated. The very term *"measure of value"* is thus a contradiction in terms. Wherever subjective personal factors come into play, wherever supply and demand, scarcity and abundance, rarity and age, durability and rapid perishability are involved, there can be no question of precise measurement as we understand it in the natural sciences.

The fact that our materialistic, technologized world believes it can measure values and believes it can use gold as a standard is by no means proof of the correctness or even the possibility of such an approach. Gold is, first of all, a commodity, and as a precious metal, a noble commodity, particularly suitable for storage due to its unchanging quality, and particularly suitable as a medium of exchange due to its special desirability. In earlier times, gold, as the *"most desired commodity,"* was certainly well-suited for this purpose.

But gold is also a monetary metal, and as a monetary metal, it acquires the peculiar dual character of both money and commodity.

Money as a function of society, money as a *"record of completed labor,"* is undoubtedly independent of the intrinsic value of the monetary tokens. Historically, cowrie shells, tea leaves, slaves, cattle, silver, and banknotes have undoubtedly served the same purposes as gold coins, and in the modern intensified economy, money has completely detached itself from its substrate and serves the economy through giro money or in the form of cashless payments just as effectively as gold.

The fixation on gold for the monetary unit today emerges as an enormous obstacle to the indispensable credit expansion necessary for job creation. Moreover, the use of gold as a measure of value, as the last months have shown us, is a self-deception of national economies that indulge in the gold madness.

What was supposed to be achieved with the golden measure of value has not been achieved and cannot be achieved, as the history of recent years alone proves. The price of gold has risen by around 70 percent in recent years, while the goods that are supposedly measured against it have fallen by 30, 40, 50 percent or more. It is crucial to recognize here that there is no uniform price movement, even though gold is supposed to possess the magical power to provide a uniform measure for all other values. One must finally come to understand that within the realm of measurements and goods, there is no absolute standard, but only a relativity.

One can only measure objects precisely in the realm of the natural sciences. One can measure the size of a pond, a house precisely. One can measure the weight of any object exactly in kilograms or grams, in pounds or ounces, units of measurement that in turn stand in a precise conversion relationship to one another. One can measure consumed electrical energy precisely in kilowatt-hours, the performance of a machine exactly in meter-kilograms or horsepower. But who could precisely determine the value of a piece of clothing, a meal, a drink of water, a medication, a political decision, etc.? In what fixed relationship should the value of agricultural production stand to the value of the products of trade, commerce, and industry? The measurement and exchange ratio of all these values depend on so many personal, human, subjective factors that an exact, universally valid valuation is impossible. One must take into account quantity and quality, time and circumstances, the distress of the one forced to sell. The interest or desire of the one determined to buy, the larger or smaller purse of the buyer, as well as countless moments of speculative kind. All these considerations show that the so-called monetary unit merely serves the function of a denominator established by the state, but that it by no means possesses fixed measure qualities. It should therefore be forbidden, for example, that goods are sold off at auctions using the alleged state standard, that in the case of natural scarcity a natural price increase occurs, or that in the case of artificial scarcity through speculation and profiteering, the population suddenly has to spend much more monetary units in order to purchase the same goods.

Certainly, it can and must be demanded that prices do not fluctuate arbitrarily. But all these fanatics who insist on an absolutely unchanging purchasing power of the monetary unit and always see the guarantee for this only in the gold backing, become elated and eagerly accept when certain goods become cheaper according to the "*gold standard.*" The goods may become cheaper; the gold backing fanatics gladly accept that. But they do not realize that they have thereby dethroned their own value measurer, gold.

The relativity of the gold standard may be better understood when one considers the following. One can say: 10 units of gold (whether Marks, Schillings, Francs, or Gulden, it does not matter here) enabled the purchase of 10 kg. wheat in 1928, in 1929 only 8 kg., in 1930 12 kg., and conversely with exactly the same justification one can say: For a ton of wheat, the farmer received in the first year 30 units of gold, the following year 23 units of gold and in the third year 36 units of gold; this proves that it deals with a value relationship between gold and wheat that is adjustable within the widest proportions, that thus the belief that one could measure values or prices with gold is completely absurd.

From a national economic perspective, it would appear more important and valuable for the future statesman to have a certain amount of bread grain available for the nourishment of his people than a certain amount of gold as the basis of the currency. Gold is not a currency foundation, is not a value measurer. Gold is a commodity like a thousand other commodities, whose value in relation to other goods fluctuates just as much, is just as relative as any other good. The price fluctuations of goods are dependent on entirely different factors and reasons than on the gold backing of a currency.

The cheaper prices for shoes and clothing, for radio devices, etc., are dependent on technical achievements. Whether the cherries and pears become cheaper is dependent on the richness of nature, but not on how much gold lies in the vaults of the Reichsbank. At what price we receive cotton, wool, copper and iron ore from overseas, in turn, is not dependent on how much gold there is in the world and how the currencies of the states stand in relation to the dollar rate, but on how production is going in the respective raw material countries and demand in the consuming industrial countries, may be dependent on the maneuvers of high finance on the cotton and metal exchanges, is dependent on the discovery of substitute materials, etc.

Where is the *"value measurer"* gold when the world's raw material prices collapse? Where is the *"value measurer"* gold in assessing political achievements or the genius of inventions? Was gold necessary as a measure of value when the Rentenmark was introduced? No! Without any gold backing, the Rentenmark was recognized as a full-value and stable currency both domestically and abroad.

Does France's enormous gold reserve today protect it from the advancing unemployment crisis? Have the fantastical quantities of gold amassed in American banks been able to prevent unemployment in America from reaching catastrophic proportions and raw material prices from collapsing steeply?

For the life of the nation, the availability of food, clothing, shelter, willingness to work, and joy in work is infinitely more important than even the largest heap of gold.

The relation of values in the exchange of goods can never be fixed. Otherwise, the concepts of *"cheap"* and *"expensive," "good value"* and *"appropriate"* would lose their meaning. On one hand, even the incentive to reduce production costs would diminish if prices were state-mandated, while on the other, a state-fixed price structure would collapse under the pressure of crop failures and catastrophes.

The highest achievable through state manipulation of currency is a relatively stable average level of living costs. The anchoring of currency in gold is entirely unsuitable for this purpose, leading only to a highly dangerous scarcity of payment means and ultimately serves only the interests of gold holders and high finance. For a National Socialist state, detaching from the gold standard is a prerequisite and self-evident necessity for the reconstruction of the German economy.

In foreign trade, the quality and superiority of German manufactured goods are infinitely more important than the gold basis for the possibility of obtaining necessary raw materials from abroad, which itself has an interest in exchanging its surplus raw material quantities for finished goods it cannot produce itself.

Gold is not world money. World money has been, is, and will always be the commodity itself. Southern thinking has placed gold at the center. The anchoring of currencies in gold has made the peoples of the Western cultural sphere tributary to financial capital. Breaking the bondage of interest would be impossible without detaching from gold.

The necessity of gold backing is a misconception. It is fundamentally wrong to believe that gold is suitable as a measure of value.

Detaching from gold is the prerequisite for a healthy economy in the Third Reich, where work must again take precedence over money, in a state where the welfare of the population comes before the profits of bankers.

CHAPTER 26

EMPLOYMENT CREATION

First published in *"Deutsche WochenSchau"* 1932

"Every people determines its own fate, toward freedom or enslavement."

Beyond political subjugation, the most terrible fate that can befall a nation is when millions of its compatriots can no longer find work. Work is the ultimate and highest life content for the creative Nordic person. Unemployment is spiritual death. As a social and economic problem, unemployment means the downfall and misery of the entire nation, the complete erosion of a people's economic strength, and carries within it the seeds of dangerous revolts that must ultimately lead to the dissolution of the entire state.

If in earlier times the state did not take care of temporarily or even long-term unemployed citizens but left these *"poor"* to public charity and private or municipal welfare, in the present day, care for the unemployed has become a problem of the utmost importance in social, state, and economic policy.

About one-third of the total German population (!) must today be sustained from public funds.

Approximately 6 million unemployed citizens, meaning including women and children and accounting for those receiving unemployment support such as dependent members of the industrial and commercial middle class, totaling about 20 million Germans, have no work. Through the most extreme fiscal exploitation of the still-employed German population, deep interventions into property assets, and ever-increasing indebtedness, attempts have been made to sustain these unfortunate people with unemployment support at a pitiful minimum level of existence, which, due to the ever-growing financial distress of the Reich, the states, and municipalities, now falls far below what is tolerable for German people even in terms of the most primitive life necessities.

Essentially, the previous governments failed because of their inability to solve the unemployment problem. The issue of job creation has become the central problem for every state government, and it will be especially so for us National Socialists, who have confronted the governments of the last thirteen years with the strongest opposition and the sharpest critique. There can be no doubt in our circle that future history will judge National Socialism based on how it has solved this issue.

However, overcoming unemployment is by no means merely a question of purely material job creation through any technical means. It is an enormously far-reaching state task that profoundly impacts trade policy and global economic relations, and is equally a matter of domestic, economic, and technical policy, as well as one that deeply affects the structural changes in our economy. It is also a task of financial technique, for without solving the financing problem of job creation, the restructuring of the entire economy is impossible. Thus, job creation requires an understanding of the main causes that have led to the current situation. These include:

1. Causes of foreign policy nature

This includes the consequences of the Treaty of Versailles, the draining of German national wealth by the Entente, and the resulting anemia in the German economic body.

2. Causes of foreign trade policy nature

The liberalist-global economic orientation allowed the main focus to shift to exploiting foreign markets, neglecting the German domestic market, and simultaneously undermining the basis of German food and raw material supply. Connected to this was the senseless and plan-less import of foodstuffs that could have been produced domestically, and of finished products that could have been manufactured in Germany at least with equal quality.

3. Reasons of domestic policy nature

These reasons are:

1. Tax-related reasons. Without regard for the ever-shrinking production base, more and more taxes were extracted to meet the excessively inflated administrative needs, new types of taxes were created, and tax rates were continually increased while overall income declined.

2. The indebtedness of the nation, both public authorities and the economy in cities and rural areas, which eventually amounted to a total debt of 95 billion gold marks by January 1, 1932, and which glaringly reveals the dominance of the interest-based economy over Germany.

3. Corruption and moral decay. Tax evasion and capital flight.

4. The fact that we are in the age of the "Technical Era"

This last factor is of extraordinary importance. A whole series of grand and essential, all-encompassing technical facilities has been completed, such as the railway network, the postal service, the electrification works for light and power, water supply systems, gas works, streetcars, etc., while the capacity of the German technical production apparatus has increased so dramatically through rationalization and technical innovations, that the ongoing required output and replacements utilize only a vanishingly small fraction of the existing production capacity.

If it is not possible to provide the industry with new great technical impulses through a transitional period (which is possible), then even with intensive job creation in the areas of land cultivation, home construction, road building, etc., we will not be able to permanently reintegrate all the unemployed into the production process.

5. The interest-based capital system

This system is fundamentally incapable of solving unemployment, as it is precisely this system with its insane loan and usury economy that has significantly contributed to the desiccation of German economic strength.

The extraordinary diversity of the causes of unemployment naturally also requires a comprehensive range of job creation measures, and these must be organically united under central leadership, and must be equally of economic policy, trade, and financial policy nature, and must at the same time be integrated into the overall framework of what National Socialist financial and economic policy must achieve in a German state of work and performance.

Therefore, some of the measures to be taken must extend beyond the broad framework of the fundamental policies of National Socialist economic strategy. Each individual measure must be placed in its proper position within the overall picture. In this context, the sequence and timing of the individual measures will also be of particular importance. Some measures must be implemented immediately and simultaneously across all of Germany, others will need to be spread out over years or even decades, and certain major specialized tasks can only be initiated after appropriate technical preparation. Other measures will be more psychological and political in nature, creating the necessary conditions for an organic economy and a mental reorientation toward prioritizing German products, foodstuffs, and beverages over foreign ones.

It is also of particular importance to recognize that a whole series of economic tasks must be transferred to state control (socialized), and that a number of economic-technical measures in the sphere of private enterprise naturally grow into conditions ripe for nationalization. This includes providing the population with light, power, and heat; the recognition that the

National Socialist state has the will to secure German bread for the German working population; and, above all, that the monetary and credit system must be placed entirely under state oversight.

When examining individual job creation measures, the following principle must prevail in the field of trade policy: agricultural products and manufactured goods that can be sufficiently produced or grown in Germany itself must not be imported from abroad.

This categorical directive does not at all mean that National Socialism intends to rigidly isolate itself from the rest of the world economy. Indeed, a National Socialist state could not do so, as a number of raw materials must, under all circumstances, be obtained from abroad. Conversely, the German export industry can rightly demand that the global market not be closed off to it due to retaliatory measures against a rigid import prohibition movement.

In the area of the food market, imports in 1928 (selected because it was a year of generally still healthy international trade exchanges, while figures from the catastrophic years of 1930 and 1931 do not accurately reflect actual conditions) amounted to 4.5 billion gold marks—a sum one-quarter of which could have provided extensive assistance to German agriculture.

The tolerance of rice imports worth 561 million gold marks at a time when agriculture in the East was collapsing because their rye could not be sold or only at inadequate prices; the fact that 755 million gold marks went abroad for fruits and vegetables, while German fruit and vegetable farming was brought to a standstill; and the further fact that 951 million gold marks (!) went abroad for dairy and egg products, while the plight of German livestock breeders and poultry farmers worsened—these demonstrate that an utterly insane, anti-national economic system was in place. According to the unanimous opinion of leading agricultural experts, there is no doubt that through the intensification of German agriculture combined with large-scale land cultivation projects, drainage of marshlands, extensive vegetable farming and greenhouse facilities, and rational poultry farming, nearly all of Germany's food needs could be met within a few years.

The import of specific tropical fruits could, of course, be stopped immediately. However, when implementing measures in this direction, consideration must be given to which tropical fruit exporting countries are also significant buyers of German industrial products. The same applies to the import of tobacco.

It must be highlighted as a particularly egregious scandal that in 1928, imports of manufactured goods reached the staggering sum of 2,459 million gold marks. Our highly developed textile industry undoubtedly renders the import of foreign yarns, rayon, fabrics, clothing, etc.—totaling 863 million gold marks— completely unnecessary and left hundreds of thousands of German textile workers jobless. The same applies to the import of foreign, especially Czechoslovakian shoes, as well as tires, motor vehicles, and watches.

The import of luxury goods to the amount of 338 million (!) into Germany seems like something out of a madhouse, and the fact that 148 million (!) worth of dyes and chemical finished products were imported is only possible if a shameless foreign bias in the purchase of perfumes, lipsticks, butter, pharmaceutical products, etc., is allowed to run rampant by the state without any restrictions.

The situation is different when it comes to the import of raw materials and finished products that our German soil either does not produce or does not produce in sufficient quantities. These must, of course, be imported, foremost among them the raw materials for the textile industry: cotton and wool, amounting to around 1.5 billion. Ores and metals at 954 million, mineral oils at 247 million, rubber at 113 million, iron ores at 243 million, copper at 376 million, hides at 324 million, furs at 235 million, silk at 145 million, as well as lead, construction timber, coal, and tobacco.

This massive contingent of raw materials, which in 1928 reached the figure of 7,243 million gold marks, naturally opens up ample export opportunities for German trade in the area of finished goods, textiles, leather goods, furs, furniture, paper, dyes, chemicals, porcelain, glass, and, above all, iron and steel goods, which stood at 1,629 million, and machinery, which stood at 1,600 million in our foreign trade balance in 1928.

Therefore, it must be dismissed as utterly unfounded when someone claims to expect damage to the German export trade from the National Socialist protectionist efforts. That the export of items essential for

Germany's survival, such as wheat (59 million), sugar (63 million), flour (35 million), must be discontinued is self-evident. That the export of fur goods, coal (472 million), salt, ammonium sulfate, chemical products, and potash will be promoted by us is equally obvious.

From what has been briefly stated and supported by figures, it is clear that the moderate protectionist efforts of National Socialism do not by any means entail a threat to German export interests, while the rejection of unnecessary imports represents one of the most important foundations for indirect job creation. It can be estimated that for every 2,000 marks of imports, one German family becomes unemployed. With an estimate of around 6 billion in unnecessary imports of food and finished goods in 1928, this means that had these imports been avoided and instead consumed domestically, around 3 million (!) German worker families would have had work and bread.

The measures to be taken here do not have to be implemented in a violent and confrontational manner. Import bans, import prohibitions, the suspension or breach of trade treaties seem to me entirely unsuitable measures here, unless political considerations in individual cases demand it. Far greater emphasis will have to be placed on education. The German women's movement will have to take the lead here in the rejection of foreign cosmetics and food as well as luxury items. In the constructive sense, the promotion of greenhouse cultivation with state funds will have to be foreseen. Particular care must be given to agriculture, horticulture, and coastal fishing. It must be prevented that, while almost the entire coastal fishing fleet lies idle, fish from Denmark is transported by truck to Berlin, Magdeburg, and Halle.

A highly effective tool and aid for the clarification of our foreign trade relations will be the creation of a currency control office, which will allocate foreign currency only for the import of goods that are essential, while it will not grant such currency for the import of undesirable items. The establishment of a state trade office seems indispensable to me, so that this office can conduct a thorough examination of trade relations with non-German countries within the framework of the points outlined above.

The measures in the area of trade policy must be matched by those within the country itself. The most important of these I would like to consider individually.

Reallocation of the Building Interest Tax

The reallocation of the building interest tax is to be described as a measure that can become effective immediately and starts at a particularly impactful point. The process is conceived in such a way that 50 percent or more of their building interest taxes are waived for taxpayers, provided they use the waived amounts for renovation work on their own buildings and submit official verifiable records of this following the exemplary model that was calculated in the Engineering Department for Baden by the local district advisor, Professor Dr. Ing. Karl Flügel of the Technical College in Karlsruhe, alone for Baden it is possible to accommodate 11,500 men in this way. When extrapolated to the entire Reich, this results in a number of around 300,000 construction workers and laborers who could be put back into activity.

It is significant that with this measure, the so-called *"second man"* will soon reintegrate himself into the economy on his own. For once the construction industry—the key industry—is set in motion, the usual commercial operations as well as the suppliers of cement, lime, bricks, iron, wire, nails, door fittings, roof drain pipes, and installation contractors, etc., will promptly receive orders again.

Special questions regarding the treatment of foreign building properties, urban housing quarters ready for demolition, and measures for houses in good condition are reserved for legal regulation at the Reich level.

Settlement and Housing Movement

The profoundly evident longing of the urban population for their own home, as expressed in the often touching care of small home gardens, and the generous population policy of the National Socialist German Workers' Party directed toward the East open up another vast area for job creation through housing construction and settlement.

Fundamentally, a distinction must be made here between suburban settlements and rural settlements. While agricultural settlement sites must serve to strengthen our production for national-political and production political reasons, suburban settlements can only be advocated and promoted to the extent that it involves fellow citizens who can themselves provide the financial means for the construction of their own homes, who are still employed or can confidently look forward to reintegration into work in the city.

The relocation of our large cities would be most simply and effectively achieved through this promotion of home construction. At the same time, this promotion will ensure that even the large mass of less affluent population can acquire the most essential asset that a person needs—their own home on their own land. Moreover, home construction will have a stimulating effect on the entire construction industry, just like the redirection of the building interest tax.

Through extensive land cultivation efforts, the yield of our agriculture can be increased by 1/8, i.e., by 1.5-2 billion marks per year. At the same time, a large part of our agriculture will be significantly strengthened. Additionally, approximately 500,000 men could be provided with work for 10 years.

Road Construction

Another vast area that can immediately be tackled at thousands of locations is road construction. The German road network covers about 220,000 kilometers, while the German railway network only has about 60,000 kilometers of operational length.

Rural road construction is the technical field that can absorb around 500,000 unemployed workers, distributed across the entire territory of Germany, at the very start of a job creation campaign. Particularly valuable is the immediacy of the work that can begin (Mussolini).

The annual scope of a rural road construction program can be set at 1 billion marks (increased scope of construction programs in the years 1928 and 1929). This could accommodate: around 4-500,000 seasonal workers, of which around 300,000 could be employed year-round beyond the season, some of whom would be utilized in adjacent industries.

A construction program for the expansion of the existing road network is a limited one. With an amount of 56 billion marks spread over 5-6 years, the current German road network can be brought into a durable condition. The construction of larger road routes (pure automobile through routes) is, by the way, not yet included in such a program. Among the necessary works is also the construction of so-called agricultural connection paths of adequate condition, which in some parts of Germany are still missing to a degree that severely hampers agriculture.

The improvement of the existing road network is less suitable for the envisioned labor service obligation, as a large number of small, short-term construction sites distributed across all of Germany must be established.

The labor service obligation shall be reserved for such works where it involves the creation of entire road bodies (e.g., bypass roads).

From a technical perspective, a more careful oversight must be introduced. The authorities must receive uniform guidelines. The research institutes must be freed from their industrial dependence and staffed neutrally. The inconsistency in road administration, the extensive state-run operations of the administrative authorities, as well as corrupt accompanying phenomena in the supplying industry, must be eliminated through an appropriate oversight body.

It should be strived for that, upon completion of construction, the costs for the maintenance of the finished roads are covered from the proceeds of the automobile tax.

Water Power Utilization, Step River Construction, and Water Economy

A field of work with still entirely incalculable possibilities for job creation arises in the three areas of water power utilization, step river construction, and water economy.

The high-water issue requires the diking of rivers and streams. The utilization of Germany's major rivers was previously considered technically impossible for power generation due to the too-small gradients. Through the so-called step river construction, which utilizes the existing high-water dams by blocking them with cross-dams at intervals of 5-10 kilometers, a long, extended system of lakes is created, allowing for excellent water retention for peak power generation. Through the Lawaczedian converters, these small gradients become technically 100% utilizable, the great rivers become navigable far upstream with uniform channel depths in summer and winter, and the high waters are safely discharged over the dam crests via syphons. In this way, 8 million kW (roughly 10 million HP) can be generated in Germany, providing the basis for a decentralized power, light, and heat supply.

Of particular importance is the possibility of achieving and maintaining uniform groundwater levels, the possibility of ensuring the necessary water levels in all river systems, which in turn is a prerequisite for technically sound bog cultivation and drainage works. Here too, we are dealing with works that can be started simultaneously along all river courses distributed almost throughout Germany, yet extending over many years, even decades. The funds needed for these construction measures can only partially be drawn from the resources of the construction and economic banks through productive credit creation: for very soon—since it involves hundreds and thousands of small water power plants forming a self-contained whole—the revenues of these decentralized water power plants will allow for the further construction of the remaining steps from the surpluses of the first-built plants. The possibilities that lie in the conversion of surplus current into hydrogen and oxygen (according to the plans of Dr. Lawaczed through pressure electrolysis) should be mentioned here only for the sake of completeness. The implementation of a nationwide hydrogen supply will provide the heavy industry, through the delivery of hundreds of thousands of kilometers of pipes, as well as the installation contractors, furnace and burner manufacturers, with work for decades to come.

Canal Construction

Canal constructions will link the individual river systems together. The expansion of the Mittelland Canal and, above all, the Hansa Canal will provide work for tens of thousands of unemployed for years to come.

Large Individual Tasks

The aforementioned Hansa Canal will become the backbone for a large-scale eastern space policy. It is little known that due to the lack of a waterway connection from the Ruhr region to the eastern seabed, German Ruhr coal cannot compete with English coal in the Baltic (Stettin, Danzig, Königsberg). A direct water route from the Ruhr region via Bremen and Hamburg to Lübeck would, in one stroke, restore the competitiveness of German coal against English coal and permanently bring hundreds of thousands of German workers in the Ruhr coal mines back to work; at the same time, it would improve Germany's trade balance.

The reclamation of old North Friesland and the land reclamation of the Jade Bay are two specific tasks of very large scale, allowing for the creation of new land the size of the Grand Duchy of Hesse (12,000 square kilometers) simply by drawing dams from iron and concrete; until the complete reclamation after decades, the tides could be utilized for power generation.

The implementation of such specialized tasks will, of course, have an extraordinarily significant impact, creating major orders for the German cement and iron industries, as well as turbine and generator manufacturers.

Expansion of Our Armed Forces

The expansion of our armed forces must not be forgotten as a driver of job creation for hundreds of thousands.

We will not allow a discussion on the question of the economic profitability of newly built battleships. If the delivery of rails in the sense of today's mercantile economy is, without further ado, viewed as a basis for issuing new Reich banknotes, then we will consider the delivery of armor plates for the construction of a battleship even more so as a fundamental basis for currency.

CHAPTER 27

"VOLK" ECONOMY

First print in the *"Voik Economy"* special issue of the *"Deutsche Sonderschul-Zeitung"* from December 1, 1923.

Today, at our German specialized schools, we are not to pursue *"presuppositionless"* science, but as Germans, we are to think, research, and shape spirit and will in the German spirit, so that as leaders we can serve our people.

When our poor people, seduced by foreign intellectualism, find themselves in the most terrible political and economic servitude and desire to be free again—and which German would not wish this with a burning heart!—it is precisely the task of the academic circles to familiarize themselves with the political and economic conditions in which we live today.

Now, the German person, as they are generally composed of extremes in their entirety, is a specialist and a visionary, brooding and rushing into the future without restraint, historically pedantic and philosophically speculative in a narrow circle, content and yet soaring into the infinite, heroically serving an idea—little suited to take the things of the present seriously and to integrate them into the overall picture of the world. Thus, the German tirelessly researches, excels as a specialist in their field, and achieves outstanding things then again, they gladly sacrifice wealth and blood for the fatherland when it calls—but strangely, the fatherland must always call them; the sense of constant connectedness with their people, which simmers in the German everyday, in the German everyday life of work and research, is missing. Here, the constant lively interplay between the nation and the individual is absent. And yet—*"The fatherland calls daily!"*, as Ludendorff recently said to a delegation of patriotic associations.

This call of the fatherland must be lively and awake, especially in our studying youth. They must not view science as an end in itself, not exclusively under the aspect of earning a living, but the thought of the nation and homeland must always be awake; the considerations during studies must always be expanded into the impersonal. It is precisely the teachers and students of our specialized schools who must never lose sight of the well-being of the people. Only from such a mental constitution will the leaders arise from our specialized schools who will be able to lead our people out of shame, need, and servitude into a better future.

The scent of the homeland's soil must permeate the halls of the universities, the entire living organism of the life and work of the people must be vividly clear above all scientific research; only then will the intellectual elite of the nation once again find the lost connection to the people.

One branch of science has particularly lost this connection with the people, where this lack is all the more striking as the field of this branch of science deals precisely with the things of the daily life of the people economics.

With *"Volkswirtschaft,"* the guilded disciples and teachers of this science ponder this foreign word, although it would be much more correct to translate it as *"people's economy."* Indeed, what is written in the old economics textbooks has very little to do with the people and their economy, their needs, and hardships. Dry abstractions and definitions about economic things, endlessly much historical ballast fill these volumes—to which the *"scientific nature"* is by no means denied—but nowhere can one feel the living breath of the life and work of the people, nowhere are considerations made as to whether what has been derived from economic phenomena is correct and, above all, serves the good of the community.

Even less has been attempted from the perspective of national economics to build creatively upon the insights gained, to point out new paths, to show what fundamental flaws exist in our economy, and how they might be avoided.

Thus, precisely in that which would first make an economy valuable for the community, the official economic science fails completely. It is not without reason, therefore, that the question is raised by men who, as practical and creative economic leaders and economists, have been and are pioneering, whether national economics even deserves the honorable name of a science.

Neither the activity of the chronicler, who brings reports of past economic conditions, nor the activity of the journalist, who records descriptions of the present state of things, justifies the claim to be representatives of a science.

National economics will only become a true science when, based on the current conditions of the people's economy in connection with the researched circumstances of the past, it has drawn broad fundamental lines. Only when it has critically examined and assessed these conditions for the driving forces, when it has recognized what mistakes were made, and above all, what abuses were perpetrated. It must consider all of this from the only possible perspective, that economic phenomena serve the general welfare – and not just the private enrichment of individuals.

But even this is not enough; national economics must also say how the entire economy must be structured to best fulfill its task – to meet the diverse needs of a nation united by history, fate, and blood.

Only when national economics is able to answer the triple great question that must always be posed in dealing with contemporary issues on a grand scale can it be recognized as a full science, called to be and to form leaders. This triple question is: What is the situation? How did it come about? What now?

It would be tempting to immediately pose this triple question in the context of the overall direction of today's economic science. To raise the question, then: Whom does this current state of national economics serve, who are the individuals who primarily act as teachers in this field, and does this state not serve exceptionally well the currently dominant economic powers?

However, although we have fundamentally and from the outset taken our purely German standpoint, we do not wish to delve further into these matters here, but purely factually, only from the perspective of whether today's economic structure serves, and can serve, the good of the community, we must examine the fundamental direction of our people's economy.

The task of the people's economy is to meet demand.

At first glance, it might seem almost paradoxical that this self-evident truth is specifically stated as the task of the people's economy. To the naturally sensitive person, it does not occur that the entire people's economy could have been redirected into a completely different fundamental orientation, namely – towards profitability. And yet, this very trait is characteristic of our entire economy today.

Not compelling necessities of the people's economy determine production primarily – but profitability. This is the natural consequence of the fact that today, it is no longer the welfare of the community but the interests of big capital that decide. What is still adapted in the various economic sectors today is done not from the perspective of pressing need but primarily from the viewpoint of whether the money invested in such an enterprise will generate a good return. Big capital makes its decisions solely based on the profitability it can extract. – Whether these profits come from a productive enterprise or a speculative venture or an entirely unproductive credit institution or from enterprises that are outright against the interests of the community, such as syndicates and trusts that extract their enormous gains from artificially created scarcity of essential goods – this is completely indifferent to the moneyed powers.

Nothing illustrates this economy-killing fact more than a glance at the enormous development of the completely unproductive people's economy banking system – while the people go hungry and the most terrible economic crises bring the healthy productive economy almost to a halt.

In the German Middle Ages, the arts of architecture, sculpture, and painting reached a height never again achieved; we still stand in awe today before the witnesses of that time – St. Stephen's Cathedral and Cologne Cathedral, Nuremberg's artistic treasures teach us this. The citizens of the imperial cities were free and proud – but money trade was a disreputable business, entrusted to the Jews. Today, the arts lie completely in ruins, having had to make way for the dullest utilitarianism of the machine age. Art and science go begging for bread and have become unfaithful to their most sacred task, to create genius works independent of the material purposes of purely economic activity. The de-deification and materialization of humanity is making rapid progress, but banks bloom and grow like mushrooms after a warm rain.

Money trade has today become solely an end in itself, focused only on the profitability of loan capital. The people-economy purpose of credit has been completely reversed. The honest banking and money mediation business, which had the important task of lending savings to trustworthy hands where greater economic efficiency through the expansion of financial means led to increased production and demand coverage, has completely disappeared. In its place has stepped the enormous network of large banks, which today completely dominate the economy in such a dictatorial manner that it depends solely on them which industries can and may operate. Small businesses have long since been impoverished and eliminated as an essential factor in the people's economy, the medium-sized enterprises are completely dependent on the banks, and even large-scale industry operates in the purely interest-capitalistic form of the joint-stock company primarily to secure bank interest. There is no large enterprise left in which the representative of a major bank does not hold a key position on the supervisory board, whose internal values are not handed over in the form of shares to the stock exchange.

Today, it is not labor, not the creative power of the mind and hands, that determines the course of the economy, but money – this tool for the production of goods – has ceased to be the servant of the economy and become its master; no longer the master and journeyman, no longer the engineer and skilled worker, but the shareholder and supervisory board member today draw the profits without effort or labor. The shareholder, who usually does not even know in which enterprise his money is *"working,"* who buys shares indiscriminately based on the stock ticker or the recommendation of his banker.

Loan capital follows only one law – the law of interest. Profitability is the sole and supreme principle. Needs coverage comes only incidentally and only insofar as this innermost necessity and task of the people's economy is the driving force and the creator and shaper of surplus value, which is then pumped out of the body of the creating peoples with the irresistible force of a suction pump into the unfathomable maw of the supranational money powers. The greater the hunger, the greater the distress, the greater the profitability of the global usury capital, the greater – the interest. The more fertile the soil bears fruit, the better the general and public welfare stands, the greater the yield of labor for the economic body itself – the less the need for borrowed money, i.e., for incurring debt – the smaller the interest.

Thus, today, two economic forms stand as fundamental and implacable enemies against each other – the interest-capitalistic economy – and the healthy and natural interest-free needs-coverage economy.

We must briefly mention here a third economic form, which in our time has revealed its destructive nature on the grandest scale – the communist economic form.

Both extremes – the high-capitalistic and the communist economy – ultimately destroy every healthy needs coverage economy because both destroy the freedom of the individual, the creative power, and responsibility toward state and people.

These questions are enormously serious and weighty; they reach far beyond the narrower economic sphere into the ultimate spiritual and national questions. Our academic youth will have the task of carrying the banners forward in this struggle of the declining West for the redemption of suffering humanity from the shackles of usury-capital and moral decline into a brighter future, in which the national idea of defense and pride in homeland and people will unite with the social idea of economic and cultural belonging among all compatriots.

CHAPTER 28

THE ECONOMIC RECONSTRUCTION PROGRAM OF THE N.S.D.A.P.

By order of Adolf Hitler on September 17, 1932, a reorganization of the economic policy department of the N.S.D.A.P. was carried out according to state-economic and private-economic perspectives. Gottfried Feder was appointed as the head of the main department IV A (State Economy), while ... was appointed with the stipulation that the two department heads must mutually substitute for each other. This was to guarantee the uniformity of the entire economic policy of the N.S.D.A.P.

As the first measure, Walther Funk, in collaboration with Gottfried Feder and the organizational leader Gregor Strasser, declared it binding for all Gauleitungen, specialized speakers, economic policy, and engineering-technical advisors of the N.S.D.A.P.

Furthermore, special attention was drawn to the fact that all publications not appearing in the party press, which deal with National Socialist economic problems, do not carry any official party character and do not gain such, even if the author holds a position within the party.

The National Socialist German Workers' Party strives for a reconstruction of the state and the economy on a National Socialist foundation, which can only be achieved through a profound transformation of the political and economic system in a total solution. The Bavarian government confines itself to inadequate individual measures, which do not have a comprehensive effect and therefore cannot lead to success. In combating the economic crisis, we proceed from the assumption that this crisis is not only of an economic nature but represents a state crisis, indeed a national crisis. We therefore fundamentally differ from the Bavarian government both in our understanding of the nature of the crisis and in the objectives set for economic policy.

The Bavarian government believes it can save the German economy by maintaining the current structure of the economy and making no changes to the present economic system.

We are convinced that the German economy must undergo a fundamental structural change, and that the German economic system cannot be maintained in its present form. Moreover, we believe that any economic reform is doomed to failure from the outset if it is not accompanied by extensive streamlining of Reich and state administration as well as municipal and professional self-administration, and if new forms and content are not provided to the economic administration. This complete reconstruction of public administration, the economy, and social life must be based on the National Socialist worldview and imbued with the National Socialist spirit. In the reconstruction of the German national economy the state-political and psychological prerequisites must first be created through the establishment of the stabilization of a strong, government power supported by the national will. Political leadership must clear the way for economic leadership to carry out a thorough renewal of the economic and social life in Germany by removing external and internal obstacles, overcoming social conflicts, and reshaping the constitutional and administrative legal foundations in the German Reich.

The supreme goal of economic policy must be the preservation and strengthening of the national power and resources, so that every German can benefit from his work again, each individual according to his performance. According to this basic principle, German economic policy must be uniformly directed.

To achieve this, a comprehensive reconstruction of both the structure of the German economy and the individual economic institutions is necessary. In this process, economic policy must proceed organically and dynamically, preserving and nurturing what is viable.

The economic reconstruction program of the N.S.D.A.P. is based on the following fundamental demands:

1. Direct employment creation for approximately two million people based on the assignment of orders for state and private reinvestments to the extent of 5 billion Reichsmarks. A special employment creation program is available.

2. Productive credit creation in the amount of 3 billion RM through the Reichsbank, which primarily issues bank money and only to the extent of 300 to 500 million RM in circulating money. These funds, after stimulating the economy, automatically return to the Reichsbank. Thus, no inflation but the restoration of a healthy currency and a healthy production-promoting money and credit economy.

3. Nationalization of the entire money and credit system, including bank money, and expansion of the state clearing system.

4. Debt restructuring of the entire German economy through decentralization of all public and private debts in a general debt restructuring institution. Liquidation of inflation damages through a pensioner welfare law debt-relations in a general debt restructuring institution. Liquidation of inflation damages through a pensioner welfare law.

5. Comprehensive reduction of interest rates in line with our major goal of breaking the interest based economy, with extensive consideration of individual economic circumstances.

6. Amendment of the Standstill Agreements and uniform regulation of foreign debts with an adjustment of interest and amortization based on Germany's foreign exchange income. The entire payment exchange with foreign countries is placed in the hands of an

7. Foreign trade office and a foreign exchange center, which should form a branch of the Reichsbank. There is no domestic and foreign currency, only a German currency and a currency bank, a federally controlled Reichsbank.

8. New regulation of economic relations with foreign countries prioritizing the necessities of the domestic market but considering the essential exports for Germany. The quota system initiated by the government is fundamentally correct but entirely inadequate because it absurdly incorporates the most favored-nation clause and lacks the foreign policy power factor and the internal political will to carry it out. We are completely isolated in foreign policy and lack unified national will in domestic politics.

9. Tax relief through mitigation or complete elimination of production-inhibiting taxes that directly influence prices. Simplification and Unification of the tax system and dynamic adjustment of tax rates according to the needs of a productive economic structure.

10. Restoration of German state credibility

- Sanitation of public finances including public insurance and considering the fact that after successful job creation, the billions spent on unemployment will cease.
- Elimination of the current unsustainable methods of budget balancing. Restoration of balance truth and clarity.

11. State protective measures for agriculture (Reorganization of the marketing of agricultural products and agricultural cooperative system, of storage, transport, dairying, processing, canning, and animal and plant breeding. Grain farming management).

12. Reconstruction of home and land ownership considering the reorganization of mortgage credit (Reich Mortgage Bank) and the tax system according to considerations of productivity and national health.

13. Planned reorientation of industrial and craft production considering state-controlled businesses and nationally particularly important industrial sectors. Provision of job creation means for the expansion of the German raw material basis and for new national industries and craft sectors as well as for technical and manufacturing reorientations (small business policy).

14. Rational transport economy. Recovery of the Reich Railway, reorientation of tariffs according to national economic necessities, unified transport policy (automobile transport, shipping), and centralized energy economy.

Reasoning

A debt relief of the economy cannot be achieved by cleaning bank balances and providing subsidies to the industry, and agriculture cannot be helped by lowering interest for part of agricultural indebtedness by 2% and negotiating with foreign countries over the reduced import of a few thousand hundredweights or even tons of agricultural products. Even the ordered suspension of enforcement must remain ineffective unless the land on which the farmer works is made healthy and productive and the future of German farmers is secured. All of this will not be achieved with the measures of the Papen government.

Fundamentally, it must be maintained that there can be no recovery of German agriculture if the entire

German economy is not healed. And there can be no effective debt relief for agriculture unless the entire German economy is freed from the constriction and entanglement in debt in which it has been for years. The structure of the German economy is unhealthy, and the system of the economy is wrong and outdated, and therefore it is necessary to take much more profound measures than the Papen government is doing to bring about the necessary reconstruction of the economy, without which every attempt to heal agriculture is doomed to fail.

In addition to the political, we must also undertake an economic general cleanup. This must proceed from the basis that the highest goal of every economic policy must be the preservation and strengthening of the national people and land forces. There can be no healthy export if the domestic market is sick. We are not so foolish as not to recognize the necessity of exports for Germany. But even for exports, a new, healthy foundation must first be created, because the current export is predominantly an export of impoverishment and squandering. The backbone of the German economy is a healthy domestic market, and the backbone of the domestic market is a healthy German peasantry.

We by no means want to destroy economic entities that are viable, but we want to preserve and nurture these entities. However, we do not believe it can be justified to drag along economic enterprises with state subsidies that are built on an outdated economic system. This applies not only to some economic forms, such as vertical concerns, but also to individual economic sectors that only force detrimental imports and whose products involve German labor in no proportion to the total value of the output.

When the Papen government directs its main focus to the sanitation of banks, we are also convinced that a healthy money and credit system must form the starting point for economic recovery. But we are of the view that the current private-capitalist banking system cannot be maintained, but that the entire money circulation must be under the sovereignty of the state and the banking system must be placed under state supervision. Only under this precondition can effective debt relief for the economy be achieved. This must extend to all debt relations.

We will not expect the state to spend billions to sanitize the banks, yet leave the execution of this sanitation to a few private individuals who are irresponsibly entrusted with the entire economic process. The rebuilding of the German economy should not be carried out by a few bank directors, but by the government, which is supported by the trust of the people and uses its power according to national and socialist principles. We do not want a state economy, nor do we want state socialism in the sense of communist and Marxist doctrines, but we want a National Socialist economy that protects the people's body from external and internal dangers and allows for a planned communal effort by all sectors and classes for the promotion of the general welfare.

From these general principles, the rebuilding of the German economy will be carried out, and these principles must also be applied in the measures to heal agriculture. Therefore, the debt restructuring will encompass the entire economy and be assigned to a general debt restructuring institution entrusted within the state monetary and credit system. However, the implementation must take place on a professional basis and not by people or institutions outside the agricultural sector. The execution of an effective debt and restructuring requires state power factors, which the Papen government does not possess at all, and a restructuring can yield no lasting success unless the interest rate reduction is also centrally carried out within a state monetary and credit system. Only under these preconditions can legal certainty in the money and capital circulation be restored, and a fair balance between creditor and debtor be created. Only a general restructuring carried out by state monetary institutions ensures that this measure does not lead to a shake of confidence or to unjustified and unbearable capital losses or capital write-downs. On the contrary, we will achieve a higher and more secure valuation of landholdings, livestock holdings, and other capital holdings than is the case today. Agriculture and the entire economy will breathe again once they are freed from the entanglement of debt and relieved of unbearable interest burdens. Then the necessary further reductions in burdens, particularly tax relief, and the protection of national production from unnecessary and harmful imports will fully take effect. At the same time, however, job creation will have to be initiated by central authorities based on productive credit creation (Feder money), which will establish a sound foundation for our currency, which is entirely lacking today. The illiquid financial bills, which currently serve as collateral at the Reichsbank, must be replaced by production bills and government securities, which will promote a healthy circulation of the economy and direct the flow of gold back to the Reichsbank at regular intervals, whereas currently it gets stuck somewhere in the illiquid, entangled economy, causing disruptions in the money and credit system and the losses of property and income due to deflationary methods. A complete new regulation of foreign debts will also be necessary, which can only be achieved in a bearable way through a reform of the entire monetary and credit system. A state regulation of money transactions with foreign countries is by no means identical to the nationalization of foreign trade. In the economic system we will build, the individual will be able to develop his initiative to a much greater extent than is the case today. The reconstruction of the economy, as we will carry it out based on a new economic structure and a new economic system, will primarily aim at the de-proletarianization of broad masses of the working populace, the peasantry, and the middle class. Real income will increase to the extent that unbearable interest and tax burdens fall away and unemployment decreases. It is obvious that such measures will also give a strong boost to production, and care must be taken to eliminate the disparity between the prices of agricultural products and industrial goods. In today's system, the credit economy leads to a general price increase, which is believed to be countered only by price controls. In our economic system, the peasant market will be freed from the burdens and fetters caused by poor public administration and misguided economic policies, and prices will stabilize without reducing purchasing power and real income. Finally, after completing the restructuring of our economy, we will ensure that saving once again has meaning, and we will also promote saving through state measures.

The Papen government has recently obtained endorsements from various economic circles, particularly from the Central Association of Banks, stating that the measures it has enacted are approved by the economy. The Papen government should not be misled by these declarations of approval, and above all, the German people must not be deceived into believing that the measures of the Papen government merely maintain a state of strain that cannot be sustained in the long run. The backlash and disappointment will then be all the more severe. The entire inadequacy of Papen's measures will be particularly evident for the peasantry. The peasant knows full well that he cannot be rescued from his dreadful state of distress with these small-scale relief measures. Ultimately, he remains at the mercy of the banks and land-alien creditors, with no guarantee that he will be able to rebuild a healthy and secure existence on his own free land. But also all other economic circles, who are discerning enough to recognize that something fundamentally new must first be created to rebuild a healthy economy in Germany, view the measures of the Papen government with extreme skepticism, unless they are indulging in a dangerous delusion due to a narrow and rigid political outlook. Unfortunately, the fear of the final decision is still as great in the economy today as it is in politics. But we cannot avoid this final decision if we do not want to hand over the German people and the German economy to Bolshevik chaos or foreign enslavement. And this final decision also includes abandoning an outdated economic system.

The world economy, as it has developed on the basis of a free money and credit system and with an emphasis on international considerations for trade between nations, has been fundamentally disrupted by the World War and the structural changes in the individual economic regions of the world. This disruption has also gripped the individual national economies, although least of all those that promptly recognized the national necessities and protected themselves through state measures. The German economy, and particularly German agriculture, have fallen almost defenselessly victim to this disruption. Now it is necessary, first of all, to reestablish a national economy. Only then can trade with foreign countries be newly regulated, and in a way that meets the needs of national politics and economy. We have sufficient national capital in Germany. And we can create new capital through work so that our people can live and continue to develop. We can and must do without international capital, and beyond that, we have the task of freeing the German economy from the fetters of international capital.

The German agriculture and, likewise, the entire German economy can only be helped by the national state, not by banks that charge international interest.

Since we do not have a national money and credit system, we must create one. The same applies to all economic entities that are subject to international influences. The reestablishment of a national German economy based on an internationally bound money and credit system, as the Papen government is currently attempting, is absurd and an irresponsible shortsightedness. The first to collapse entirely under this system will be the German farmer. But industry, trade, and craft will follow. The necessary reconstruction of the German economy can only be carried out by a government that, supported by the trust of the people, implements unstintingly the national and socialist principles that today are exclusively held by the National Socialist movement of Adolf Hitler.